Albert J Thomas VII
02 VIII 72

THE POLITICS OF GOD

Related books by
Hugh J. Schonfield
THE PASSOVER PLOT
THOSE INCREDIBLE CHRISTIANS

THE
POLITICS OF GOD

HUGH J. SCHONFIELD

Henry Regnery Company, Chicago

To
H. HUGH HALLER
*who arrived in this world as the last
chapter of this book was being completed,
and whose parents named him after me.
It is my hope that what I have written
will one day be an inspiration to him
and to the generation to which he belongs.*

Contents

Prologue

THE world of today is full of knowledge, but largely empty
of wisdom. The skilfulness of man has been remarkably
sharpened, but his sensitivities in respect of many effects of
his skills have been strangely blunted. The capacity to save
life has greatly increased at a time when violence and
brutality has been intensified and the wholesale destruction
of living things from plants up to humans has become a
commonplace. While abundant means exist to raise character
and behaviour to their highest level the spectacle presented
to the young is that of a society governed by self-interest and
power-seeking, cunning and duplicity. Both the eggheads
and the boneheads are made the creatures of the wolfheads.
Where peace and harmony might reign there is noise and
strife, the spread of noxious fumes and substances and
noxious thoughts and policies, the poisoning of mind and
body and environment. Where heaven on earth is practicable
mankind seems bent on contriving a hell.

To have come to this pass, is this the sorry end of the long
and painful process of evolution? Have all the noble hopes
and dreams, the sufferings and the gallant sacrifices, been
vanity and delusion? Has our species to be written off as
inherently faulty and incapable of attaining the higher
reaches of its ideals? If the only reality of which we are
aware is that which is determined by outward appearances
and the limited extent to which we are able to probe
beneath the surface by scientific means there would seem to

be substantial grounds for pessimism. Sitting in judgment as our own gods few would fail to deem our race deserving of extinction. Even with spiritually-minded people there are many now, as in past ages, so overwhelmed by human turpitude and contrariness that they have turned away from belief in any future earthly paradise. To an extent, of course, they are right. Perfection is not to be looked for under physical and temporal conditions. Yet it could be possible for there to be very great improvement, and for some part of humanity to progress so much that it would be able to help and influence the majority. It could be possible for a nucleus of more advanced persons to initiate a further stage of evolution and give rise to a race approximating much more closely to the ideals humanity has cherished. We must not ignore that there are many recorded instances of individuals who have exhibited the graces of worthiness, and who can doubt that there have been countless others of whom no record has been preserved? There is no lack of such people living in this very day and age.

Therefore we should not be overwhelmed by what is brought more prominently to our attention, so that we are deceived in our estimation of how much positive good exists and is in active operation. Neither should we be driven to the conclusion that our plight is beyond remedy, that the forces which are adverse to our deliverance are unconquerable.

In this book I am arguing the case for a more confident interpretation of our contemporary circumstances, not on any basis of superior learning, but in the light of insights which have affected my whole life, and which have been confirmed by study and experience.

My theme is the message of Messianism for modern man. It is not one which is widely apprehended and canvassed; for although it has been prominent in past periods, especially at a particular epoch, it has been so much misunderstood that it has been brought into disrepute and neglect. Yet, as I shall endeavour to show, what has largely been despised and rejected of men alone affords the means of our salvation.

To explain how I came to acquire comprehension and thus to embark on the task with which my name is associated it is

needful for me to refer to aspects of my personal history
which are only known in part to very few. These relate to
spiritual and paranormal happenings, certain of which were
so intimate that even now I cannot bring myself to reveal
them in their entirety. Apart from this, there were considerations which dictated caution about what I made public,
particularly when I was a much younger man. There was
the risk to myself and to others that I might be deemed to be
someone of special worth and consequence, whereas I am
neither a sage nor a saint. Cults have been founded on
experiences akin to my own, and what was called for was not
a new religion. I was anxious not to attract to myself those
who delight in the mysterious, and love to feel they are
sharers in strange secrets. The message with which I was
charged demanded sober and responsible action. What
mattered was not how the revelation came but whether it
made good sense. It could be most detrimental if I was
thought to be a crank, a crackpot or a charlatan. Therefore,
as in this book, I have endeavoured all along to appeal to
reason and intelligence, seeking out evidences that lent
support to the proposition for which I contended. It would
not increase its verity that I had obtained it in a peculiar
manner.

If I am now breaking a silence of more than thirty years
it is not because I have ceased to think these considerations
to be important. What weighs with me with advancing age
is that those to whom the message has come and will come
have a right to know how it originated. It could be a means
of strength to them in their resolve to heed it and to act upon
it. There also prevails that in humble gratitude I must
openly give thanks for the inspiration which has guided and
sustained me and made it so worthwhile to be alive and so
creatively employed. The enrichment I have received in
being permitted to see and enjoy the world and the society
of my fellows with love and in confident faith has been
beyond all expectation.

And so here I will begin, somewhat diffidently, to introduce
you first to a very small Jewish boy in London town who
started to puzzle his parents at an early age with his solemn

questions and his strange dreams. He was on the whole a cheerful smiling child, who asked his questions very naturally and for whom God was very real. He bore the Hebrew name of Joseph, and like his Biblical namesake disturbed his family by reporting what happened in his sleep.

One of his dreams was of an unknown seaside place. It kept recurring for many years. Sometimes he went there by train, sometimes by air or on foot. Gradually he got to know it so well that he would draw pictures of it, and yet it was unidentified. When the boy became a man and married he and his wife went one year for their holiday to the seaside town of Folkestone. To his astonishment it was the place of his dreams, which physically he had never before visited. Putting his dream recollections to the test he was able accurately to tell his wife in advance what buildings and features they would encounter before they became visible. The family had had no connection with Folkestone, and there seemed to be no reason why it should have figured so continually in the boy's dreams. One fact did come to light, which he had known nothing about as a child. On the Folkestone-Sandgate border for many years an author had had his home where he wrote many of his books. Some of this author's books were to exercise a powerful influence on the boy's thinking in later life. His name was Herbert George Wells.[1]

A different seaside resort was the scene of another dream experience. My wife and I knew nothing of the place or the hotel we had selected. When we arrived with our small daughter the building seemed to be a pleasant late nineteenth century structure, and we found that we had been allocated a bedroom on the ground floor. That night I dreamt that there was a hollow place beneath us in which monks were moving about. The dream was so vivid that we decided in the morning to question the manager. It transpired that the hotel had been built on the site of a monastery, and that blocked up now was an underground tunnel which the monks had used and which had led down to the shore. There had been no reference to this in the brief description of the hotel which we had seen.

Such experiences are by no means uncommon, and I have selected these two out of several happenings—some of them in the daytime when I was fully awake—simply to illustrate a psychic sensitivity which has been part of my make-up and which I accepted in childhood as being just *me*. Of course I was intrigued that I had these capacities and they led me to take an interest in the whole subject of psychic phenomena and extra-sensory perception. But I never became very deeply involved. Only once, about twenty years ago, I experimented with automatic drawing. Banishing images from my mind, I sat at my desk with a pencil loosely poised over a blank sheet of paper. After some minutes the pencil began to move with great rapidity and quickly created a remarkable but perfectly coherent picture. In all five illustrations were produced on different occasions, and then I stopped. Each was quite different in style, but all were highly symbolic.[2]

There is so much that we cannot yet grasp or rightly understand, and the mysteries even of our own 'being' are so extensive, that we can never come anywhere to a point at which we can say, 'Here we have reached finality.' With awe we have to acknowledge that we belong to the Infinite. It came quite naturally to me to make that acknowledgment when I was six years of age, standing in my bedroom at the open window and gazing up into the night sky. Frankly and unreservedly I gave myself to God.

It was a boyish gesture, but it reflected the sensitiveness I have indicated and the disposition I had to open myself to the intake of everything relating to the joy and wonder of being alive. I delighted also in being able to leap high and run very fast. It will be judged that I was very impressionable, and had I been otherwise I could not have served as a receptive instrument.

Very soon as a schoolboy I began to be aware of guidance, of being prepared for a task which one day would be revealed. I did not feel that this was at all strange, and the knowledge was not in the least obsessive. I was in no way a lonely or a brooding type. The chief effect of this inner conviction was that I became a voracious reader, setting myself to acquire both information and aptitudes which did not always fall within the school curriculum. I delved into the remote past to learn all I could of the story of our planet and of the ancient civilizations. When I became a pupil at St. Paul's I remember buying books in the secondhand market at Farringdon Street so that I could begin to study Egyptian hieroglyphics, and I went in for a competition for public-speaking because I knew that one day I would need to be able to speak. I may say that I did not acquit myself very well.

What was to be the nature of my task was not disclosed, but I did receive the intimation that it would be of a Messianic character connected with my own people and with humanity at large. My wife to be, who was a childhood friend, was one of the few recipients of my confidences. For the most part I accepted the influence on my life as a matter of course, and it did not continually engage my attention. But when I came to manhood I could and did observe from time to time how this and that circumstance was forming a needful part of my preparation. My wife and I used to remark on these things quite unaffectedly.

At the age of sixteen I read the New Testament for the first time, because I gathered that Christians held Jesus to have been the Messiah. I came in due course to the same conclusion; and having very little acquaintance with Christianity I was disposed to take a great deal on trust. The disclosure of my belief to my parents brought a time of great suffering, mercifully ended in a few years. But in those years I really grew up. In the event, the more discussion I had with Christians and opportunity seriously to consider their teaching it became progressively apparent to me that there were two Christianities, one inside the other. The inside one was Jewish relating to the Messiahship of Jesus, while the outside one was largely Gentile reflecting the major doctrines of the Church. As soon as dialogue went beyond the inner Christianity there were difficulties; for the Christians I knew, some of whom were of Jewish origin, mostly spoke the language of the Church and expected one to subscribe to their faith and employ their terminology. It was in fact another, and to their way of thinking a much more exalted and necessary Jesus, who was the object of their devotion and worship. For them the matter of his Messiahship was a relevant incidental, while for me it was paramount.

I sensed that there was something radically amiss with Christian teaching, which had taken Christianity out of the proper orbit of Messianism and made it alien. But I could not detect how things had gone wrong, and how they might be put right, without embarking on an elaborate and protracted study of Christian origins. To this I became committed while at the University of Glasgow in circumstances which I have related in the Introduction to my book *The Passover Plot*.

After leaving College I married, and held down a job during the day and worked at my studies in the evening. I wrote and published a number of books on a variety of subjects; but since I was still ignorant of exactly what was my mission in life there was nothing I could do consciously to prepare for it beyond profiting by every opportunity to acquire more knowledge and competence.

My engagements, however, were made more purposeful in the Thirties with the development of Fascism and Nazism and the growing threat of another world war. How could the dangers be met and overcome? I could not be idle in this situation, and it came to me that what I should do was to launch a Peace Publishing Company with a Book Club to give currency to what prominent persons might have to offer in devising a solution. This enterprise I launched at the end of 1935. The Club had as its distinguished Selection Committee Dr. A. Maude Royden, Vernon Bartlett, M.P., and Professor C. E. M. Joad. The outcome was a spate of literature, books and pamphlets, to which the well-known and the comparatively unknown contributed. Among prominent names were those of Cordell Hull, M. Van Zeeland, President Benes of Czechoslovakia, H. G. Wells, Sir Norman Angell, J. Middleton Murry, A. Ruth Fry, Dr. L. P. Jacks, Professor G. M. Stratton, and Emil Ludwig. If combined insight and erudition could have found a remedy it would have been made manifest in all the documentation. I personally read every line of it, and derived much from it which afterwards stood me in good stead. But what I could not find was any proposition that appeared to be sufficiently fundamental in its approach, not so much to the immediate situation as to the whole life of mankind.

It was while I was exercised with these matters, which I could see later were making my mind operate in a much wider context, that the moment came for which I had so long been waiting. Nevertheless, I was taken quite by surprise.

I was thirty-seven years of age. In 1938 we had rented a house at Staines, not very far from London, and on September 26th, at two-thirty in the afternoon, I was strolling in the garden when it happened. Suddenly I was in the midst of a stream of lights which poured upon me from every direction, all the colours of the rainbow, so that my surroundings completely disappeared. Inwardly I heard words which came from the book of the Hebrew prophet Zechariah, 'Not by might, nor by power, but by my Spirit.' At the same time it was conveyed to my mind that what was needed for the deliverance of humanity was a servant-nation. It was the building of this nation to which I was required to address myself.

My first reaction was one of dismay. How did one begin to create a nation? I could see that service was the only valid answer to mastery, but to call a nation into being was a task for which I felt totally unqualified. Yet the revelation was clear, and I accepted in faith that since what was to be done had been made known so amazingly the manner of realization would also become evident. I went indoors and informed my wife, and said to her, 'You know what this means. We shall not have a private life any more.' We would no longer belong to ourselves but to mankind.

I did not expect, of course, that ordinary existence for us would be wholly disrupted. Neither in fact has it been. But at the time I was so overwhelmed that I could not imagine what might befall, and had to be prepared for anything. The account of what followed, so far as it concerns the task, I have reserved for description in outline in the last chapter of

this book. What I have wanted to bring out here is what led
to my being embarked on it. Patently, as I quickly appreci-
ated, the enterprise had its foundations in the Bible, in the
history of the Jewish people and in the Messianic mission of
Jesus. It now became evident why I had had those youthful
premonitions, and why I had had to make contact with
Christianity and carry out an investigation of its beginnings.
I could also appreciate why the story of mankind had always
meant so much to me, and why latterly I had been so deeply
engaged with world problems.

The mandate received did not go into details. I had in any
case to augment my studies to get a clear picture of what lay
behind the terms of the message, and how it met the contemporary need. I was greatly concerned not to concentrate
attention on myself, so that it could be imagined that I was
someone of consequence. It seemed sufficient, therefore, to
communicate the effects of my researches; for if the theme
did not convince on its own merits would it make a greater
impact if I disclosed how the inspiration had come to me?
Naturally, I could not claim for my exposition, and I do not
now, that it represents more than the fruits of my own quest
for enlightenment. But I must insist that what is not mine is
the key with which I was furnished, and therefore I have now
put the facts on record.

The task is neither cultic nor egoistic. It is one for sensitive
but very level-headed, competent and practical people.
Since Christians are more particularly affected, as regards
their beliefs, I have had to prepare the way with two previous
books *The Passover Plot* and *Those Incredible Christians*, which
have enjoyed a very large world circulation and have
attracted in church circles both favourable and hostile
comment. Though my inquiries were without any polemical
intention it was unavoidable that the results should give
offence to the conservative.[3] I may now have to face further
attacks. Yet I venture to hope for greater charity and
understanding when all that is set down in this volume is
carefully studied, because it is those who claim to have the
spirit of Christ who should be most forward in bringing the
next stage of the Messianic purpose to fruition.

Those who identify themselves with the Politics of God should be prepared to face scorn and suffering. I dare not underestimate the difficulties, which will call for love, patience and determination, and especially for harmonious relations with fellow-workers. It will be on the inside that strength of character will chiefly be required, to maintain coherence, to resist the temptation to retaliate, never to despair of success, or to be turned aside to pursue other aims which seem to promise speedier results. But at least those who will come in now have the advantage of the foundations which have already been laid.

This book could not have been written until the right moment had come. Much had to be thought out and to happen. The way had also to be prepared by the prominence which has only recently come to me as a result of the success of my writings.[4] These have now introduced me to millions who previously had never heard of me, and so enabled the present even more consequential book to reach the multitudes for whom it is intended.

My mind works in an orderly and logical fashion, and therefore I have endeavoured to present the Politics of God in a rational manner in keeping with a modern approach, and in line with recent events and developments. The implications can in fact be apprehended much better today than in any earlier period. Strictly the book is neither a religious nor a political treatise. If it had been the one or the other I would have had to write very differently. What I have explored and built upon is a tradition that sees religion and politics as interrelated, and a Divine Plan being unfolded in the affairs of men. Not everyone will be in agreement with the thesis in its entirety, but I am confident they will get something out of it. What I have particularly sought to keep in mind is the variety of positions from which readers would be setting out on the road towards a common destination.

Spiritually inspired, the effect of the whole work is nevertheless pragmatic. It defines what is to be done in the light of a definite purpose and directive, which represents an explosive revolt into sanity.

Because of its momentous import, this is not a book which

having been fathered is to sink or swim as fortune and comment determine. All to whom it will speak, being thus made messengers as much as the author, have it laid upon them to spread the word for the sake of mankind in this time of its greatest need.

It may fairly be said that the work has had a number of authors, for the meditations of many have helped to frame it. It will be found that a great many others in many lands have expressed themselves just as appositely on various points as those whose words I have requisitioned. Having had to make a choice, largely of documentation in English, I have taken most of my quotations from those whom it has been my privilege to have known personally, or with whom I have been in contact in my reading and correspondence. It is a pleasure to acknowledge how much they have assisted me in stimulating my imagination and lending weight to my contentions.

Among my own materials I have employed some passages from a short study of mine entitled *By What Authority?* published in a small edition while the second world war was still in progress. I have also borrowed the language of certain of my speeches, mostly unpublished.

Finally, I would ask all who may consider writing to me to bear in mind how fully my days are occupied with so much yet to be done in the time that remains to me. I am also anxious not to burden my publishers with forwarding a large amount of mail. Letters of support and help will be welcomed gratefully, and these should be directed to The Mondcivitan Republic, 27 Delancey Street, London, N.W.1. Where a personal reply is deemed essential communications should be sent to me at the same address enclosing an International Reply Coupon obtainable from any Post Office.

In the nature of things I cannot expect to witness the major outcome of the message with which I have been entrusted. But fulfilment calls for a collective enterprise, and not any individual accomplishment. To build a world people for the service of all peoples, unlike any other in type, purpose and commitment, is a task for many hands, of those who are here now, and of those who will come after. They have to furnish the will and the skill to create that community of mankind on the Earth which has become even more imperative by the extension of man's realm to the heavens.

H.J.S.

NOTES AND REFERENCES

1. I did not meet H. G. Wells until 1939, and I helped to publicise his New Declaration of the Rights of Man. On the hundredth anniversary of his birth it was an honour to be chosen by the H. G. Wells Society as Chairman of the Centenary Committee.

2. I still have these pictures. The first depicted a planet in space with curving lines converging upon it and coming away from it and also going off at a tangent. At the time I entitled it *Fiat Lux*; but looking at it again now it seems rather to have been an anticipation of the Space Age.

3. A typical evangelical reaction was that of Dr. Billy Graham who syndicated an article in the Press in which he confidently announced that I had a closed mind into which even God could not enter.

4. A great many years ago two seers independently predicted what would happen. The second, an Indian, stressed especially the period from 1965 onward in terms which I cannot publish.

Part One

I

God and Man

THE assertion that religion and politics don't mix is an old and familiar one. Partly it is a reflection of the age-old power struggle between monarchies and hierarchies. But it also conveys an incompatibility due to a basic difference of function, politics being supposed to be concerned with the practical and the here and now while religion has to do with the metaphysical and the hereafter. The business of politics would be frustrated and rendered nugatory if affected by ideas of terrestrial perfectionism. Ideals are all very well and have their place, but a distinction must be drawn between the possible and the unattainable.

This kind of pleading offers an excuse for and a justification of behaviour which is inconsistent with the affirmations of religion in respect of laws of God applicable to men, and where there is a religious profession gives rise directly to a frequently unconscious hypocrisy on the part of both clergy and laity. Either a compromising form of religion manifests itself, or an extraordinary feat of compartmentalism which enables the individual to give allegiance to opposing principles, to love and worship both God and mammon, to love and succour his fellows and to hate and destroy them. For those capable of realizing this the alternatives have seemed to be to withdraw from society, to act humanely in defiance of its unethical demands, or to repudiate religion as unrealistic. Only a comparative few honestly believe that religion has the task of redeeming politics and therefore has

3

its own inescapable and uncompromising political aims informed and guided by a Divine design for ultimate human harmony.

Religion has not in fact divorced itself from politics; but hitherto it has largely surrendered its redeeming influence. Advocates of the Great Faiths, Hinduism, Buddhism, Judaism, Christianity and Islam, have interfered and some have formed political parties often for unspiritual ends; but they have not acted either independently or in concert to introduce and promote a world order consistent with their noble teachings. The teachings remain, to incite and to baffle, but the religions themselves, judged by the majority of their adherents, stand condemned out of their own mouths. Undoubtedly the religions have inspired, helped and transformed many, and to this extent have rendered useful service which has been beneficial to mankind, but they have shown themselves to be incompetent to overcome their competitiveness and to apply themselves unrestrictedly to the welfare of humanity as a whole. Always a declaration of authority has been combined with subservience to procure privilege and self-perpetuation.

It is a lame argument that religion works by changing individuals and that therefore it has to be left to them to change society. On this basis there should by now exist world conditions incomparably better than those which actually prevail. Neither in such progress in certain directions which has been made can it truthfully be said that religion has been the primary cause. It is all too easy to illustrate that religion has continually been a factor which has as much retarded enlightened development as it has sponsored it. By emphasis of personal preparation for an afterlife there has been a tacit acknowledgment of defeat of a comprehensive endeavour to transform the earthly scene. There are religions and religious denominations which do embrace activity to build a world of peace and righteousness, but it is not easy to find one which is pursuing a definite plan to this end. And without a plan there can be no concentration of endeavour.

The question has therefore arisen acutely whether the

religions really speak for God, if God is to be supposed to have a purpose in creation and to be operative in history? Mankind stands in the greatest need of illumination, overwhelmed as it is by the problems which have been multiplied as a consequence of unprecedented advances in science and technology. Plainly the religions, which have spoken much of contact and communication with God, are today without seership. They have received no clear message worth listening to, and are themselves confused by events and the progress of knowledge. Their theology is in disarray: their dogmas are in tatters. Their chief concern appears to be with salvage and reinterpretation so as to find some justification for survival and some means of retaining a hold on defecting and disillusioned congregants. This is a terrible plight in which to be placed. For organized religion it spells out in letters of fire 'weighed in the balance, and found wanting'.

But does God go overboard with his hierophants? This is what the discrediting of antique religious positions conveys to multitudes. Of course there has been a strengthening of an atheistic humanism. Let us face realities, it is said. Let there be an end to mumbo-jumbo. Man has only himself to think of and depend on. Interestingly enough, and indeed significantly, the humanist and that bugbear the communist have espoused the cause of human progress towards the ideal which the religions flinched from. Thus atheism could be said to be closer to the mind and will of God than the theism of his proclaimed devotees. In this upsurge of man's assertion of his entitlement to work and plan for a worthier future it may be that God unacknowledged is speaking very definitely as the greatest revolutionary of all. A God who does not act is an impossibility. It is not only men who will reject such a God: he is self-rejected, and thus we would have the paradox of the Divine Atheist.

The religions are the product of men's quest for understanding of the meaning and purpose of existence in relation to their earthly and celestial environment and to the phenomena of time and space. They have endeavoured to bring the operations of the Unknown within the bounds of at least partial comprehension by systematic conceptions which have involved various kinds of God-theory. In many aspects and representations their findings have been questionable, and this has been demonstrated in the history of religious thought by progressive changes of expression and the discarding of more primitive views. Religious knowledge has followed the same evolutionary road as other branches of knowledge. The causes for particular religious formulations can be determined by the anthropologist and also now by the psychologist. But such science is not equipped to pronounce on the worth of the spiritual inclination, or to judge whether this reaching out from within is idle or the effect of an intentional 'pull' emanating from a higher state of consciousness. All the propensities of man have objectivity, and there is no reason to suppose that his spiritual inclinations are any different. The evidence of our most used senses may assist convictions. This is why we can readily accept now the pull of gravity and the fact that man can communicate with, guide and control his created machines over many millions of miles. But the old adage that 'seeing is believing' is wearing very thin in these days, and nothing could be more absurd than to deny the possibility of Agencies of an indeterminate nature guiding and communicating with man, or to assert categorically that man possesses no built-in equipment for reception. The religions may be very wide of the mark in their creeds and dogmas, but they concur in testifying to the reality of message transmission of a spiritual order.

The religions themselves are no longer essential: they have served their purpose in catering for the spiritual needs of infant humanity. Their disciplines and their myths contributed importantly to the education of the race at the nursery stage. They will continue to be useful to the backward and immature. But what they pointed to in our involvement in a plan and design which called for our existence is still relevant, though we have to take it forward, so to speak, from simple arithmetic to higher mathematics. On this I shall have to enlarge as we proceed. We have to apprehend that we have not dispensed with God, any more than we can dispense with Zero. We will have to exercise more care, however, in stating what God signifies for us, so that we are not furnishing a misguided rationalism with ammunition. I am myself using the term as expressing within the limitations of human competence what man is able to sense and experience of operative Being implicated in all phenomena but inevitably beyond definition and description.

The ancient Israelites made one of the great advances in spiritual thought when they accepted that God must be so totally different from anything in the observed natural order that it was nonsensical to depict or define him, or to suppose that there were any states or conditions of being, as we know it, with which he could be compared. His Otherness had to be taken for granted, and it had simply to be said of him 'I am what I am.'

I must confess that for me, as a Jew, theology has held no appeal. It has never entered my head to want to imagine what God might be like, and as to his existence, doubt would have been ridiculous. I was fully conscious of him, affecting me, illuminating every kind of contact of mind and body, making life almost unbearably exciting. For me, to love and wish to serve God was not just an injunction to be obeyed, it was a profound joy.

This may seem a rather naïve statement of faith, but I have to make it. I would commend what Herberg has written: 'The efforts of contemporary scientists to "prove" that God is to be inferred from the course of organic evolution or the strange phenomena of subatomic physics is on a par with the efforts of the older philosophers to deduce God from the nature of pure being or the requirements of cosmology. These "proofs" are dubious at best, but even if they were to succeed in making their case, it would be a case irrelevant to our purpose . . . If the word "God" is to have any relevance to our problem, we must recognize that God is not a "something" the existence of which can be established by the simple expedient of pushing scientific investigation or metaphysical speculation just a bit further. The very attempt to do so is a mistaken and delusive enterprise, for, at bottom, it treats God as just another object in the world of objects, not as the transcendant Subject who cannot be encompassed within the material of reason and experience. Very much the same may be said of the attempt to "deduce" God from history or the inner depths of the human consciousness, in which, after all, are mirrored our own confusions and limitations. God creates and sustains nature; God works in and through history; in the human mind we come upon something that points beyond itself to the dimension of God—but all this is visible only to the eyes of those who have *already* found and affirmed the God of faith.'[1]

One may take the view, as many are prone to do, that even to postulate God is folly. He is a hypothesis, an invention, to transfer to the Beyond or Above or Around that which is unaccountable to man and which idealises a father-figure which can carry responsibilities and exercise powers which exceed man's strength. Man is thus fortified to contend with his problems by reliance on superior aid: he can make a virtue of his inadequacy manfully to shoulder his own burdens.

This position is perfectly tenable as a recognition that there can be no validity in any attempt to prove God's existence, since what is demanded to be proved falls outside the capacity of our finite minds. Progressive theologians are now disposed to admit this, and accordingly the trend is towards emphasis of the God-within-us. The Christian doctrine of incarnation is given a new twist.[2] Humanist and deist are drawing nearer to each other in concentrating on those faculties in man's make up which insist on both his increasing acceptance of responsibility, in the exercise of wisdom in what pertains to his self-development, and on his inherent compulsion to evolve. In keeping with this, H. G. Wells makes one of his heroes use a big phrase, when he speaks of our race 'moving necessarily in the direction of its innate promptings.'[3]

There are certainly faculties in man's nature which are extra to his normal requirements and which conceivably are related to his betterment and self-fulfilment. The God-within-us view offers only a partial explanation. It does not allow for our being affected by 'external' spiritual influences

as we demonstrably are by external physical ones. As
rational creatures we naturally dislike the idea of the
indeterminate. We wrestle with notions such as time and
space and the multi-dimensional, and find ourselves balked
by the thought of infinity. Thus it is helpful to some, theologi-
cally, to speak of the Absolute or the Ultimate Reality,
because wholes are something which our minds can grasp.
But as Koestler has pointed out,[4] all the wholes we are able
to contact turn out to be subordinate parts, and therefore
there can be no detectable cessation, no eventual finality.
The mystery of Being is endless and cannot be compassed.
As relating to the existence of God whatever may become
explicable will by that very fact contradict that we have
attained access to what Godness may be.

But if it is fruitless to speculate on whether God is or what
God is, it is by no means fruitless to have an apprehension of
what may be described as Godness functioning within the
sphere of the order in which we have a place. Personally, I
am assured of God's being, but what I can experience of that
being is confined to Godness in manifestation.

Provided, then, that we refrain from supposing that what
we can learn about Godness affords any precise information
about God, there is nothing irrational in a God-for-us
concept which Godness conveys. What would be irrational
would be to ignore the abundant indications that Godness is
present and active in the universe. So long as we acknowledge
our limitations and respect that God-for-us has to suffice we
can use the word God meaningfully and legitimately. We
can ascribe to God in this context qualities and intentions,
since through Godness we meet with God in realized activity
in the created universe.

Therefore there is no harm in speaking of the Divine
character and attributes, so long as we refrain from imagining that by such descriptions we are defining Godness. By
such language we may indeed be creating God in our own
image; but this is because we find need to set before ourselves
standards, goals and objectives towards which we must
strive. Idealisation and aspiration are aspects of the Godness
in us. The more we progress in consciousness, it would seem,

the less inclined we are to seek to bring God down to our
level. With increasing knowledge our level is continually
rising and being refined. This is why the old doctrines of
God can no longer content us.

But Godness is never going to be capable of scientific
explanation any more than of theological explanation, since
we can only contact it at our end, a shallow end. Almost
immediately in moving forward we are out of our depth. We
have the impression in the universe of heavenly bodies
receding from us at enormous speeds into space, and
Godness similarly passes beyond our ken. As our capacity is
enlarged we shall penetrate a little further, but it must ever
be only that much of Godness which is within our range
which will become evident to us. Wonders upon wonders lie
ahead as we gain access to more of the secrets of the universe.
Yet even so, as graphically but crudely expressed of old, man
will not have seen more than God's back parts.[5]

There is a multiplicity of questions philosophical and
metaphysical with which man has long busied himself, and
he will continue to do so with increasing lucidity as his
equipment is enlarged, for it is a necessary part of his nature
that he should be a question-asking animal. But even if, as
certain expressions of religion maintain, he can move out of
the physical body into a less inhibited state of being, it will
still be denied to him that he can obtain answers which are
more than fractional and microscopic.

But there is not denied to man in the universe greater
access to Godness, because this would deprive him of all
incentive. Not only has he been endowed with a capacity to
investigate, which argues that he will be benefited and
rewarded by investigation and exploration: he has also been
given the power to employ imagination and reasoning to
pass beyond the boundary of appearances and enter the
realm of concepts, ideas and theories. Through his creative
capacities it is as if he possessed rudimentary Godness. Thus
it is possible that a manifestation of God-for-us could be
responsible for an ungodness partaking of Godness. This
might help to explain what we call evil. Over all, Godness
could be directing and impelling being towards the highest

achievement of Godness of which ungodness through its
participation in Godness is capable. The religions have
tended to be much too specific in their God-formulations,
but they have witnessed to a concern of Godness to aid man
by a demonstration of what it holds out of potentiality, and
lending as it were a boost to man's Godward advancement.

We cannot omit from consideration all that is embraced
by the word revelation. We have to ask ourselves whether
mystical experiences, intuitions, premonitions, flashes of
insight and illumination, would be continual ingredients of
the human story unless man was wide open at some part of
himself to all the mysterious winds that blow, unless he was
equipped with a kind of radar screen which could receive
images and impressions from beyond his ordinarily effective
range? We do know that progressively man has been able
to find and contrive means to supplement, amplify and
extend the employment of his mind and senses, both
mechanically and with the aid of drugs and intoxicants.
Would this be so if there were no requirement that man
should be able to be the recipient of higher instruction and
guidance? We have, therefore, to allow that although man's
ability to interpret must often be at fault for a variety of
reasons it is practicable for him to have more of Godness
and what it calls for imparted to him, and that he is indeed
constituted to acquire it.

This is far from saying that at any time or in any manner
anyone has been put in possession of *the* Truth. Quite
elementary thinking rules out that there can be any such
possibility. The sudden extension of the context in which we
are able to see things, the startling falling of diverse pieces
into place to form a coherent design, may often give the
illusion that truth has been obtained; but we ought to know
that what our comprehension has embraced is heavily
restricted in its validity and conditioned by the particular
texture of our personality. Even in our human relationships
it is virtually impossible for two minds to think absolutely
alike about propositions or ideas which ostensibly they are
holding in common. Every human being is seen differently
not only in the two categories of himself and others, but

more widely in the interior awareness of a variety of selves comprising his personality, any one or combination of which he may disclose in his contacts, and in the impression of him further affected by the individual minds of those associated with him both intimately and remotely.

Since we cannot experience integrity without qualification we are incapable of judging what in a total sense any event or circumstance really signifies. Thus we are not constituted comprehensively to know the meaning of evil and apparently needless suffering, which makes many question whether there is a God, and if there is why he does not intervene. We have to say with Isaiah, 'My thoughts are not your thoughts, neither are your ways my ways, saith the Lord. For as the heavens are higher than the earth, so are my ways higher than your ways, and my thoughts than your thoughts.'[6] We have to exclaim with Paul, 'O, the depth of the riches both of the wisdom and the knowledge of God! How unsearchable are his judgments, and his ways past finding out!'[7]

But we may surely accept that it is not without meaning that we have been equipped with certain powers of judgment and appreciation, so that we can be moved by feelings of love and compassion, conduct ourselves with altruism, and create for ourselves standards which reflect ideals of perfection. There does enter our consciousness, to whatever cause we may attribute it, that we are being prodded in the direction of a nobler conception of what is worthy. The road ahead may be far longer, more beset with perils, than the more optimistic suppose; but the driving force in man insists that he pursue it at all risks and costs because it is in his nature to aspire to greater achievements and greater happiness. The deist asserts that these propensities are not due to blind chance, and he is able to conceive that man originated on earth by Divine design for the accomplishment of a purpose which ultimately will come to fruition.

Humanists will readily allow that man is a purposeful animal, that he thinks things and does things to obtain results, end products of his activities, that he has a considerable foresight and imagination which enables him to plan, frequently quite effectively and on a major scale. They will also allow that man is deliberately selective, and to a degree can make choice of what appears to be for his best interests and welfare, not only as the outcome of experience and experiment, but also in visualising what has never previously been tried, by operating a creative faculty. What atheists and many humanists are not so ready to entertain is that these characteristics suggest that there is a purpose for man which has been predetermined. Consequently evolution is treated as if it were a process which is fortuitously working its own way out rather as a stream finds its way to the sea, getting over and round obstacles in its path, recruiting strength from tributaries, gaining increasing volume and capacity to advance.

This would be a tenable interpretation of the circumstances only if man with his developed consciousness had no inkling of where he wanted to go, had no desire to lend purpose to his existence. We could then say, as Wells did, that our race was 'moving necessarily in the direction of its innate promptings.' But even so evolution in our case would have ceased to be blind as a stream or a worm, and would be governed by intention rather than chance. How and why is man being prompted? We cannot dismiss that man is both a purposeful animal and a religious animal. There is ample room for discussion of the factors which have shaped man's convictions, but it cannot be denied that he has believed himself to have been put in possession by spiritual intimation of some knowledge affecting his destiny.

The experiences of man have taught him that effects are attributable to causes and that ends are achieved by means. There is a reason why things happen. Continually he has added to the causes he has been able to discover, and to the means he has been able to employ. Sometimes his hypothesis of the nature of a cause has proved to be incorrect and has had to be revised or discarded in the light of further information. Similarly, a means has been found to be inadequate and a better one has had to be devised, or a new end has called for a novel means.

The natural inference, therefore, is that as well as within

man's intelligence so beyond human intelligence there is
operative planning power responsible for all phenomena, for
there are vast areas already known to man in which objectivity uncontrolled by man is evident. This objectivity
appears to be exhibiting and exercising qualities which we
associate with mind, and individuals can sometimes recognize its intervention in their own affairs. This happening is
not susceptible to the explanation of chance or coincidence.
Additionally, through those channels termed psychic it is
conveyed to us that what we have called God-for-us, in
whatever form it may present itself, has definite intentions,
and that our species in one element of its make-up is responsive to what this 'mind' wants. We are linked with its
requirements as by a spiritual umbilical cord, by which we
imbibe inspiration and instruction and can be motivated to
predict or to work for objectives which are not directly
dictated by anything which has come under our consideration; which may indeed be contrary to our views, desires,
and believed interests.

We are familiar with the fact that in our universe there
are plenty of exceptions to the rules, and that human
behaviour is among them. Exact science does not function
in many connections, and certainly does not apply to what
anyone is going to think or do in his conscious state, because
man has a higher degree of autonomy. Of course man can be
conditioned and controlled to a considerable extent, for
example by hypnosis and brainwashing, so that he obeys
directives where his will has been subjugated. The brain
gives directives to the body, and the child gives obedience
to parent or teacher. But even so, in no instance is there
absolute dictatorship. We have, therefore, to be very careful
not to ascribe to the Godness with which we are in contact a
dictatorial authority, so that willy nilly its commands must
be obeyed. An ungodness has been generated which militates
against automatism, and predestination is not in conflict
with free will.

John Macmurray has explained the position in this way.
'God acts in history as Creator of Man. The intention of this
creation is known—a universal community of persons, with

freedom and equality as its structural principles of relationship . . . And since God cannot fail to realize his own intention, this will to community is necessitated. But if man is to
be free to will freedom, he must be free to reject it . . . May
not this rejection go on for ever, and result in the final
destruction of man by man? No. This is impossible. The
negative will can never destroy the positive will, since it is
sustained by the positive. The will to community is the real
will of Man; its rejection is unreal . . . The negation is
necessarily limited.'[8]

   The proposition for which I am arguing is therefore this:
first that Godness is at work in our universe, and secondly
that this work involves a plan for the accomplishment of
which our active cooperation is essential. In so far as this
plan affects mankind it is progressively being revealed, so
that it may come to have for us a character and intention
with which we have identified ourselves as if it were our own,
and as if it arose directly from our experiences as a race. We
are being both wooed and equipped to carry it out, and our
time sense is not a factor in determining when fulfilment will
take place. Individually and even sectionally we can opt out
or retard, though allowance will have been made for this.
What man cannot do is to prevent the plan's realization,
because in the end he will have been won to bring it to pass.
God's will must be done on earth, since of man's own free
will it will inevitably become his own will.

NOTES AND REFERENCES

   1. Will Herberg, *Judaism and Modern Man.*
   2. The incarnation stories in all religions are myths, but the Christian
version has sublimity and a strong emotional and didactic appeal. To
regard it, however, as coming within the sphere of a real and unique
happening is to indulge in unwarranted literalism.
   3. H. G. Wells, *The World of William Clissold.*
   4. Arthur Koestler, *The Ghost in the Machine.*
   5. Exod. xxxiii. 20–23.
   6. Isa. lv. 9.
   7. Rom. xi. 33.
   8. John Macmurray, *The Clue to History.*

2

Towards the Theocratic

THERE is complete clarity in my own mind that I have been given insight into what has now to be done in accordance with the Divine Plan for mankind. I could, therefore, proceed immediately to set out the details without concerning myself with any further preliminary discussion in support of my contentions. But I do not regard this as desirable. I see reason as necessary to the acceptance of revelation, as the means by which we become able to discern that what is designed for our good makes good sense. Since it is we who have to carry out God's will for us our intelligent assent is essential. A God who reveals is not the same as a God who dictates. We may not previously have entertained what has been brought to our attention, but when it is presented it must appeal to us as not less right than if it had originated purely as a result of our knowledge and experience. The course of action suggested should not be felt to have to rest for its implementation on the possession of a religious conviction. It ought to commend itself as advantageous no matter where it came from, though faith can assist vision and comprehension.

I do not see Godness as despotic, but as motivating man to seek fulfilment of himself in a manner which corresponds to an intention for him. The process has been twofold, calling for the equipment of man with the desires and capacities to work towards his destiny, and a Divine feeding-in progressively of information conducive to man's coming up with answers to his problems. In the past it was not as easy to apprehend this intellectually as it is today. We know now something of the programming which operates in the natural order, and our own skills have enabled us to do many things comparable in character to what religion had asserted of the activity of God. We have not only devised machines capable of doing our bidding: we have equipped them with a built-in power of response. We take programming in our stride, and think nothing of communicating over great distances, transmitting voices and visual images.

Thus our science is drawing us nearer to the ways of God with man. A major effect of evolution so far as man is concerned has been his increasing competence to discover the secrets of nature, its component elements and modes of operation. Armed with this knowledge man has been enabled to produce articles, substances, applications of natural resources in almost infinite variety which his requirements called for. Man has been invested with imagination and constructive abilities which have conferred upon him a creativity of his own. But he can make nothing for which nature has not supplied the essential ingredients. The building blocks were there aeons before man appeared, and without them he would have been helpless.

We see, then, functioning in man a delegation of qualities of Godness which has made him independent to a degree, but not to an extent which could procure for him more than a very limited detachment from the physical. He can change his physical environment with remarkable facility, but cannot create for himself one which is totally unphysical.

Among the great characteristics of the human being are his developed self-consciousness and the measure of autonomy conferred by it. Consequently he has been enabled to assume a control over much in nature which constitutes a radical departure from the pattern of the animal state. It is as if another source of authority had begun to manifest itself on earth as soon as evolutionary progress permitted. While animality is still operative in man and necessary to him, qualities of a higher order have progressively assumed direction. There has been brought into play at man's level a boosting factor which indicates that to what we commonly think of as natural resources we have to add another dimension which may be described as spiritual resources, and which have raised man above the animal kingdom while not divorcing him from it. The being of man has demonstrated the existence of these spiritual resources, otherwise he could not be the creator he is, and given evidence that he has already some access to them as well as to the natural resources of which he is principally aware.

It is man's spiritual equipment which has taught him how to put questions and obtain answers, and how to penetrate ever more deeply into the area of ideas and abstractions.[1] It is the same equipment which has enabled man to realize that just as he is receptive to communications in the sphere of his normal contacts so is he also to communications from beyond their range.

Let us look briefly at the subject of history. In modern times this has been expanding with quite extraordinary rapidity. It has had to include social, economic, religious and cultural developments, as well as political. It has pushed back the frontiers of the so-called historical period by thousands of years, while also filling in many of the gaps in our information. At the same time it has had to move out to sweep into its concerns the prehistoric, all that relates to the emergence and advancement of man, to the evolution of life on our planet, to the formation of our planet and of the universe around. All the multiplying sciences are playing their part with the records they are able to discover and read in revolutionizing our understanding of what the experiences within the framework of the narrower idea of history really signify.

It is as if we were exploding into a time-dimension which affords us an increased facility not only to look back much more meaningfully, but also to look ahead. The area which we are beginning to be able to survey affords possibilities which could not previously be envisaged for guiding and controlling the future. In the past it might appear, so far as we were concerned, that things were just happening to us; but now we are beginning to acquire the power to draw history in the direction of conscious choice. That power previously was largely latent, employed to a limited extent and by a relative few. Its serious and systematic exercise is now becoming one of the *musts* for mankind. From our new vantage point we have to discern what we are looking at, how we are looking at it, and what we are to look for. The revelation to ourselves of our world in a whole sense, to which has now been added its visual image by cameras directed from outer space, is giving us a new perspective.

It is beginning to be possible to see the present as extending indefinitely backwards and forwards, as the spectrum extends into the infra-red at one end and into the ultra-violet at the other. In seeking understanding we are as much compelled to become time-travellers as adventurers into space. Spiritual thinkers of old obtained some impression of what was to be discovered in postulating a succession of ages, which some identified with the Earth's progression through the signs of the zodiac. We are now placed where Pisces merges into Aquarius, and according to this interpretation each age is distinguished by the characteristics of its ruling sign as the parts of the spectrum are distinguished by their colour.

There is great complexity in the observable movement in Time, as J. W. Dunne showed in his books *An Experiment with Time* and *The Serial Universe*. According to Dunne, we are both individual observers and also part of a composite observer representing all men. 'The picture you draw shows the real world in its relation to yourself—shows, that is to say, how the world is capable of affecting you. If drawn as the composite effort of many observers, it shows how the physical world is capable of affecting Mind in general. The most important fact which emerges is that you prove to be the immortal part of an immortal composite observer.'[2]

Through capacity for composite observation we have the potential to become increasingly identified with 'Mind in general'. As a consequence the Godness affecting us and our recognition of what is called for can move towards agreement. We are being given the benefit of drawing upon the vision of 'an immortal composite observer' with whom we have an individual and corporate relationship. We must not, of course, equate the collective mind of man with Godness, for our 'Mind in general' is itself subordinate to Mind in the spiritual sphere with its infinitely greater powers of observation. As our 'Mind in general' can be affected by the physical world, so also is it capable of being affected by the spiritual world, and thus being no passive onlooker but having a hand in what is happening, willing it in the direction of destiny.

It is, therefore, not inconceivable that an overall Plan can exist simultaneously with lesser planning which apparently could defeat it. In this case, in the end, what may seem shortsightedly to be adverse and negating would be shown to be a contribution to the Plan's achievement. 'All things work together for good to them that love God.'

The more attuned the individual observer can be to 'Mind in general' the better prospect he has of comprehensive understanding, though much will still be blurred. And the more spiritually conscious he is the more he should be able to grasp that a Plan is in operation. This heightened consciousness was anciently attributed to the Divine spirit coming upon the seer. Mystics and people under the influence of certain drugs have had the experience of a state in which it has seemed that in a blinding flash the whole riddle of the universe was resolved. We have many records of individuals who have found themselves detached from their physical bodies, able to look at what was happening while they lay unconscious or in trance, and even to visit and see what was going on in places far away. Persons in mortal peril have had their life story unfolded to their minds almost instantaneously in the way we can speed up action in a motion picture. We should, then, be able to allow that history may be far more meaningful and purposeful than is commonly supposed.

It cannot be denied that we do allow our minds to range with great rapidity over a series of happenings which took hundreds of thousands of years to accomplish, and in so doing we perceive much more of their significance. As one illustration among many we may think of man in relation to his tools.

The tools employed by primitive man were initially things used just as they were, bits of stone, wood, skin, bone and sinew. But in time he was chipping and carving and shaping them, and tying different things together, to create real tools made or adapted to serve specific purposes. With knowledge of the use of metals and of certain principles of mechanics man was enabled to evolve in increasing variety actual machines with elementary articulated structures which could be manipulated to perform needful functions and thus augment man's control of nature and his capacity to diversify and extend his own activities and way of life. Later man learned about dynamics and could endow his machines with power within limits to operate themselves: something corresponding to being alive was communicated to them, and they could become capable of movement by self-propulsion and of internal self-adjustment. The consequence was the increasing mastery by man of time and space. The stage was reached when the machine could be equipped with sensory organs and some of the characteristics of a brain. Electronics and cybernetics are still in their infancy, but machines can now do many things in many respects more effectively than their creators. Will they ultimately constitute a challenge to man's own sovereignty?

Looking to the future it is therefore clearly demanded that man himself should evolve further to assure that he is a step ahead of his creations, so that they do his bidding, and not he theirs. He has to move up into a region to which he has an access which they do not have, and utilize the higher power thus conferred to bring them into conformity with purposes that makes them only instruments for good. There is a parable here, which could be repeated in other connections, such as the meaning of the evolution of society.

Pierre Teilhard de Chardin has put the position in this way: 'When we consider the increasing compression of elements at the heart of a free energy which is also relentlessly increasing, how can we fail to see in this two-fold phenomenon the two perennial symptoms of a leap forward of the "radial"—that is to say, of a new step in the genesis of the mind. . . ? A new domain of psychical expansion—that is

what we lack. And it is staring us in the face if we would
only raise our heads to look at it.'[3] Surely the need for such
an expansion is now underlined in red as we contemplate
the awful weapons we have contrived for our self-destruction.
We have now lifted off into space. Why should we not also
advance into the spiritual?

Evolution takes place because nature has both the urge
and the capacity to meet the challenges of existence and in
so doing to produce forms of life of greater complexity and
competence. Environmental changes have contributed some
of the stimuli, and there have been many other factors.
Proverbially, 'necessity is the mother of invention.' The
subject of stimulation crops up continually in modern
thought, observation and experiment in the quest for better
understanding of behaviour. The biologist offers his findings
from the study of lower forms of life to assist us with our
human problems, and he has been joined by the psychologist.
Undoubtedly there is much in our natural inheritance which
can teach us more about ourselves; but we have also to allow
for the evolution of consciousness through which we are
persons in our own right with an advanced power to make
independent decisions.

There is no need to enlarge here upon the evolution of the
individual and collective consciousness. But the view we are
taking is that such evolution is neither accidental nor
fortuitous, and has been designed to qualify us for greater
participation in a preordained purpose. In the context of a
Divine Plan for mankind selfhood can be seen as a more
acute and complex mechanism for intensifying progress, to
ensure not only that the process of becoming will not be
halted, but that it will gain momentum by the garnering and
sharing of more knowledge and corporate experience. It
enables the will to survive and improve to take the form of
conscious effort and organization. Selfhood has to keep the
ball of development in play. Otherwise both for the individual and for the institutions he creates rigidity and fossilization
would set in, and they would be out of the running.

For collective selves, whether religious or political,
evolutionary progress is much harder to maintain. The

inclination to stand still is greater by reason that some creed or code is deemed to be of permanent validity. The tendency is to emphasize conformity. Revisionism becomes a crime, and those who challenge the system have to be suppressed. But the wind of change does not cease blowing. The rigidities have to be broken up by new thinking and new awareness. Persons have to arise within the community to counter the inflexibilities of governments and priesthoods with their monolithic and monopolistic attitudes. 'Who art thou, O great mountain? Before Zerubbabel thou shalt become a plain.'[4] Real progress is ever the work of enlightened and forward-looking minorities, and not of any mass of humanity. The principle of natural selection is against remedy by mass movements, a fact which we find it extraordinarily hard to face with our emphasis of the power of numbers.

Far back in the days of the primeval monsters we have a glimpse of this principle in operation. We may see how a concentration on defence, the creation of barriers, hardening and crystallization is a sure sign of decadence. 'He that will save his life shall lose it.'[5] With the dinosaurs and other gigantic armour-plated creatures of the mesozoic the Life Force had nearly spent itself. The future lay with the insignificant, unprotected, unregarded little creatures, ancestors of the mammals, nimble, alert and sensitive.

Gerald Heard has shown how the principle has continually applied. 'As among all animals, as again among all mammals when at last they dominated, so now when man of all animals and all mammals alone dominates, the same process of selection is at work among his races and stocks. The vast majority, we must expect, will specialize, play for safety and security, defend themselves—even more than against their fellows—against the intolerable strain of persisting in sensitiveness, in awareness, in sympathy and understanding. They will shut down, and from being defensive become offensive and finally parasitic and so extinct. One strain will find the more excellent way and seeming to be set on losing its life will alone gain it.'[6]

The static is forever overcome by the dynamic, the mailclad giant Goliath is defeated by the nimble unprotected boy David. The feeble plant breaks through the concrete. The wind and the rain and the flowing water wear away the massive rocks. Solidity and security spell out death. Life is with the free adventurous pioneers, with those who are born of the Spirit.

The way of the Spirit has to mean that the world is to be saved not by the many but by the few. If this is so, it affects fundamentally our whole consideration of the manner and method by which mankind can be brought into harmony and peace. 'Perhaps,' writes Vera Brittain, 'you feel that a minority so small, surrounded by powerful forces so adverse to its growth, is unlikely ever to achieve its purpose of leavening the lump. But you must remember that nearly all the great revolutions of history not only started as minority movements, but seldom became anything else even when they had succeeded . . . In the same way the movement to abolish war is likely not only to begin, but to end, as the achievement of a minority which ultimately persuades the majority to adopt its view. The elimination of war and the building of permanent peace differ from other great movements for the liberation of humanity from the evil within itself, only because the sphere of action is so much wider and the problems involved far more complicated.'[7]

The dynamic behind individual and minority action must always be a spiritual one. It is the super-sentience that comes from alignment with the purposefulness of evolution that lends daring to the weak and insignificant. It is the keener perception of the meaning of the contrasts and conditions of life which strengthens the fibre of human beings for further adventures. The ends of the self have to be unselfish. The development of self-consciousness would be a blind alley, as with so many cults, unless it is understood to be the athletic training of the soul-force for direct and active involvement in promoting the welfare of mankind.

What happens to the individual, with man as with lower forms of life, has to be discerned to be of contributory consequence. The individual has to count in relation to other individuals, to the collectivity, especially as with man the realization of brotherhood is vital to a preparation for further evolution. We have to get past teaching which accentuates the personal and group ego as if this was an end in itself. Selfhood is indeed consequential as the instrument for agitating the mass and moving it forward towards the fulfilment of the purposes of Godness. We have to treat the soul or personality as achieving its function within those purposes, and in our world individually and in combination as augmenting the prodding of mankind towards its goal. Primarily consciousness is aimed at intensifying the potentiality of participation by the continual transformation of the present-passive into the present-active at all stages of growth. The superiority of man lies in his enhanced faculties by which mind-force and soul-force has supplemented and will in due time supersede brute-force.

The pressures of the next stage of evolution are already beginning to be felt, and attitudes which prove incapable of adaptation to the new conditions will decay and ultimately disappear. Inevitably there will be opposition and resistance on the part of those whose attitudes are being replaced. They can and will fight to maintain their status and authority, and those who belong to the New Age will have to exercise their qualities to reduce tensions and the destructive effects of conflict. They will require constantly to remind themselves that 'the wisdom from Above is first of all impartial, then peaceable, reasonable, persuasive, laden with mercy and beneficial fruits, free from favouritism and insincerity. For those who make peace the fruit of righteousness will be sown in peace.'[8]

What is called for on our part is therefore a more acute consciousness. We have the equipment for it, but hitherto it has been exercised by very few. It is at this crucial stage in our evolution that it has to begin to function more comprehensively and successfully by the application of a boosting agency which can furnish the appropriate stimulus. One of its effects has to be a more enlightened love of humanity, a personal identification with all mankind. Our dichotomies and our preferences are utterly alien to the Godness which has to manifest through us.

The road ahead would be neither bleak nor uncertain if

we had accomplished that identification. As Lionel Curtis
wrote: 'No society can learn to think of itself as a whole
which does not believe in its own future. Still less can it
realize its own capacity for improvement and the structure it
ought to attain, and so work on a plan. The growing confusion of the world is due to this failure, and will only be
ended by those who face the question where it is going or
ought to go. We talk of planning as the great panacea; but
intelligent planning can only begin when men have asked
and answered the question, what is the ultimate structure
they mean to attain for human society? It is only by reference
to such a conception that the steps which practical statesmen
are taking from day to day can be judged. No political
science can guide men far on their journey through life
until it can say what is the goal to which the journey should
lead.'[9]

To think concretely in terms of the whole, especially as
regards ultimates, is one of the hardest essays in imagining.
Who can tell what life will be like even in a few more
generations? But we can know what ought to be the principles governing our relationships. If we have the right
attitude towards our fellows we can direct our policies away
from segregation and segmentation and programme them
for the attainment of harmony and peace. There is our goal,
and to plan for its realization becomes practicable as we are
able to apprehend more of what Godness requires.

Across all the barriers and artificial distinctions spirit
must call to spirit. This spirituality that is more than us, and
is in each of us, we inescapably share. In the ultimate it is
upon this that we build and plan more complex relationships, and which gives us a title and incentive to do so. We
shall wish more and more to revolt not against what is
different, and can so easily be deemed to be hostile, but
against our own limitations. Whatever is narrow and
sectional in our programme will be relegated to second place
in our esteem and allegiance, and what is comprehensive and
universal will be promoted to first place. We shall become
more civilized, that is, more expressive of the Spirit in
organization for community.

Some people, who regard themselves as evolved personalities, dislike organization and favour anarchy. That is because in human experience organization has often brought with it dogmatism and repression. But antipathy to all organization is a failure of understanding. Nature teaches us that inorganic life is rudimentary and unevolved, lacking a high degree of sensation and power of participation. The more life develops the more highly organized and complex does it become, and with correspondingly greater attendant risks to itself and all about it. By the conversion of instinct into will the capacity for harm is magnified a thousandfold, and it is only by conversion of self-will into the will of the Spirit that the capacity becomes one of infinite good. Again and again there will be partial failure through the weakness of the flesh; but failure will not be complete. Some lessons will have been learned leading to improvement and adaptability in performance. *Per ardua ad astra.* The anatomy of a brave new world cannot be modelled on a jellyfish.

Arthur Koestler makes much of hierarchic order. 'A part,' he says, 'as we generally use the word, means something fragmentary and incomplete, which by itself would have no legitimate existence. On the other hand, a "whole" is considered as something complete in itself which needs no further explanation. *But "wholes" and "parts" in this absolute sense just do not exist anywhere,* either in the domain of living organisms or of social organizations. What we find are intermediary structures on a series of levels in an ascending order of complexity: sub-wholes which display, according to the way you look at them, some of the characteristics commonly attributed to wholes and some of the characteristics commonly attributed to parts ... The members of a hierarchy, like the Roman God Janus, all have two faces looking in opposite directions: the face turned towards the subordinate levels is that of a self-contained whole; the face turned upwards towards the apex, that of a dependant part. One is the face of the master, the other the face of the servant. This *"Janus effect"* is a fundamental characteristic of sub-wholes in all types of hierarchies.'[10] Of course, so far as we are concerned, no apex, no full stop, can ever come into

sight. Always there is a Beyond. But for our Earth and all that
is upon it there must be a termination when their purpose
has been served. What is important in the existence of
hierarchic order is that its presence does afford some
evidence of purposefulness. We can therefore make the
assumption that our own purposefulness reflects a more
comprehensive purpose which is in operation, testified to in
nature, and which has a bearing on our human development
and human affairs.

What we can observe should accordingly not impart to us
a feeling of helplessness, as if we were no more than puppets
on a string, or alternatively create in us an arrogance, as if we
were wholly in control of our destiny. We are obliged to rule
out both chance and an arbitrary determinism, and have
more consciously to quest for insight into a higher planning
in which we are directly involved as progressively more
competent, responsible and active partners. We have to move
up in the direction of a greater grasp of superior policy and
what is required for its implementation.

Slowly we are beginning to realize this, beginning to grasp
that our sectional concerns have to be subordinated to a
greater wholeness. This is where revelation comes in at our
level of consciousness. Revelation is frequently experienced
when suddenly, whether in sleep or wakefulness, a solution
has been obtained to a problem which has baffled us. A
variety of circumstances may have been instrumental in
pushing the right buttons in our brain, but the answer was
there when the data were correctly assembled as a meaningful whole. What has appeared to be essential to getting
results was the direction of the self towards the idea of
wholeness, or its becoming involved in a whole which
brought the subordinate parts into relationship.

We have, of course, to distinguish between problems. We
could only expect to receive adequate solutions to those
lying within the sphere of our human capacity for comprehension. The more exact and familiar are the facts we have
to go on, the more likely we shall be to obtain correct
answers. If the programming has been wrong the result will
be faulty.

Revelation is something that really takes place because of the coordinating resources upon which man is able to draw. The idea of greater wholeness is embraced by these resources. Consequently the practical possibility is there for man in his great need to acquire the insight which can enable him to solve his social and political problems. What is called for is that some part of mankind should bring to its thought a care and concern which is inclusive, and by a deep desire for the welfare of all obtain revelation of a more excellent way to promote the attainment of a united world.

Obviously we cannot look to the generality of statesmen and politicians for universalist solutions. Where there is power-seeking, sectional interests and loyalties, the requirements are lacking to produce ideal policies for the good of the whole. The failures of the United Nations, as of the League of Nations before it, have been due to the fact that only to a very limited extent has the collectivity of the members concentrated on the well-being of all peoples everywhere without bias or discrimination. Something beneficial has emerged only where the impediments did not intrude too formidably, where mutual interests were able to prevail.

Evolution is bound up with the idea of greater wholeness because it represents a continuing expansion into the more complex: the hierarchic system operates in it. Revelation begins to make its appearance as evolution advances far enough for unconsciousness sufficiently to give rise to consciousness. Consciousness itself is evolutionary, and in its activities has added spiritual selection to natural selection. At the level of man selection works more positively as a choosing as well as a being chosen. An element in evolution has been a change of environment and of living conditions. Progressively with man there has been both a choosing of environment and the creation of environment, so that an adaptation of the conditions of living has been in evidence even more than an adaptation of man himself to them. Through the capacity to draw upon spiritual resources, man has been enabled to be much more selective on his own account. His consciousness has been extended by increased knowledge and application of knowledge. His awareness of

greater wholeness has accordingly grown both spiritually
and materially. But a selection not entirely of man's devising
has nevertheless continued in operation in that with certain
individuals and groups a faculty to perceive a wider and
deeper meaning in wholeness has been apparent. In advance
of the rest of mankind there is always the more sentient
minority.

We have considered revelation as the experience of
phenomena becoming suddenly meaningful when we are
devoted to discovering their significance. To solve our
terrestrial problems, therefore, we have to be in a state
which gives access to their solution.

We cannot, however, get into that state without genuine
desire, and in mundane matters part of the evidence of that
desire is that we should reach out to wholeness by giving
value to everything conceivable that is pertinent to the
problem. We have to seek to identify with the whole.
Naturally, some will be more ready for this than others,
and in the scheme of things will be chosen because in certain
respects they are more ready and thus have in a sense chosen
themselves. But their fitness does not imply that they have to
be powerful or peculiarly meritorious.

The question then arises, whether in man's experience of
revelation there is operative a Divine intention which
enables him—and is meant progressively to enable him—to
participate more consciously in bringing the purposes of
creation to fruition?

Answering the question affirmatively, we should be able
to discern in the sphere of history the dawning comprehension of a design of Godness for mankind which has been
communicated. And not only so. We should, with the backing
of what we learn, be able to receive an indication of how we
are to proceed towards the implementation of that design.
Religion, notably in its expression in the Bible, has certainly
asserted that revelation has been given to this end.

John Macmurray has stated the theocratic thesis in these
terms: 'The knowledge of God and the knowledge of history
are inseparably bound up . . . To think history as the action
of God is to think of it as the realization of the intention of

God. Since God is absolute it is nonsensical to think that his intention in history will not be realized. For this reason any statement of what the intention of God is in history is also a statement of what *will in fact be realized* in the future. Thus the spiritual understanding of the will of God for man (which is what we represent as an "ethic") is *ipso facto* an understanding of what will happen to man in the future— our "apocalyptic". The two are one and the same, necessarily. But what is wanting to complete the picture of religious knowledge is the connecting link between the two—the understanding of *how* the intention of God in history is being realized. Until we know this we cannot partake intelligently in its realization. At the most we could allow God to use us, without understanding what was happening to us. The master-servant relation would be the only possible one. But that would mean that we did not ourselves act and could not ourselves be responsible agents. The attitude of complete submission to orders which it is not for us to understand is an effort to will away our own wills, not an effort to bring them into harmony with the will of God. It is indeed a subtle way of refusing to accept the will of God by which we are persons.'[11]

This is a legitimate argument if we guard ourselves against speaking of God too glibly, as if we know exactly what Godness is and how it works. It has been the error of Christian theology that it has been too much concerned with revelation as the means by which God communicated knowledge of the character of his own Being. There is nothing within man's experience which could permit him to know what, as to his nature, God is. God 'is what he is', which no human could fathom or represent. We can only glimpse God-for-us as this concerns us.

What men have deemed to be the self-revelation of God qualitatively is the progressive raising of the standards of man to the heights man is intended to attain as he is able to perceive them, and attune him to the recognition of God as Sovereign of the universe.

Arthur Cohen, explaining the views of Abraham Heschel, emphasizes that 'the Hebrew Bible discloses the history of

God's concern for man. It is not, as disengaged criticism would have it, a document of man's efforts to record, texture, and sophisticate his apprehension of God. "The Bible is primarily not man's vision of God, but God's vision of man. The Bible is not man's theology, but God's anthropology, dealing with man and what He asks of him rather than with the nature of God." What the illuminated man, the prophet, experiences is consciousness of being exposed to the presence of God, an awareness of being called upon.'[12]

What is open to us, in questing for what we have to do for our own good, for what is the will of God for us, is to dispose ourselves to be receptive to what God intends. The solutions to our human problems exist: they are there in the Divine Plan for mankind. But we can find out about them only as we are tuned in to what God wants, as we expose ourselves through our own longings and positive concerns to being 'caught up' into a dimension which can to a degree survey humanity from the commanding position of a Godness outlook, and become invested relatively with a Godness insight.

Since there is in us a propensity to govern it is our business to acquire the art of it by becoming more aware of its intrinsic requirements in the light of our apprehension of Godness. To this end it devolves upon us to become better acquainted with the significance of much more than the sciences bring within our range. The call of our blood is to adventure and to pioneer: it must be discerned to be also the call of our spirit, and we have to dare to let it pursue its promptings in the spiritual medium, confident that what is learned will contribute effectively towards the illumination of our down-to-earth affairs.

NOTES AND REFERENCES

1. See Arthur Koestler, *The Act of Creation*.
2. J. W. Dunne, *An Experiment with Time*.
3. Pierre Teilhard de Chardin, *The Phenomenon of Man*.
4. Zech. iv. 7.
5. Mk. viii. 35.
6. Gerald Heard, *The Source of Civilization*.

7. Vera Brittain, *Humiliation with Honour*.

8. Jas. iii. 17–18. Schonfield's translation in *The Authentic New Testament*.

9. Lionel Curtis, *Civitas Dei*.

10. Arthur Koestler, *The Ghost in the Machine*.

11. John Macmurray, *The Clue to History*.

12. Arthur Cohen, *The Natural and the Supernatural Jew*, expounding the thinking of Abraham Joshua Heschel in *God in Search of Man, Man is not Alone*, and *Between God and Man*.

3

In Fear and in Anger

IF a Divine Plan is operating in human history, this is of much greater consequence for mankind than the utmost wonders of scientific discovery. It would be a tremendous thing if we could have intelligence of a purpose at work in our affairs; for then there would no longer be doubt and darkness in our minds as we survey all the grim tokens of our folly and inadequacy, and contemplate the awful perils which beset us. We would know that man will win through because it is intended that he shall by a Godness which cannot be gainsaid.

The proposition is one which emotionally we would wish to accept. It is so much more satisfying than that which deems us to be the product of a blind and blundering activity of nature giving rise to higher forms of life quite irresponsibly and motivelessly. For us the notion of belonging somewhere by right is very real, to have home and family and a place in the scheme of things. We have pity for the lonely and the outcast, and for those whose life is mere aimless existence, or who by accident or sickness have substantially been shut out from participation in what life has to offer. Deprivation of hope is a terrible condition. And so just to be whirling briefly in an awful void on a minute speck of cosmic dust with no Being who cares a damn is a horror from which instinctively we recoil.

But is our reaction more than an emotional response? Can we have evidential conviction that what we can equate with

Intelligence is at work? There are arguments which can be used, such as those I have employed in the preceding pages, which favour an affirmative answer. There are noted religious thinkers who have made outstanding contributions in this connection. Yet it must honestly be said that there is widespread uncertainty. Doubt and denial have not been overcome. To have assurance, most of us need to be persuaded not by theology and metaphysics but by a very realistic perception of how the asserted Plan can be demonstrated to be in action.

Men have never willingly been unbelievers. The history of religion shows how passionately men have been ready to believe. But the increase of knowledge of the universe has progressively made untenable theological propositions based on notions of the scheme of things which have been discovered not to correspond to reality. One by one the props which supported faith in the Divine have been knocked away, and the considerations which formerly seemed to guarantee that all was well because God was there now appeared to tell heavily against any such consolation. What was there left to make existence tolerable? Only, so it could be argued, an atheistic humanism. Man without God must still go on trying to cope with his problems, not merely out of sheer desperation or because it seems the sensible thing to do, but because inwardly the acceptance of defeat is inadmissable.

Saying this, however, are we not still in a backhanded way acknowledging a spirit in ourselves which savours of the divine? Otherwise would we continue to strive manfully and altruistically, and devote our energies to the pursuit of ideals and noble causes? If man's unconquerable spirit sometimes falters in moments of despondency, does it not readily revive? Is it no more than a reflex action when people sing out defiantly, 'We shall overcome'? Self-preservation is a natural instinct; but we are equipped to ask ourselves, to what end should we trouble to preserve and to improve ourselves? The very fact that we set before ourselves goals and standards which we consider to be worthy of our utmost travail points to a dimension of consciousness which embraces far more than merely a will to survive. Our motivations are not just

animal and physical: they are spiritual as well. We are
persons, which means that we are much more than bodies
with certain chemical constituants. We have powers and
purposes which extend into the unknown. We have meaningful relationships in the present, and contemplate and plan for
a future we shall never see. There could be much more to our
being than as yet we know, linking on to higher states of
being, and atheism can only be maintained by wilfully
ignoring what it finds inconvenient. It has to sit tight within
its three-dimensional world, affirming its disbeliefs while
movement goes on into areas waiting to be further explored.

Admittedly, pragmatic atheism with its narrow range
could plead some justification in opposing facile religious
dogmatism. In many respects the contradiction has been
obvious to the openminded that assertions regarding the
nature and activities of God involved incredible inconsisten-
cies, so that it often appeared that man was capable of be-
having better than the God he was invited to worship.
Of course, at the heart of the religious attitude of mind there
has ever been a sense of a realm of Spirit which was there for
contact, for guidance, help and inspiration. But organized
religion and systematic theology, especially in claiming
custodianship of mysteries and authority to define and
prescribe, tended continually to make the jewel in the lotus
inaccessible and to pander to human ignorance and credu-
lity. The elevation of Godness and its debasement were so
intermingled as to offer inducement for total rejection.

It was impossible that Godness in its profound Otherness
and superiority could reflect qualities which men had learned
to regard as inferior. The ancient Greeks tired of gods and
goddesses who were lustful, quarrelsome, envious and
vindictive. Their philosophers took refuge in converting God
into little more than a convenient symbol covering the
operations of the universe. What was left to man were his
ideals, his virtue, that at any rate he might be happy, living
and dying with nobility, courage and dignity. What else was
there, except withdrawal or heedlessness, a demand to 'Stop
the world. I want to get off'?

Rationalism and dropping out of the running can be

understood. There are those who are self-sufficient and those
who cannot put up a fight. But for the generality of men it is
repugnant that they should be alone and unaided, play-
things of a capricious fate. They have insisted that there are
Powers able and ready to lend their superhuman strength to
supplement man's own resources and effect his deliverance.
Godness can and must come to the rescue.

The ancient mythologies are not necessarily devoid of
truth; but in what man has expected of God there are grave
drawbacks. It has been desired of God that he should take
short-cuts to get results, that he should exercise autocratic
power benevolently and deal summarily with injustice and
iniquity. He should not be able to tolerate what man finds
intolerable. The idea of Divine incarnation incorporates the
demand for a short-cut. In man's impotence God must take
the law into his own hands and intervene decisively in
human affairs as redeemer and deliverer. 'He saw that there
was no man, and wondered that there was no intercessor;
therefore his arm brought salvation unto him.'[1] In versions of
the ancient myths he is sown in weakness and reaped in joy:
he appears as feeble man and yet is revealed as the unconquerable captain.[2] The teaching of Christianity remains
akin to that of the national or hero-god who performs
marvels to save his people in their extreme need when they
call upon him.

The belief is not readily given up that God is there to
perform miracles. Much of the argument between sceptic
and believer is still occupied with this issue. The believer will
not be denied his miracles. For him they do happen no less
today than of old. He can point to evidence of this. What is
wrong in his position is not his conviction that there are
spiritual resources which circumstances can and do bring
into operation—though attributing them to particular
persons or divinities arises from individual religious affiliations—but his assumption that wonder-working is the
special function of Deity, which may be delegated or conferred, and which determines that God exists.

Faith, though not to be despised, is at a very low level
when God means primarily the supreme performer of

magical acts, and it is not greatly enhanced when accompanied by the affirmation that God is Love and consequently that all the actions are beneficent. For at once there arises the concept of the Great White-Magician who, if he is to be worth his keep, ought to be employing his power to transform the earthly scene like the Good Fairy in a pantomime. Everything by this time should have been lovely, the poor and the suffering relieved, and the arrogant and selfish toppled from their seats. On an arbitrary power basis, God being Almighty, the persistence of evils and the martyrdom of man does not make sense. On this basis the sceptic feels fully justified in discarding a God who is so heedless and insensitive that he does not use compulsion.

It is no come back to say that the power of God operates only where faith is present, and that faith itself is a gift. For why could the gift not be bestowed universally so that all would benefit? No, we are told. Each must come forward to accept it, and no one is compelled to do so. This neatly puts everything back in square one. Man has to request what God has to offer. Otherwise he cannot be a beneficiary of God's charity. This is offensive to human dignity, and invites no esteem for a God who will not open his purse unless men beg.

So there is a dilemma. Either there is a God who could do things for men but deliberately refrains, waiting to be asked properly. Or there is no such God, and men must act for themselves. In which case how are they to obtain the competence to act wisely?

Of course we do not have to be impaled on the horns of this dilemma. There could be an alternative if we are able to rid ourselves of our power-complex. As yet this complex remains in the forefront of our thinking. We are bedevilled by the attraction of the proposition 'ye shall be as gods.' Our gods mean the exercise of mastery. So we have Great Powers, politically and economically, mass-power, military-power, money-power, white-power, black-power, student-power, etc., etc. Yet it should be evident that very rarely has despotism gone hand in hand with pure and comprehensive benevolence. Said Lord Acton, 'All power corrupts. Absolute power corrupts absolutely.' The 'gods' who have been placed in the seats of power have proved no better than those whom the Greeks placed above them on Olympus, betraying many of the same undesirable qualities. Man's inhumanity to man has been intensified by the recognition that while having magical means to transform the earth into a paradise the 'gods' have employed their awesome might to wage war more destructively, to persist in reckless conflicts, and to aggravate disorder, so that fear and anger have arisen in those who are threatened.

Let us by all means join the atheists if the gods we make for ourselves are conceived as power-wielders and miracle-workers. One of the contemporary 'gods' has given expression to this sentiment: 'The seizure of power by armed force, the settlement of the issue by war, is the central task and the highest form of revolution.'[3] We have not come very far in our apprehension of Deity if this is what it means for us. There is still very little realization that those who trust in power put themselves in bondage to power, and that to dominate is deadly for those who wield dominion. To meet power with power, and force with force, is no way of salvation: it is the way of slavery for both victor and vanquished. A true God, and those who worship him, should not have the disposition to use the lightning and the thunderbolt.

Fortunately for us God is not man magnified X times, otherwise our plight would indeed be desperate and our human race could well destroy itself. Neither at any epoch has he conformed himself to the terms and conditions of our existence. It is by opening more of his realm to our spirit that he is providing us with the capacity to bring our realm into conformity with his Spirit. If we are a long way yet from reaching the goals of our implanted aspirations it is not because we have been neglected and forsaken, but because we have not yet learned enough of the manner in which God works in us and through us to do what he intends for us.

'Not by might, nor by power, but by my Spirit, saith the Lord of hosts.'[4] It is in the Godness which embraces 'the spirits of all flesh' and which therefore sees history as the process of becoming Sons of God that we have to find that which moves us towards greater perfection.

'As I see it,' Olaf Stapledon has written, 'the thing that is
dawning on us is simply a new purged realisation of the
"spirit". . . . The spirit, the spirit, the spirit is the essential
thing in us. Everything else in us is but a confused, drowsy,
somnambulistic approximation to the spirit, the fully awake
and coherent spirit which each one of us at his best and in his
own particular style of living hesitantly manifests . . . In an
important sense there is something about it far older even
than the human species. Of course, man's apprehension of it
did not begin before man began: but the truth itself, the *fact*
which man's idea can never more than vaguely, misleadingly
express, is far older than man, older than life on earth, older
than the stars, old at least as the cosmos itself. This great fact
is involved in the very stuff of our bodies, which is at bottom
identical with the stuff of the remotest stars and galaxies.
For in the very substance of our bodies, and therefore of the
stars, it is implied that ultimately the way of life must be the
way of intelligence and love and creative action . . . It is the
essential nature of man, and therefore of any self-conscious
and other-conscious species, to grope toward ever clearer
feeling and conception of this truth. To say this, believe me,
is not to indulge in fantasy or groundless faith or wishful
thinking. It is plain commonsense . . . We must feel the unity
of the spirit in all its diverse modes. Only in this way can we
avoid being passionately faithful to one aspect of it while
betraying the rest. We must feel its identity also in all human
beings, its identity underlying its manifold, lovely, particular,
personal idiosyncracy in each man and woman.'[5]

It would be foolish to say that nothing has been learned in
the course of human history except greater skills and insights
into natural processes. There have been advances in thinking
of what is right and just and what is held to be worthy, and
there has been progress in the sense of personal and corporate
responsibility and the duty of mutual aid. The ideals of
peace and harmony have continually spurred us to fresh
endeavours. Many of our challenges to authority have
sprung from our feelings that what we are pleased to call the
Rights of Man have been inhumanly violated. If we have
been unduly impatient, and sometimes restlessly aggressive,

it is because we are intensely conscious of our mortality. It does not satisfy us if we cannot see results. Often we have used the wrong means to achieve good ends because of our haste. Possession of power offered the possibility of taking short-cuts, and the temptation to seize it has proved too great to resist.

What has been most difficult to learn is that God does not work under our pressures, so that he is obliged to perform miracles and intervene in a positive manner by direct action. When we take this view, which is inherent in incarnation doctrines, we are saddling him with our own time-consciousness and limitations. We have not been prepared to allow that what we have supposed would speed things up might well be retarding them. It has been well said that without faith we could not exist, we could not carry on. But now it has to teach us more of the ways of Godness, so that we have the certainty that in our affairs a Divine Plan is functioning, not independent of us but through our instrumentality. In that case, also, it must be practicable under guidance of God's Spirit in us that our information of what this Plan calls for should be augmented.

Such knowledge at this critical period of human history would be an enormous asset, for those who possessed it would be stimulated to look very differently at the problems to be overcome and thus be in a position to perceive what actions they must take to solve them.

I may here recall how at the beginning of the second world war the International Consultative Group of Geneva deliberated on the 'Causes of the Peace Failure 1919–1939.' The Group did not neglect the spiritual factors, and reached this conclusion. 'As it becomes increasingly evident that the crisis of Western civilization is in the last resort a spiritual crisis which is due to the absence of great common and compelling convictions, and that none of the ideologies which are at present in control can pretend to be able to bring about a true integration, men everywhere are searching for a new universalism. It is rightly believed that international society has become so interdependent that it will only be able to live in a harmonious and orderly fashion if

some fundamental common convictions concerning man and
society are held by all nations, however different they may
remain in all other respects ... The gravity of the present
situation is precisely that, humanly speaking, we do not see
how our disintegrated civilization may come to a new
unity.'[6]

Must we then say that when a cry of man is raised because,
as H. G. Wells expressed it, we humanly find *Mind at the End
of its Tether*[7] there is no possibility of any response: the signal
reaches nowhere and is unanswered? If so, then we are
flying in the face of the long and overwhelming record of
spiritual experience.

It is true enough that many have been put off by the out-
dated notion that God is located somewhere in space. We do
now have to think of Godness differently, and only by being
ready to do so can we learn more of how this activity
operates in our sphere. In our cosmic studies we have long
ceased to be impeded by antiquated ideas of a flat earth or a
geocentric system. So why should we be retarded in our
spiritual growth by ancient theological representations?

We have therefore to believe that the answer to our cry
was there before our problems arose. God is not conditioned
by our time sense, so that he goes along with us from day to
day making decisions and taking action as circumstances
occur, with, so to speak, his life running parallel with ours.
When we say that God hears and answers this has to mean
drawing by ourselves to ourselves the spiritual resources
which are available to us. If, then, our hearts are set on a new
universalism we shall be made aware of what it will call for
to achieve it. We shall be introduced to the reading of history
which will enable us to become associated with God's
intention.

To ask for what is best for us and for all humanity is to ask
in accordance with God's will, and in the manner and to the
extent that God's will can be done by us so will it be revealed
to us what we should do. It may be a dramatic image to see
man defiantly shaking a clenched fist at a brazen and
impotent heaven, but such an image has no justification in
reality. To employ it we have wilfully to ignore all that is

intuitive and creative in our composition, and the whole history of ideas and discoveries.

It would be foolish to deny that there has been a correspondence between needs and the finding out of the means to meet them. The operations of nature were going on millions upon millions of years before man appeared on Earth, but only as man developed a greater complexity of organization and requirements has he been able progressively to learn about them and utilize them. The chief moments of individual discovery have been those when a problem was pressing acutely on the mind or external conditions and circumstances created an urgent necessity. It has also been the periods of great social change which have been most productive of new thought. It is when the established order is shaken, and there is doubt and uncertainty, that fresh propositions have emerged to seek to deal with the situation. It is only a step further, but a vital one which faith has to take, to conceive of a Divine Plan in which provision has been made to give us enlightenment when we make claims upon it in our sore distress.

It may be asked, what difference would such a belief make to the worth of the ideas which present themselves as solutions? If what is concerning us is the state of world affairs and we are questing for a new universalism it must make a very substantial difference. It would no less make a difference in personal affairs. The difference would arise from our attitude of mind. A genuine turning towards God would involve on our part an acute desire to see things from a God-ness viewpoint, free from selfishness, enmity and discrimination. If our desires should be contaminated by dislikes, hatred and self-interest, what we will come up with will be at best palliatives and at the worst the replacement of the evils we wish to remedy by other and perhaps graver evils. This is why, as the International Consultative Group of Geneva put it, 'none of the ideologies which are at present in control can pretend to be able to bring about a true integration.' Any idea which carries with it the use of force or coercion, lying and misrepresentation, or the favouring of any group, party, section, state or race to the hurt or detriment of any others, is

thereby excluded from the possibility that it can furnish any
true and comprehensive solution, for none of these things
could enter into a Divine Plan.

It may be pleaded that none of us is perfect, so how can we
hope to obtained a perfect answer to our problems? We
cannot hope to do so. But we can try to obtrude our in-
firmities as little as possible by directing our minds towards
the ideal. In this way we could expect to learn more help-
fully what would contribute to the common good. We would
be moving in the way of the Spirit in our own time and
generation within the limitations of what has so far accrued
to us of knowledge and experience. The requirements of the
Divine Plan could only be imparted progressively and
selectively, in the way evolution functions, as human
consciousness extended and developed. We are aware how
some men in their apprehensions have been in advance of
their time while yet conditioned in many respects by the
circumstances and the knowledge of their time. Of this order
have been the prophets and reformers and often the scientists. But we could not in general catch up with their insights
until conditions were ripe for these to register sufficiently to
be acted upon. Because both our problems and our conscious-
nesses are now attaining world proportions, and we can more
readily look backwards and forwards, it must be more
practicable for us to discern what the Divine Plan requires of
us at this stage, since on the one hand the desperation of our
situation demands such a revelation and on the other hand
our equipment better prepares us for it.

A fact to be observed is the very considerable engagement
of thought with a philosophy of history, the attempt to discover from man's story taken as a whole, united with the
study of trends, what is its purport and what must be done to
promote mankind's future well-being in every aspect of
individual and corporate life. There have been periods in the
past when there has been an explosion of interest in universals, but with our predicament and obsessive fears of self-
extinction it has become magnified and intensified as never
before. We know what it may mean if we fail to find the right
answer, and in the young especially there is an upsurge of

almost uncontrollable anger against the stupidity which has placed their future in such jeopardy. Most pitifully they will go along with any creed that preaches revolt, or alternatively become apathetic or seek the stimulus of drugs, or live it up to get the most out of the fleeting hours. For the most part they are not turning to religion, since that is discredited as belonging to the system which has landed them in such peril. Yet still there are those of all ages and backgrounds who are earnestly seeking illumination and remedy, and who shall say that there is nothing to encounter which can give it to them?[8]

But where shall they go for guidance? Obviously not to any doctrine which turns away from history, since it is in the sphere of the historical that the remedy has to be found. It has to be discovered what we must do to be saved, here rather than hereafter. And this means going to the Hebrews, the people who beyond all other peoples have held before mankind that there is a Divine Plan operating in history to which they are witnesses, and which assures that ultimately the world will come under God to peace and harmony.

NOTES AND REFERENCES

1. Isa. lxiii. 5.

2. 'For it became him (i.e. God) . . . in bringing many sons unto glory, to make the captain of their salvation perfect through sufferings' (Heb. ii. 10). 'And it came to pass, when Joshua was by Jericho . . . behold, there stood a man over against him with his sword drawn in his hand: and Joshua went unto him, and said unto him, Art thou for us, or for our adversaries? And he said, Nay; but as captain of the host of the Lord am I now come' (Josh. v. 13–14).

3. Mao Tse-Tung, *Problems of War and Strategy.*

4. Zech. iv. 6.

5. Olaf Stapledon, *Beyond the 'Isms.*

6. *International Conciliation,* published by the Carnegie Endowment for International Peace, No. 363, October, 1940.

7. This was not the last word of H. G. Wells, but the title of the last book published in his lifetime. It expressed the author's anxiety that man might prove unequal to what was required of him.

8. See Norman Mailer, *The Armies of the Night* (New York, 1968).

4

Messianism

THE quest for a new universalism cannot be conducted in a vacuum. It can be pursued effectively only in the context of historical experience, and only as that experience is viewed as an evolutionary discipline. We readily accept history as evolutionary in relation to the sciences and to various branches of knowledge. We love to trace the development of this and that 'Through the Ages'. But when it comes to the grand view of history taken as a whole we tend to jib at the implication that its progress is significant; for then it would appear that necessarily it has been going somewhere, making towards some greater attainment, some fulfilment which would justify the succession of experiences. If we were to admit this we would have to think of the story of man as part of a plan, which it could only be by bringing God into the picture. If history has meaning and purpose it is because what we have described as Godness is at work.

'An authentic conception of history,' writes Berdyaev, 'was foreign to Hellenic consciousness. Its origin must be sought rather in the consciousness and spirit of ancient Israel. It was the Jews who contributed the concept of the "historical" to world history.'[1] Leading on from this, Herberg points out that 'the Hebraic mind, as we find it in Scripture, sees all history as a great and meaningful process under the control of the God who is the Lord of history . . . History is of one piece, a single great drama, under one Lord: thus emerges the idea of the unity of history as *world-*

46

history. Because history is under the control of God, it has purpose ... God's ends are effected with time, in and through history; the salvation that is promised as the ultimate validation of life lies indeed beyond history but it lies beyond it as its fulfilment and consummation. It is conceived not as the negation of time but as a "new time" in which historical life will be redeemed and transfigured. From this point of view, earthly history takes on a meaning and seriousness that are completely absent where the Hebraic influence has not been felt. But above all it is the sense of the future that creates authentic history ... With this living, vital sense of the future, the true idea of history is born.'[2] This sense, as the author states, was the product of the Hebrew prophets. The prophets were the first authentic 'philosophers of history'.

But the Hebrew vision of the future, except for some extravagant millennarians, was not directed to the unattainable and purely imaginary. It concentrated upon an outcome of history which could be deduced from the traditions and records of past experiences and aspects of the contemporary situation. Primarily, therefore, it concerned itself not with unpredictable ultimates, but with what was requisite to rectify what had gone wrong and had moved away from the potentiality to proceed towards what was equitable and could legitimately be required by God of man. Thus it heavily underlined social and political behaviour with reference to a God of righteousness, justice and compassion, and foresaw the rule of God *of* the world being endorsed by man's conformity with its character *in* the world. Thus the Kingdom of God would come on Earth because God's will would be done there. That would be the climax, but not the finale, of history.

The Hebrews could have their conviction of the unity and purposefulness of history only because of their faith in God, a God who was the Father of all mankind. It was this faith that lent to history both coherence and meaning. But what was implied went very much further than history just happening along lines of evolutionary development. Man was not going to advance inevitably towards his goal in obedience to an innate prompting. His much higher degree of autonomy called for guidance and illumination so that consciously he would choose to follow his star because he was convinced that it was in his best interest to do so. Progressively man needed and was entitled to know what was proposed for him so that he could cooperate, and to be advised of what provision had been made to assist him towards success. There must be increasing access to the Divine Plan, and insight into its *modus operandi*.

We may ask, then, was it only fortuitous that the Hebrews should have arrived at 'an authentic conception of history'? Might it not be that they were given it so that the Divine Plan for mankind could be promoted through them? It could be, as so many who are not Jews have believed, that the mystery of Israel holds the key to the solution of the problems which face us today.

'The history of Israel,' says Joseph Jacobs, 'is the great living proof of the working of Divine Providence in the affairs of the world. Alone among the nations, Israel has shared in all great movements since mankind became conscious of their destinies. If there is no Divine purpose in the long travail of Israel, it is vain to seek for any such purpose in man's life.'[3]

The whole Jewish story is so strange, so exceptional, that no secular interpretation of history can adequately explain it. The Jews have been a perpetual challenge and rebuke; so that no society bent on self-aggrandisement and acting with intolerance and injustice has been able to stomach them. Their otherness, their confident assertion of Divine claims upon them which made them necessarily different, has been a constant irritant. Always and uniquely as a people they have moved through time as enduring the present for the sake of the future, a future which was to be not only their vindication but that of all mankind. Their only imperialism was to claim the world, not for themselves, not for any partisan interests, but for the God who made it, to whom it rightfully belongs.

A Jew, therefore, could write naturally in terms of objectives unlike those of normal national self-expression. 'When the harp of Judah sounded, thrilled with the touch of inspiration Divine, among the echoes it waked in the human heart were those sweet sounds whose witcheries transport the soul into the realms of happiness. That melody has been our source of courage, our solace and our strength, and in all our wanderings we have sung it. It is the music of the Messianic age, the triumph-hymn to be one day thundered by all humanity, the real psalm of life as mankind shall sing it when Israel's world-task of teaching it shall have been accomplished. Its harmony is the harmony of the families of the earth, at last in peace, at last united in brotherhood, at last happy in their return to the One Great Father.'[4]

A dweller in many lands, a citizen of many states, the Jew who is true to his Jewishness must above all other earthly loyalties be a world citizen. His whole outlook and ideology identifies him and his hopes with the whole world community. If we are to insist that the existence of a Divine Plan for mankind must be demonstrated, then it is to the Hebrews that we have to turn, for it is their tradition, their understanding of history, which peculiarly and specifically affirms this proposition. They alone have the heritage which can enable us to carry out a test.

But we do not merely have to thumb through the ancient records noting what presented itself to the minds of other ages. Their prophetic insight could see certain things in their time under the conditions of that time. Accordingly, they spoke in the name of the Lord, giving out what they saw. But we have to look at the spirit of what was said, at its basic implications, and not be so foolish as to treat prediction as if it was forecasting exactly what was going to happen in time to come, so that literally and automatically it must be fulfilled. This would be a denial of man's God-given autonomy, and reduce faith to the level of superstition, which the prophets themselves declaimed against.[5] What they discerned was the movement in history, where and to what ends it would lead, and what intention was indicated by the processes of change and the means to effect them. We can now, looking back, find in what they said both things which they could not fully appreciate and things which they inferred mistakenly. All inspiration has to be mediated through the

personality of the recipient, and how it is projected can thus
be influenced by it. We have to seek a conspectus, which does
not exclude high-lighting distinctive features which are
revealed.

If we are to give a name to the Hebrew 'philosophy of
history' that name must be Messianism, and if we wish to
be more definite about Messianism we may describe it as the
science of the Politics of God.

It is pertinent that in our present time of crisis the consideration of Messianism has greatly increased. This in no
small measure is due to the eschatological element in
Christianity, which seems to chime with the catastrophic
state of world affairs. Second-Adventist belief has extended
beyond sections of the Christian Church to adherents of other
Faiths. But on the whole both Jews and Christians are without
any positive Messianism which directs their activities. Since
Nazism the Jews have been primarily concerned with
survival, which has largely directed concentration of effort in
creating and maintaining the state of Israel, while the
Christians have chiefly been wrestling with their theological
problems, also with the objective of a new coherence which
would save Christianity from extinction.

Here I would like to quote Father Lev Gillet, a very
perceptive Christian thinker of the Orthodox Russian
Church, who specially devoted himself to the Messianic
question. These are his words.

'The Christian attitude in relation to Messianism is rather
strange. Christians believe in a personal Messiah. Notwith-
standing this belief, they are far less Messianically-minded
than the Jews. Their lack of Messianic consciousness takes
two forms. They have largely lost the sense of Jesus' Messiahship. And they have, largely also, lost the Messianic vision.
The Greek name *Christos* means "anointed" and is the literal
translation of the Hebrew *Meschiah*. Now the idea of the
Anointed is a specifically Jewish idea. It fell decidedly into
the background when Christianity left its Palestinian home
and became a Gentile religion ... Christians who think or
speak of Christ almost always forget the Semitic word and
the ideas which this name translates; in fact, they forget that

Jesus is primarily the Messiah. The very idea of Jesus'
Messiahship has passed away from their minds ... Having
lost the original sense of the word "Christ", Christians (or,
to be exact, most of them) have also lost the Messianic
vision, i.e., the expectation of the divine future, the orien-
tation towards "what is coming" ... It is true that an
important revival of eschatology has recently taken place in
theological thinking, but this revival has hardly affected the
Christian masses and their practical piety.' He goes on to say
that 'nevertheless, a real "Messianic communion" would be
possible between Jews and Christians if both were inspired
by a common Messianic hope and expectation ... And
perhaps more easily than through the medium of thought,
this "Messianic communion" could express itself through
the way of practical cooperation of "life and work." Much
could be achieved by Christians and Jews messianically-
minded and acting together.'[6]

What we have to consider, then, is that the world problem
appears to be without remedy essentially because the two
basically Messianic Faiths, Judaism and Christianity, have
largely opted out of their Messianic tasks and responsibilities. They have become self-centred, and have no words
of comfort and inspiration for mankind because they have
lost track of what positively they were supposed to be doing.
They now have their last opportunity to return to their
mission, which involves their coming together as a single
entity, not by the fusion of two religions, but by reunion as one
People of God. If they should fail to do so, this will not
frustrate the Divine Plan, but it will mean that their part in
it will be transferred to those who give evidence of response
to its demands.

The dichotomy of the People of God goes back to the
early days of Christianity, and was brought about by circumstances and events which I have fully described in my
previous books *The Passover Plot* and *Those Incredible Christians*.
These books have to be read to learn the nature of Messianism as understood and expressed by Jesus, and how the
Church rejected his vision and replaced it with a new
religion in which he was worshipped as God. The Jews also

rejected the implications of Messianism as Jesus had borne witness to them, which called for an outgoing love of all humanity rising above nationalism and the consideration of anyone of any race as an enemy no matter what the provocation.

Reunion will obviously, therefore, be attended by very grave difficulties. Christianity as a religion will have to go, and Jewish nationalism will have to go. There is nothing which can make these changes possible, except the rediscovery of the real character of Messianism and what it can achieve to deliver mankind from disaster. There must come such a passionate desire to help in the manner called for by the Divine Plan that nothing will be allowed to stand in the way. The beginning of the restoration of the unity of the People of God and its reengagement in its appointed function has to be signalized by deep contrition and repentance. Both Jews and Christians have Messianism in their heritage, and thus, if they will it, the capacity to bring it to the fore. They can exercise it, or go on as they have been doing. The choice is theirs.

The ancient vision of the Kingdom of God among men will not fail to be realized, for it has in it a dynamic which can burst through the confines of statecraft and priestcraft, and inspire men to do and dare in the cause of human betterment with the goal before them of a world united and transformed.

But since the vision has for so long been obscured as to what it calls for, Messianism must again be made explicit, so that its requirements for our time can be clarified. In speaking about a Divine Plan we have to know essentially what it is. Therefore we must concern ourselves with its peculiar features and evolutionary development in coming into operation. Messianism takes its name from the Messiah, a Jewish leader who at a certain stage had to make an important and necessary contribution to the progress of the Plan. But the Plan was never centred on him, so that he might be supposed to be the sole and unique saviour of the world. The Plan involved, as we shall see, a long-extended programme, centred on a People of God as the vehicle by which all peoples would be brought into harmony with the will of God. The Messiah for his part, would stand in relation to this people as the people itself was designed to stand in relation to all mankind.

There has been much friction and needless controversy between Christians and Jews, because Jews have tended to emphasize the collective Messiah and Christians a personal Messiah. In fact, the task of the Messiah is to restore his people to consciousness of its Messianic obligations. What the Messiah has to do for Israel is to stimulate its faithfulness to the Divine mandate, the effect of which will be to save humanity. Thus the Messiah does become the saviour of mankind, but through the People of God. The Messiah is personal for his people, and his people is personal for humanity.

The earlier stages of the Plan are reflected in the Bible. It is through this collection of books that we are introduced to its character. In these books at various times men spoke in the name of the Lord, for it appeared to them that what they experienced and what they discerned was due to a relationship between the Unseen and the Seen, between God and Israel. There was a fellowship arising from a choice, a partnership for the fulfilment of the purposes of God on Earth. This is why the contents of the Bible have continued to be electrifying.

> 'Listen! the world is rising,
> Seeking, unquiet, thrilling.
> Awakens the new century
> To new hopes and new visions.
> Men hear upon the mountains
> Strange and life-giving voices;
> Every soul seems to wait,
> And from that Book the signal
> For the new day shall come.'[7]

The Bible stands apart from other Sacred Books of the great religions with its extraordinary intermingling of religion and political history, its world outlook, and its coverage from the dawning to the ending of time. Anciently, there were other peoples of the Middle East who related religion to the march of events; but they did not endure as

Israel and its Bible have done. Comprehensively the Bible came to be regarded as the Word of God.

Unfortunately, with many, veneration of the Bible has gone to the length of idolatry, so that it could not be allowed that it had any fault or blemish, or contained any errors and contradictions. Even today the Bible has a multitude of worshippers, who resent and turn aside from the cogent evidence which has increasingly accumulated that the Bible bears all the marks of human weaknesses and failings. It is not a book, but a collection of books dating from different periods and of varying merit, with many mistakes in the transmission of the texts, and subject to a great deal of editorial activity. Each document in the collection calls for separate study and evaluation. There is much that is legendary and tendentious, and even bogus.

The significance of the Bible does not lie in the false notion that it is the perfect embodiment of unalterable Divine Truth; but in the manner in which there marches through its pages the theme of an unfolding purpose which gives history a meaning. To have discerned that there was such a purpose, so that from generation to generation events were being connected with it and viewed in the light of it, this is what sets the Hebrew tradition apart from other records of antiquity.

Revelation comes in through the perception that One God was at work in the changing pattern of human affairs. Because of God-consciousness there could be assurance that man's destiny was sublime, and that his halting steps were being guided towards it by progressive illumination of the road ahead. It is this recognition which constitutes the Messianic ideology, and it is this ideology which gives the Bible its coherence and its chief claim to fame.

When, therefore, we speak of a Divine Plan we are implying a definite intention on God's part that mankind should come to fulfilment of its destiny, and the manifestation of a means to attain it. Necessarily, the process does not end with the Bible, since we are still a long way from the goal. Neither can revelation have terminated some two thousand years ago. We must be able to know more now than could be detected by any of the prophets of old, more than Jesus in the role of Messiah could see. The validity of the Plan will not have changed, but for its progressive implementation fresh factors will be in operation. Indeed, we must say that the only guarantee we can have that we are not being misled by the Biblical intimations of a Divine Plan is if we discern how it applies in our time and for our time. We must be able to cope with our present predicament in the light of it, and the history of the past two thousand years must be relevant to it.

We must not be conditioned by the partial perceptions of long ago, so that we go to the Bible as if it was exactly fore-seen by its writers what would happen many hundreds of years later. This would be to treat the Bible as an oracular Book of Fate, and it is nothing of the kind. At various times down to the present day people have approached the Bible in the belief that it would enable them to predict the future if they employed some peculiar method of exegesis. By twisting and turning the text they have extracted information to their own satisfaction which could be fitted to the circum-stances of subsequent history. This is a folly highly gratifying to those who lend themselves to it, who only reveal how hard it is to eradicate superstition in human nature. But the real seership we find in the Bible is of another order, in seeking to depict the logical outcome of contemporary policies and behaviour taken in conjunction with what was understood to be the Divine Plan. Where the more remote future was delineated the descriptions were largely utopian, not so much forecasting the shape of things to come as creating images in line with the Plan to be held before rulers and people as ideals and incentives. Revelation does not involve Divine dictation, as we should by now be able to appreciate, but the stimulation of our minds with their diverse capacities and equipment to interpret phenomena, and in an exalted sense to learn something of the will of God.

We have not, therefore, to wrestle with texts as exact and consistent predictions which can be placed in a correct sequence and will automatically be fulfilled at more or less precise times. We have to consider with the Hebrew prophets the great sweep of things, the purposeful onward movement of human history, in its relationship to an agency chosen for the furtherance of God's design.

Messianism first made its appearance concretely in the period of the Hebrew monarchy, a period lasting some four hundred years (from about 1000–586 B.C.). When the period opened the tribes of Israel had only recently achieved the character of a nation and were still rather loosely combined. Under King David a state was created with its capital at Jerusalem. The United Kingdom did not last long, and after David's son Solomon it was divided into the two kingdoms of Israel and Judah. Israel was extinguished in 722 B.C., but Judah continued down to 586 B.C.

The existence of a monarchy and a large measure of religious centralization had the effect of creating a status comparable to that of other sovereignties of the Middle East. Commerce and diplomacy augmented communication, and it became appropriate that the Hebrew kingdoms should now have their own national libraries and archives. This called for a developed literary activity, the writing and editing of records, the collecting of songs, hymns and proverbs, the preparation of histories, the setting down of laws, the keeping of annals of the reigns of kings, the preservation of the utterances of prophets. There were some writings and traditions from the past which were available, and a fund of folklore orally transmitted. There were literary resources of neighbouring peoples which could be drawn upon.

Thus the period of the Hebrew monarchy produced a flowering of literary expression, and a substantial part of what was to become the Hebrew Bible, including most of the material in the books of Moses, took form in this period.[8] When, therefore, we use quotations from the Pentateuch, we do not have to think of them as long antedating the words of Isaiah and some other prophets. Messianic thinking owed much to the position of the small Hebrew kingdoms sandwiched between great powers like Egypt and Assyria. The Israelites found themselves in a world in which might and militancy flourished, a world of pride and arrogance with strong class distinctions.

The Hebrews were unused to the complexities of state-hood, the pomp and the stratified structure of civilizations. They were still in essence nomads, to whom the sophistication of dwellers in great cities was alien. Their inheritance was the code of the wilderness with its simplicity of faith and its concern for every member of the tribe. There was temptation and distraction in the religious and political environment of a settled existence. To be a nation like the other nations had pitfalls and problems which had not been anticipated. The Hebrews discovered that with all their efforts to conform to the prevailing pattern they did not really fit in. Their clan type of monotheism did not square with the mythology and ritualism of their polytheistic neighbours, though they borrowed much from them. In their own tales of the past, which had been handed down, the heroes were not great lords and rulers but people distinguished by a simple piety whose adventures were mainly within the sphere of tribal life and custom. These people as a consequence were much more real, much more genuine human personalities, unmistakably different from urban types, and the contrast is exhibited in their relations with other cultures. The Hebrew stories of Creation and of the beginnings of the nation reflect a refreshingly delightful intimacy with God and an honest appraisal of the behaviour of men.

It was imperative for the Hebrews to have understanding of their place in the scheme of things. Their folk memories when assembled pointed to an answer to their questioning which explained why they were not as other nations. It was because they had been chosen by God to accomplish his purposes in the world. They saw themselves not as better than others, but as making a singular contribution to the betterment of all nations. Power and great wealth was not to be their portion. Their strength would be in their weakness, their glory in what they could teach about God and his ways.

In the times when this Messianic philosophy took shape the surrounding nations were struggling for mastery or forming alliances to combat imperialism. The monarchs of the Hebrew kingdoms were embroiled in these aggressions and intrigues. Armies were constantly in motion; bitter battles were being fought. To the Hebrew prophets it was revealed that this was not what God intended for mankind. A vision far in advance of contemporary imagination emerged, so noble in what it contemplated and proclaimed that men have never ceased to be inspired by it.

NOTES AND REFERENCES

1. N. Berdyaev, *The Meaning of History*.
2. Will Herberg, *Judaism and Modern Man*.
3. Joseph Jacobs, *Jewish Ideals*.
4. H. Pereira Mendes, American Rabbi, quoted in *A Book of Jewish Thoughts*.
5. Deutero-Isaiah, xliv. 25, xlvii. 13.
6. Lev Gillet, *Communion in the Messiah*.
7. *The Bible*, a poem by David Levi, 1846, translated from the Italian by Mary A. Craig. The quotation is of the last verse.
8. See the Introduction to the Old Testament by Professor H. H. Rowley in *A Companion to the Bible*, edited by Dr. T. W. Manson (1950 edition).

5

The Priestly People

THE Bible is something more for Jews than it is for others, since it tells the story of their own ancient history and has preserved relics of their early religion and culture. It belongs to them as it can belong to no one else. Christians regard it primarily as the unfolding of spiritual ideas leading up to the self-revelation of God in Christ, an account of the way of salvation by faith by which Paradise Lost becomes Paradise Regained. The place of the Jews in the scheme of things is seen to be a special one, but necessarily preparatory to the full expression of the means of redemption open to every man. The Old has to give way to the New.

The difference of approach has a bearing upon what Jews and Christians look for and find in the Hebrew Bible, the so-called Old Testament. The one is thinking in terms of a social and political salvation which will bring humanity into harmony, while the other is dwelling on how the individual can be made fit for heaven. Of course the positions are not totally opposed, and in some respects overlap. But the emphasis, nevertheless, is distinctive.

When I read the Bible in my youth, being a Jew, what engaged my interest was the setting out of a Divine Plan by which my people were being schooled for a mission to mankind the achievement of which under a Messiah would one day bring war to an end and unite the world under God. I was a natural Messianist. It was because of this that I came to study and finally to understand Jesus in a way which few

Jews have done, and few Christians also. For me he emerged
not in the terms of Christian doctrine, which betrayed his
Messiahship, but as a Jew who had the root, heart and spirit
of Messianism in him. I was so much drawn to him that I
could joyfully enlist under his banner without subscribing to
the creed of Christianity as I became more fully acquainted
by protracted research with the causes of its errors. It was
the witness of Jesus which put me on the road to comprehension of what Messianism called for in our time, and thus
helped to prepare me for the illumination which came to me
in the vision of a Servant-Nation, which this book has to set
forth as I have been able to work it out.

Following the experience I had, which I have described in
the Prologue, I turned in the first instance to the Bible, and
was rewarded by observing some things which had not
previously registered as significant. My attitude was one of
objectivity. I was well-acquainted with what modern
scholarship and archaeology had disclosed, and not therefore
disposed to indulge in any fanciful reading of the Biblical
records. I gave every attention to the historical situations and
circumstances. So in what I wish to speak about I have
striven to be faithful to available information and avoid
extravagances.

There is something personal about nations. They exhibit
individual self-expression and marks of character. They have
moods. A small nation can think just as highly of itself as a
big one, and have its own ambitions. It can assert a right to
rule others by reason of a superior quality or competence,
and when aggressively it attempts to give effect to its claims,
sometimes deemed to be divinely or ideologically sanctioned,
this is what we call imperialism.

In the Thirties of the present century, which was the period
when I was deeply concerned to obtain enlightenment, there
was widespread anxiety over three outbursts of national self-
aggrandizement. Italy under Fascism was nurturing dreams
of reviving the glories of the ancient Roman Empire, and had
proclaimed an ideology of the state. 'For the Facist,' wrote
Benito Mussolini, 'everything is in the state, and nothing
human or spiritual exists, much less has value, outside the

state. In this sense Fascism is totalitarian, and the Fascist State, the synthesis and unity of all values, interprets, develops and gives strength to the whole life of the people.'[1]

The Germans under Adolf Hitler had produced the *Herrenvolk* doctrine of Nazism, of which Master Race thesis a German Christian theologian could say, 'A new movement, full of life, has broken out in our midst, to which not world citizenship and universal culture is the ideal, but a culture bound up with the people ... What it can contribute in spiritual value it gives best by developing its own inherent culture, which springs from blood and soil, and by killing as poison all that opposes it.'[2]

In the Far East the Japanese enunciated a 'Great Japan World-Teaching'. It was declared that, 'The people and gods who are centralized in the doctrine of *Kodo Omoto* are only working to accomplish this greatest and loftiest task of unifying the world under the sway of the Emperor of Japan ... We are only aiming at making the Emperor of Japan rule and govern the whole world, as he is the only ruler in the world who retains the spiritual mission inherited from the remotest ancestors in the Divine World.'[3]

In the Bible, however, the operation of God in history as the Hebrews saw it was of quite another order. It involved no claim to racial superiority or world rulership by conquest and subjugation. The spokesman of Israel did not parade their people's virtues: they denounced their vices, because these hindered the fulfilment of God's designs for mankind. This people had been chosen, so it was affirmed, not to exercise domination over other peoples, but to lead them to the One God and Father of all mankind. If Israel was discharging its appointed function the nations would voluntarily come to Zion to learn the ways of peace and righteousness.[4]

Looking back from the period of the monarchy, the sages of the Israelites saw in the beginnings of the nation the evidence of a singular purpose, which had first been expressed in a Divine call to its progenitor Abraham to leave Mesopotamia and journey to the land of Canaan. There he was told that he would be the ancestor of a great nation through which 'all the nations of the earth shall be blessed'.[5]

Here long ago a novel concept was revealing itself, that of a nation whose greatness would lie in ministry, in the performance of priestly duties for the benefit of mankind. The concept was emphasized in the word of God to Moses on Mount Sinai, 'Ye shall be unto me a kingdom of priests, and an holy nation.'[6]

Israel was distinguished from other nations as a people *chosen to serve*. Therefore its very preparation for nationhood entailed the bitter experience of bondage to one of the Great Powers of the ancient world. There could be no harder apprenticeship; but it underlined that the service of God is not as the servitude of men, degrading and humiliating: it is manifested in disinterested love. Specifically it was laid down in the laws of Israel, 'Thou shalt not oppress a foreigner: for ye know the heart of a foreigner, seeing ye were foreigners in the land of Egypt,' and again, 'The foreigner that dwelleth with you shall be unto you as one born among you, and thou shalt love him as thyself; for ye were foreigners in the land of Egypt.'[7]

If we look in this light at the economy of ancient Israel we can see in it a structure having relevance to the whole world community. In this structure, which appears in the books of Moses, Israel is depicted as a microcosm.

We learn that out of the twelve tribes of Israel one of them, the tribe of Levi to which Moses belonged, was chosen for priestly duties. To restore the number of tribes to twelve that of Joseph was subdivided into Ephraim and Manasseh, the tribes of the sons of Joseph. Just as Israel was chosen to be a priestly people for the nations, so Levi was chosen to be a priestly tribe for Israel. The pattern of Messianism is foreshadowed in this dispensation, and accordingly Aaron and his sons were *anointed* for their priestly office.[8] Israel is described as God's beloved son and firstborn, and all the firstborn in Israel were to be dedicated to God. But we are then told that in place of these firstborn God took the Levites, who were to perform the service of God in his Sanctuary. Unlike the other tribes the Levites were to have no territorial possession in the Promised Land. 'At that time the Lord separated the tribe of Levi . . . to stand before the Lord to minister unto him, and to bless in his name ... Wherefore Levi hath no part nor inheritance with his brethren; the Lord is his inheritance.'[9]

When the sacred Tent of Assembly was pitched in the wilderness the Levites were to camp around it, while the other tribes were to encamp three to the north, three to the south, three to the east, and three to the west.[10] In this arrangement a Messianic significance can be perceived, in which Levi represents Israel as the chosen priestly people, and the tribes of Israel represent the inhabitants of the world who are being blessed in the four quarters of the earth.

In another passage, Balaam the heathen seer looks down from the hills on the tents of Israel and exclaims, 'Lo, the people shall dwell alone, and shall not be reckoned among the nations.'[11] It is a strange idea this, a nation isolated and distinct from all other nations, having a function which is not theirs and existing to bless them.

To be a holy nation and kingdom of priests, dwelling in a holy land as in a temple zone, sanctified by obedience to divine laws and communicating to mankind God's will in love and righteousness, such was the ancient vision set before the Children of Israel. In these terms was the Divine Plan first apprehended.

What it called for could be absolutely right, but the accomplishment presented enormous difficulties. Israel existed amidst idolatrous warlike peoples, and its contacts and concern for survival exposed it to great strains and temptations. It seemed to be asking too much to be required to be a people apart, unlike everyone else.

We read in the Bible how the Hebrews came to their aged prophet and judge Samuel and demanded a king of their own. They were informed how Gentile kings treated their subjects, and what they were to expect. But they insisted, 'Nay, but we will have a king over us; that we also may be like all the nations; and that our king may judge us, and go out before us, and fight our battles.'[12] The people got what they asked for, but those who reported the circumstances recognized in them a repudiation of God's sovereignty. The

Divine Plan had to go forward, in its texture unchanging, but under changed conditions.

The prophets of old, at the time of the greatest testing of Israel under the monarchies of Israel and Judah, had to admit that for the present there was no prospect of persuading the people to come into line with the function God had assigned to them. Looking back on this period the Chronicler sadly reports: 'All the chief of the priests, and the people, transgressed very much after all the abominations of the heathen; and polluted the house of the Lord which he had hallowed in Jerusalem. And the Lord God of their fathers sent to them by his messengers ... because he had compassion on his people, and on his dwelling place: but they mocked the messengers of God, and despised his words, and misused his prophets, until the wrath of the Lord arose against his people, till there was no remedy.'[13]

If ever the vision was in danger of being blotted out, given up as hopeless and totally unpractical, that was the time for it. How could it possibly have a future in these circumstances? The wail of the prophet Elijah is typical of a mood of surrender. 'I have been very jealous for the Lord God of hosts; because the children of Israel have forsaken thy covenant, thrown down thy altars, and slain thy prophets with the sword; and I, even I only am left; and they seek my life, to take it away.' But the answer that came to him declared, 'I have still left me seven thousand in Israel, all the knees which have not bowed unto Baal, and every mouth which hath not kissed him.'

A mere seven thousand, truly a tiny minority! But such a faithful remnant challenged defeatism: it certified that the vision would not perish. As another prophet put it: 'It is yet for an appointed time, but at the end it shall speak, and not lie.'[14] Clearly, if there was a Divine purpose for mankind faith in it could never be obliterated. Somehow the knowledge of it must be preserved, so that it should come to fruition when a people should be ready to carry out what it demanded of them.

So now the seers began to turn to the emphasis of a new microcosm, the patient, faithful and suffering remnant of

Israel. Their task it would be to exemplify the priestly people in miniature, to nurture the conviction that with the penitence of Israel there would come restoration, and to proclaim with ringing confidence and in sublime language the ultimate triumph of the will of God. To their aid, and indeed as their spokesman and chief exemplar, there would come an ideal king of the line of David the servant of God.

The doctrine of the Remnant was developed after the return of the Jews from the Babylonian captivity. It came as a timely solace and incentive to the disheartened and dispirited thousands restored to their land by the Medo-Persian kings. The chief exponent of the doctrine was Deutero-Isaiah,[15] but it progressed through the centuries that followed, culminating—as we shall see—in a fully fledged Messianism built upon the concept of Elect Messianic persons and the saints of the Most High as the Elect people.

The Remnant doctrine has been described as 'the revelation of Messianism to Society,' and as 'the very opposite of the mass movement idea.' In the words of T. W. Manson, 'The Remnant—which is the Son of Man collective as applied to the residuary faithful—is committed to a present role of service and sacrifice, not as something to be endured until better times come, but as something to be embraced in order that better times may come.'[16] In this respect the doctrine was to advance from the static to the dynamic; but it still incorporated as of yore the belief that salvation was of the Jews.

In Deutero-Isaiah the Suffering Servant of God, a strange and poignant figure, is both individual and collective. The Man of Sorrows is inseparable from the People of Sorrows. 'I believe,' wrote Max Margolis, 'that Israel was chosen by God as His anointed servant to proclaim unto the families of mankind His truth; and, though despised and rejected by men, to continue as His witness until there come in through him the Kindom of Peace and moral perfection, and the fullness of the knowledge of God, the true Community of the Children of the living God.'[17]

What are we to make of all this? The Jews to this day are still powerfully affected by the Remnant doctrine. In the light of it they have endured agonies from century to century, hatred, persecution and destruction, never giving up hope because they knew they were indestructible and that their survival was linked with the purposes of God for mankind. Always before their eyes was the vision of a redeemed world the realization of which would justify the long drawn out nightmare.

But there is another side of the picture, represented by what the Bible also reveals of revolt against being chosen, against having to be a people apart. Whenever opportunity has offered, many Jews have been ready to abandon their Jewishness as an intolerable burden, only to find themselves driven back into it by some external hostility. Rationally, the Choice has seemed to be a myth. Why should Jews remain distinguished from Gentiles (all the rest of mankind)? Of what use to be separate from others just for the heck of it, a living anachronism?

To Gentiles also the continued existence of the Jews has posed a problem, especially since Christianity proclaimed that it had superseded them as the People of God. It cannot help being resented that the Jews should still hug to themselves a claim to hold the secret of humanity's deliverance from its grievous problems. And yet there is unsureness, discomfort. Surely the Jews should be justifying their claim by collective engagement in solving those problems! They have given evidence for a great many aptitudes for individual success in so many branches of knowledge and enterprise; but in these days when it comes to setting up a state of Israel, what becomes of their wisdom and humanitarianism? They behave as badly, as stupidly, as aggressively as other peoples. It is an insult to mankind to pretend any longer that the Jews as a people have any other interest than in being left to go their own way and in being treated decently and without prejudice.

But mankind is not willing to leave the Jews alone while they remain in any way wedded to a special status, to a beneficial purpose for the world which they refuse to put into practice. Antisemitism is not exclusively rooted in the fact that Jews are different, but in the disappointment that they have failed to justify the difference by leading the nations into the paths of peace. The world, as it has seemed, has been left to its fate, victimized by an unfulfilled promise. The Jews gave mankind a vision of what could be, and then retreated from its obligations and rejected what it demanded of them.

But we can look at things in yet another way. There is no getting round that the call to Israel, as set out in the Bible, did not have as its objective the bringing into being of a religion called Judaism. The Divine Plan committed to Israel, as there described, was to be a light to the Gentiles, a priestly people ministering to the nations, communicating and *demonstrating* the will of God for mankind. History records the failure of the Jews as a people to accept responsibility, except for a particular effort to which we shall refer later. But this failure does not imply that the Plan was wrong, only that it cannot be fulfilled until there is a people ready to carry it out. Israel remains as the medium through whom the Plan had its first expression, and should there be a willingness to do so Israel can still be associated with its more comprehensive development today. In the meantime the survival of the Jews has been essential. It has assured that the Plan would be kept alive.

Christianity, which has had its own part in the promotion of the Plan and no less than the Jews failed to implement it, has contributed greatly to the universal circulation of the Bible. But without the living continuance of the People of the Book the Book itself would not have counted for so much. It is because the Jews were there as a present reality that the Bible could be apprehended, not as the dead story of a long dead past, but as a vital force which was always contemporary and governing the future. Jews could be met and watched, abominated or admired, and what happened to them be always of interest, even of prophetic excitement, as a sign and portent. The Church might emphazise the otherworldly, but would continually be pulled back to the earthly purpose of God for mankind while the Jews endured.

They were the emphatic and agitating evidence that the workings of a mysterious Providence in human affairs was no old wives' tale. They were also the inconvenient but salutary reminder that Jesus the Christ was a Jew.

NOTES AND REFERENCES

1. From the Article 'The Doctrine of Fascism' by Benito Mussolini in the *Enciclopedia Italiana*.

2. Kittel, *Die Judenfrage* (the Jewish Question). Communism can express itself in much the same language, and no less find Jewish universalism an obstacle.

3. See Holton, *The Political Philosophy of Modern Shinto*. He is quoting here from the *Taisho Nichi-Nichi Shimbun*, Osaka, 1920.

4. See Micah iv. 1–5; Isa. ii. 1–4, and cp. Zech. viii. 20–23.

5. Gen. xii. 3, xxii. 18, xxvi. 4.

6. Exod. xix. 6.

7. See Exod. xxiii. 9; Lev. xix. 34.

8. Exod. xxviii. 40–43.

9. Deut. x. 8. On the theme covered by the paragraph see Exod. iv. 22; xiii. 2, 12–13; Num. i. 48–50, iii. 6–9, 41; Hos. xi. 1.

10. Num. i. 52–ii. 31.

11. Num. xxiii. 9.

12. 1. Sam. viii. 19–20.

13. 2. Chron. xxxvi. 15–16.

14. Hab. ii. 3.

15. See Isa. xl–liii.

16. T. W. Manson, *The Teaching of Jesus. Studies of its Form and Content*.

17. Quoted from *A Book of Jewish Thoughts*, Selected and Arranged by the Chief Rabbi (the late Dr. J. H. Hertz).

6

The Holy King

THE return of the Jews from the Babylonian Exile bore little resemblance to the great ingathering visualized by the prophets. Their land now formed part of the Medo-Persian Empire, and while they had a considerable measure of autonomy they were not independent. The people were in a subdued mood, and though they gallantly and doggedly set to work to restore and rebuild Jerusalem and the Temple and repair the country's ravages they were all the time conscious of departed glories. Prophets, priests and scribes did their utmost to encourage a religious revival, but the remnant of the nation was too cowed and depressed to make more than a halfhearted response. The circumstances did not favour strong convictions and hopes. The yoke of the Persian rulers was light, and material prosperity not difficult to acquire, but there was nothing to reawaken any collective sense of purposefulness. The old dreams and visions were there in the sacred books, now lovingly collected and edited as a national heritage. Their store was added to by new writings; the Hebrew Bible began to take shape. But the future was very much left to take care of itself.

One century passed, and then another. The Jews were content under internal priestly government. There was interest in literature and learning, cultural pursuits and philosophical speculations. Jewish thought was affected and enriched by ideas from East and West. There was a taking in more than a going out of beliefs. The sense of mission was lulled almost to the point of unconsciousness, and reminders that ahead there lay the great and terrible Day of the Lord went largely unheeded.

From the viewpoint of the movement of God in history this was by no means a barren period. It sparkled with new wisdom, science and human self-expression. Zarathustra and Gautama had made their contributions in the East. Greece and Egypt were mingling their knowledge and their artistry. Jewish horizons were being widened as never before. An expanding and much more communicating world was being created. A narrow tribalism was on the way out.

The Medo-Persian Empire was now crumbling, but it had brought East and West together in a new synthesis. Then suddenly there was the meteoric Alexander the Great with his dramatic conquests and universalistic thinking. Plutarch wrote of him, 'Alexander desired to render all upon earth subject to one law of reason and one form of government and to reveal all men as one people, and to this purpose he made himself conform. And if the deity that sent down Alexander's soul into this world of ours had not recalled him quickly, one law would govern all mankind, and they would look towards one rule of justice as though toward a common source of light.'[1]

Socrates had thought of himself as a world citizen, for wisdom overstepped all national frontiers, but Alexander went further and sought to unite mankind politically in a democratic world order.

The world was far from ready for any such development. But in the context of Hellenism the Jewish vision was turned emphatically outward to embrace an enhanced consciousness of the contribution of other peoples and of what constituted human worth and dignity. This was an age which elevated the idea of virtue in the individual and sought to define the characteristics of the good man. The stressing of ethical values had a great appeal to the Jews, and by reason of it they became eager not only to share with the Greeks their own concepts of man under God, but also to participate to the full in the Hellenic civilization and way of life.

The Jews had supported Alexander, and he in return had favoured them and encouraged them to settle in his domains, notably in his new city of Alexandria. Hellenism thus created for the Jews an enlargement of contacts and a great temptatioi. to believe that the Jewish mission could be fulfilled by a less arduous process than the discipline the Torah called for. Why be a priestly people set apart when being like others offered such opportunity to build a brave new world? There were real advantages in a turning outward if it were not accompanied by the delusion so often entertained down to the present day by believers in the unity of mankind that there was some easier means of reaching the goal than by dint of sacrificial dedication and the accepting of exacting personal responsibilities. Human nature has always been prone to pursue policies that offered a way of escape from the strain of total commitment, and again and again such hopes have been frustrated.

Salvation for mankind can only come about in God's way. It is a way which men want to avoid having to follow if they possibly can, and they are always on the look out for a method which will be speedier, less strenuous and more gratifying. In particular they are hypnotized by the mass idea, since for them the command of numbers means power.

Because their witness had to be maintained, the Jews, therefore, were in for a severe shock. It was delivered by one of Alexander's successors Antiochus IV, called Epiphanes. He took the position that to unite humanity a single universal religion was necessary, and for him this meant the common worship of Olympian Zeus. The land of the Jews formed part of Hellenic Syria, and accordingly he insisted that the Jews must abandon their ancestral faith and customs, and he proceeded to convert the Temple at Jerusalem into a shrine of Zeus. Many Jews conformed, but others refused and suffered intense persecution.

The king's agents, we read, 'built altars in the cities of Judah, and burned incense at the doors of the houses and in the streets. The books of the Law which they found they tore to pieces and burned with fire. Where the book of the covenant was found in the possession of anyone, or if anyone adhered to the Law, the decree of the king condemned him to death . . . According to the decree, they put to death the women who had their children circumcized, and their families and those who circumcized them; and they hung the infants from their mothers necks. But many in Israel stood firm and were resolved in their hearts not to eat unclean food. They chose to die rather than to be defiled by food or to profane the holy covenant; and they did die. And very great wrath came upon Israel.'[2]

In this crisis, which developed in 167 B.C., the priestly family of the Hasmoneans succeeded in organizing armed resistance under the leadership of Judas Maccabaeus and his brothers. The revolt was joined by the puritanical Chasidim, a body of Jewish pietists which had long been denouncing the Hellenising apostates in Israel. After a series of bloody encounters Jerusalem was regained and the Temple purified. But it took many years and much suffering before the Jews obtained not only their religious but their political liberty. The Hasmoneans created a new dynasty which held both the high priesthood and the civil authority, and which achieved its zenith in the reign of John Hyrcanus I (134–104 B.C.).

The bitter struggle triggered off a Jewish religious revival, which I have described in my previous volume, from which I quote the following extract. 'Extremist sects flourished. Loyalty to God and the Torah became paramount, and with this loyalty there was brought to the fore a fresh consideration of what it meant to be the Chosen People. The Law and the Prophets became the subject of acute study to discern the character of the Jewish mission, the circumstances of the Last Times, and the coming of the Messianic Age when all idolatry would be abolished and the nations would be converted to the worship of God . . . From this time the Jews became ardently missionary. Many passages of the Scriptures spoke of the illumination of the Gentiles, and these were now seen to impose upon Jews an urgent and positive role in winning the heathen for God. Devout bodies like the Pharisees especially espoused this cause.'[3]

But zealous and devout as the Jews might be, they still failed substantially in their external relationships. While many Gentiles came through knowing them to become worshippers of God, there were also aroused in many areas strong antisemitic feelings which, perhaps, more active love of all peoples might largely have prevented, or at least greatly modified. There was much emphasis on Divine wrath and judgment, but too little reference to disinterested benevolence and humanity. The Divine Plan called for the ministrations of a Chosen People, but it must be a people with a transcendent love of mankind. This too was written in the Book. The trend instead was to draw acute distinctions between Israel and the nations. The book of Daniel, for example, contrasts the devoted saints of the Most High with the heathen imperialisms. These are likened to ravening brute beasts, while the saints are depicted as one like a Son of Man (*homo sapiens*). To him collectively is given 'dominion, and glory, and a kingdom, that all people, nations and languages should serve him.'[4]

After Daniel there was an outpouring of eschatological literature emanating mainly from the Essenes and Pharisees, filled with exhortations and predictions, and surveying events from the viewpoint of those who regarded themselves as the loyal Elect of the Last Times. As conditions in Judea worsened again in the first century B.C. so did this literature intensify its warnings and admonitions. The rise to power of the Romans, and their intervention in Jewish affairs from 63 B.C., confronted the saints with a new world power and enemy of the Kingdom of God. Accordingly, the propaganda directed to the heathen, prophesying a Day of Judgment unless they repented of idolatry, now singled out the Romans for special denunciation.

Roman sponsorship of Herod the Great as king in succession to the Hasmonean rulers was regarded as another punishment of Israel for failure to follow the way of the Law of Moses. It was just that there should be a new tyrant. The *Assumption of Moses* declares: 'And an insolent king (i.e. Herod) will succeed them (the Hasmoneans), who will not be of the race of the priests, a man bold and shameless, and he

will judge them as they deserve. And he will cut off their
chief men with the sword, and will destroy them in secret
places, so that no one may know where their bodies are. He
will slay the old and the young, and he will not spare. Then
the fear of him will be bitter in the land. And he will execute
judgments on them as the Egyptians executed upon them,
during thirty and four years, and he will punish them.'[5]

The saints insisted that the people's plight was due to
failure to adhere rigidly to the commandments and lead a
holy life. The doctrine of the Remnant was brought to the
fore, a remnant which by obedience to the Torah was
performing an atoning work and making it possible for the
redemption to take place. The situation called for Messianic
personalities, not only to fulfil ancient prophetic words as
now newly interpreted, but because it was felt that only such
commanding dedicated figures could be sufficiently effective.
There was reminder of the perpetual covenants with Levi
and Judah, which promised the emergence of such figures as
the Great Day approached. Especially with the arrogant
Romans dominating the world and their despotic puppet on
the Jewish throne was popular expectation directed to the
advent of a holy king of the line of David, who at the climax
of history would convert Israel into a holy nation and in the
name of God take control of world affairs.

So by the Jewish propagandists the *Sibyl* was made to
announce, 'But when Rome shall rule over Egypt, though
still delaying, then shall the great Kingdom of the immortal
King (i.e. God) appear among men, and a holy king shall
come who shall rule over the whole earth for all ages of the
course of time.'[6]

A description of the holy king is given in the pre-Christian
Psalms of Solomon, where it is said of him, 'And a righteous
king and taught of God is he that reigneth over them (the
Jews); and there shall be no iniquity in his days in their
midst, for all shall be holy and their king is the Lord Messiah.
For he shall not put his trust in horse and rider and bow, nor
shall he multiply unto himself gold and silver for war, nor by
ships shall he gather confidence for the day of battle . . . For
he shall smite the earth with the word of his mouth even for

evermore . . . He himself is pure from sin, so that he may rule a mighty people, and rebuke princes and overthrow sinners by the might of his word. And he shall not faint all his days, because he leaneth upon his God: for God shall cause him to be mighty through the spirit of holiness, and wise through the counsel of understanding, with might and righteousness.'[7]

The concept harks back to the Old Testament, where we find in Isaiah, 'And there shall come forth a rod out of the stem of Jesse, and a branch shall grow out of his roots: and the spirit of the Lord shall rest upon him, the spirit of wisdom and understanding, the spirit of counsel and might, the spirit of knowledge and of the fear of the Lord; and shall make him of quick understanding in the fear of the Lord. And he shall not judge after the sight of his eyes, neither reprove after the hearing of his ears; but with righteousness shall he judge the poor, and reprove with equity for the meek of the earth. And he shall smite the earth with the rod of his mouth, and with the breath of his lips shall he slay the wicked.'[8] He would be a second David of whom it was said, 'I have found David my servant; with my holy oil have I anointed him: with whom my hand shall be established: mine arm also shall strengthen him . . . I will set his hand also in the sea, and his right hand to the rivers. He shall cry unto me, Thou art my Father, my God, and the rock of my salvation. Also I will make him my firstborn, higher than the kings of the earth. My mercy will I keep for him for evermore, and my covenant shall stand fast with him. His seed also will I make to endure for ever, and his throne as the days of heaven.'[9]

The coming of the Messiah was thus seen as marking both the End and also a new beginning, the commencement of the era of the Kingdom of God made manifest throughout the world. These would be the days when God would make a new covenant with Israel. 'After those days, saith the Lord, I will put my Law in their inward parts, and write it in their hearts; and will be their God, and they shall be my people . . . In those days, and at that time, will I cause the branch of righteousness to grow up unto David; and he shall execute judgment and righteousness in the land.'[10]

There has to come home to us how closely fitting together were the expectations which associated the holy king with the nation brought into holiness. The very idea of a king involved the existence of the people he would rule. To effect the redemption of mankind king and people had to be one and act as one on behalf of God. There could be no Christ who by himself was the saviour of the world.

This is why it is said further in the *Psalms of Solomon*, 'And he shall gather together a holy people, whom he shall lead in righteousness: and he shall judge the tribes of the people that hath been sanctified by the Lord his God. And he shall not suffer iniquity to lodge in their midst; and none that knoweth wickedness shall dwell with him. For he shall take knowledge of them that they be all sons of their God, and shall divide them on earth according to their tribes . . . He shall judge the nations and the peoples with the wisdom of his righteousness.'[11] We are again here in contact with the microcosmic arrangement of the Assembly in the Wilderness, where at the centre the priestly tribe of Levi represents the priestly Israel, and the twelve tribes camped round about represent the rest of mankind.[12]

In the scheme of things as now envisaged, and before the Messiah's advent, a priestly figure would appear as reconciler in the person of the returned prophet Elijah. 'Remember ye the Law of Moses my servant, which I commanded him in Horeb for all Israel, with the statutes and judgments. Behold, I will send you Elijah the prophet before the coming of the great and dreadful Day of the Lord: and he shall turn the heart of the fathers to the children, and the heart of the children to their fathers, lest I come and smite the earth with a curse.'[13]

The Messianism of the time set a very high standard in what it demanded in the way of fulfilment both as to conduct and circumstances, and surrounded the predicted developments with an apocalyptic aura, so that they were to be accompanied by miraculous signs and portents and cataclysmic manifestations. It was a time when faith was mingled with strong superstition, the heroic with the near hysterical, so that we do not have to take seriously that any reality could approach what imagination depicted. Yet the imagination itself was remarkable and conveyed that something was bound to happen to reflect the widespread sense of a turning point in history. And something did happen in the appearance of the Elijah-like person of John the Baptist son of the priest Zachariah and in the appearance as Messiah of Jesus son of Joseph, descendant of King David.

The Christian Gospels, while painting an exaggerated picture of Jesus in line with the ideas of the period, and imposing upon him a reflection of later quasi-pagan concepts and various Christian concerns, have nevertheless preserved very strong traces of his relationship to the Messianism we have described; and this applies also to the material about John the Baptist. The nativity stories of both, for all their legendary embellishments, introduce them as the embodiment of the contemporary Messianic hopes and convictions.

Jesus is the subject of angelic announcements. In Luke his mother is told, 'You will conceive in your womb and have a son, whom you are to call Jesus. He will be a great man, and be termed son of the Most High,' just as David and Solomon were, 'and the Lord will give him the throne of his ancestor David: he will reign over the house of Jacob forever, and his sovereignty shall be without end.'[14] Similarly the shepherds of Bethlehem are informed by an angel, 'I bring you news of a great joy which will be shared by all the people (i.e. of Israel), that today in David's town a deliverer has been born to you, none other than the Lord Messiah.'[15]

The primary function of the holy king was to bring his people back to God, so that through the holy nation mankind would be led to peace and righteousness. Therefore in the annunciation to Joseph in Matthew (i. 20) it is not said that the Messiah directly will save all men, but 'he will save *his people* from their sins.' In keeping with this view Jesus himself declares that he is not sent except to the lost sheep of the house of Israel, and instructs his twelve apostles (symbolic of the twelve tribes) to go only to them, not to the Gentiles, not even to the Samaritans.[16] The initial work of the 'Elijah' forerunner is identified with the activity of the Messiah in the

prophecy attributed to Zacharias father of John the Baptist
(Lk. i. 68–79), and Zacharias too is informed about his son
by an angel, 'And many of the children of Israel will he turn
to the Lord their God. He will precede him in the spirit and
capacity of Elijah . . . to make ready a people prepared for
the Lord.'[17]

Both John and Jesus applied themselves with complete
dedication to their Messianic tasks and attracted large and
responsive crowds. The call to Israel was sounded out,
'Repent, for the Kingdom of Heaven is at hand.' John the
fiery prophet, warned the people of the wrath to come, and
those who were contrite he dipped in the Jordan as a token of
repentance. Jesus, the sagacious and perspicacious leader,
taught the ethics of the Kingdom in proverb, parable and
wise saying, and demanded of his people absolute commitment to the perfection the laws of God required of members
of the holy nation.

Jesus enacted methodically and in all sincerity the part
which current interpretation of prophecy had assigned to the
Messiah, as I have fully explained in my previous book *The
Passover Plot*. But what concerns us here is whether he
contributed anything of worth which reveals a Messianic
insight. Did he offer some fresh understanding of the
requirements of the Divine Plan?

It is notoriously difficult to determine which of the
recorded sayings of Jesus are genuine; but there are some
which are so closely related to a Jewish environment of
thought and to conditions in Palestine in his day that, though
altered in certain cases by the Evangelists, they are unlikely
to have been invented by a Church with a different background and another way of thinking about Jesus.

Among those sayings which ring true are a number which
are found in the so-called Sermon on the Mount. The
behaviour of Israel as the People of God is not to be as that
of other nations. The Kingdom of God is to be their first
concern. Hostile actions against them are not to be resisted.
Enemies are to be loved, not hated. No one is to harbour a
grudge. There must be ready forgiveness and active well-
doing. In all connections Israel is to set an example. Else-

where Jesus stresses the principle of service. The rulers of the Gentiles wield authority over them, but the followers of Jesus are to regard themselves as servants.

It took great courage to say such things in an occupied country dominated by Roman might to a people greatly wronged and illtreated, seething with unrest and on the verge of revolt. But if Jesus was the Messiah it was his duty to say them, since the Chosen People could not fulfil its mission on any other basis. Israel could be no light to the Gentiles if it followed the ways of the Gentiles. Jesus, like Moses, proclaimed a doctrine of perfection, which meant bringing all conduct into line with what was consistent with the Fatherhood of God. How otherwise should the Kingdom of God commend itself to mankind? It was useless to speak of the world-saving ministrations of a holy nation without plainly spelling out what these involved.

The advent of Jesus, therefore, did mark a great moment of change, not in the intention of the Divine Plan but in the reaffirmation of its requirements. The holy king had done his part in recalling to his people the inescapable demands upon them of their priesthood, and offering them the testimony of his life as their example.

But there was more than this. In the coming to a head at this juncture of the Messianic vision there was shaping itself a new development of the Chosen People which would increase its potential in an evolutionary manner. The development had been initiated before the appearance of Jesus on the stage of history by the enlargement of the Jewish diaspora, so that the geographer Strabo could write, 'This people has already found its way into every city, and it would be difficult to discover any place in the habitable world that has not received this tribe and in which it has not made its presence felt.'[18] As a result a great many non-Jews had been attracted by Jewish monotheism and ethical principles. The Messiahship of Jesus was to set in motion a considerable propaganda about him which reached the world at large initially through the synagogues throughout the Roman Empire. By this means thousands of Gentiles were enlisted to be his followers.

Jesus probably had no inkling of this process and prospect. But those who as Christians looked back to him in his life and teaching credited him with knowledge that the holy nation must have a new expansion of its membership by the incorporation of multitudes who were not born in the house of Israel. Therefore, in their reports, he was made to say, that many would come from the east and west, and sit down with Abraham, Isaac and Jacob in the Kingdom of God, and to tell those who refused their service that the Kingdom would be taken from them and given to a *nation* bringing forth the fruits thereof.[19]

NOTES AND REFERENCES

1. Plutarch, *Moralia*, tr. by F. C. Babbitt (Loeb Classical Library).
2. See I. Macc. i. 51–64 (RSV).
3. See Schonfield, *Those Incredible Christians*, p. 25f and also p. 37.
4. Daniel vii. The equation of the Son of Man with the Messiah, as the ideal Israelite, came much later.
5. *Assumption of Moses*, vi. 2–6, tr. by R. H. Charles.
6. *Sibylline Oracles*, Bk. III, tr. by H. N. Bate.
7. *Psalms of Solomon*, xvii.
8. Isa. xi. 1–4.
9. Ps. lxxxix. 20–29.
10. Jer. xxxi. 31–34 and xxxiii. 15.
11. *Psalms of Solomon*, xvii.
12. See previous chapter and Deut. xxxii. 8.
13. Mal. iv. 4–6.
14. Lk. i. 31–33 (ANT).
15. Lk. ii. 10–11. The King James version wrongly translates 'all the people', meaning Israel, by 'all people' implying persons in general. The Greek has the definite article.
16. Mt. x. 5–6 and xv. 24.
17. Lk. i. 16–17.
18. Strabo, quoted by Josephus, *Antiq.* XIV. vii. 2.
19. See Mt. viii. 11–12 and xxi. 43.

7

Conflicting Claims

WHAT stands out from the reading of the early Christian literature, if the documents are simply allowed to speak for themselves, is that the Christians, known as Nazareans, did not present themselves as the adherents of a new religion, but as the Israel of God of the Last Times, the faithful who had given their allegiance to their God-sent Messiah.

We can by no means understand Christian beginnings unless we are capable of entering into the state of mind of people who believed they were living in the Last Times, and that very shortly the Kingdom of God would come in power heralded by a Judgment Day and the return of the Messiah from heaven.

It is not our business to allegorize or to seek to bring inconvenient ideas into conformity with later religious persuasions. We have to look at what is there honestly. It is abundantly evident that Jesus and his followers subscribed to Jewish eschatological teaching. Without it, as it was believed, there was no necessity, no imperative, that a Messiah (a Christ) should come at all. According to prophetic interpretation he must come, and the only time for his coming was the End of the Ages. This was the determined time for God to intervene decisively in human affairs.

So great was the conviction of the Jews that not only were they deeply stirred and agitated by what they anticipated; they circulated their beliefs throughout the Roman Empire. We have ample material testifying both to their doctrine and

to its effects.[1] From a Messianic viewpoint, therefore, as
seen by Jesus and afterwards his adherents, the crucifixion
fitted into the scheme. It was necessitated in order to assure
that there would be a redeemed Remnant, and also to
assure the survival of the Messiah by his entry into a new
condition of being, for otherwise the further course of
Messianic expectation could not have fulfilment.

A dead Messiah could not be victorious, could not judge
and reign throughout the Messianic Age. But a Messiah
made immortal while still retaining a human body, temporarily absent from the world while events shaped themselves
to complete what was called for prior to his return, was
wholly appropriate. The Messiah must come into the
presence of God on high, there to have bestowed upon him
the crown he had earned, and there to await the signal for
his second advent in triumph with the legions of heaven at
his back. Not resurrection only was demanded, but the
Messiah's bodily ascension into the skies. Standing at the end
of his life before the high priest, we are told that Jesus
declared, 'Hereafter shall ye see the Son of Man sitting at the
right hand of Power, and coming in the clouds of heaven.'
The key to the circumstances was found in the frequently
quoted words of Psalm cx, 'The Lord said unto my lord (the
king), Sit thou at my right hand, until I make thine enemies
thy footstool. The Lord shall send the rod of thy strength
out of Zion: rule thou in the midst of thine enemies. Thy
people shall be willing in the day of thy power ... The
Lord hath sworn, and he will not repent, Thou art a
priest for ever after the order of Melchizedek (i.e. king of
justice). The Lord at thy right hand shall strike through
kings in the day of his wrath. He shall judge among the
heathen, he shall fill the places with dead bodies: he shall
wound the heads over many countries.'

We are to look at what transpired in the context of first
century belief, and have to accommodate ourselves to the plain
fact that Jesus was a man of his time. Those involved easily
took everything in their stride, all kinds of miraculous
occurrences, all kinds of naïve notions, with a simplicity we
now find it necessary to excuse or disregard rather than

accept. It in no way detracts from the greatness of Jesus, nor from the Messianic part he played in the providence of God, to face up to his mental limitations. Of course it has been the Church's identification of him with God that has created a problem, since our ideas of God are different now. We no longer think of God as being 'up there', as having a location in space. Neither do we think of him as quite properly exhibiting the defects of our humanity as people in the past could do. So if we still hold to the Deity of Christ we have to busy ourselves with face-saving and credit-saving, and questing around for how to patch things up for the satisfaction of our more sophisticated religious needs.

Instead, we should embrace the reality that the period in which Jesus lived produced its own peculiar and significant Messianic outburst. It matters that this occurred and had certain important consequences. But it does not matter if Pauline and Johannine Christology is dated and bears the marks of antique speculation, often beautiful and penetrating but highly unreliable. Neither does it matter that what Jesus and the Messianists in their day supposed about God, about the cosmos, about the imminent climax of history and the sudden transformation of the earthly scene after a Divine Judgment, was quite wrong.

Let us then accept that for the early Christians a miracle had been wrought in the bodily resurrection of the Messiah from the dead and his bodily ascension to a place in the skies where God and his angels are. Let us accept with them that the term of his absence from the earth would be brief, since some who heard him would at that time still be living, and that then he would return in flaming fire to judge the sinners, bringing with him a host of angels and the immortalized saints who had died, restore the kingdom to Israel and set up his throne in Jerusalem. From thence with his people he would minister to mankind in the name of God, and usher in peace and justice which would endure until there should be Time no longer.

The temporary lodgement of the Messiah in heaven would be marked on earth by many signs. For the believers there would be the pouring out upon them of the Holy Spirit as a foretaste of the powers of the New Age, and as a cogent demonstration to unbelievers. The saints would endure much tribulation which would test their professions severely, but those still alive at the Messiah's return would be rewarded by the instantaneous immortalization of their bodies. Evil would come to the zenith of its intensity. An antichrist would seek to have himself worshipped as God in the Temple of God, and delude the nations. There would be wars, earthquakes and famine, and numerous wonders and portents in heaven and on earth. All these things and many more would confirm that this was indeed the Time of the End.

This was a highly superstitious and credulous age, and what people looked for they did not fail to find. There was the attempt of the Roman emperor Gaius to set up the statue of himself as Jupiter in the Temple at Jerusalem. There was the great famine in the reign of Claudius, the Great Fire of Rome in the reign of Nero. Josephus the first century Jewish historian devotes a long passage to the signs that preceded the Jewish war with the Romans. He tells us that a star like a sword hung over Jerusalem, and a comet appeared for a whole year. In the night on a Passover eve a brilliant light suddenly shone on the altar of the Sanctuary. At the same Passover in the Temple a cow gave birth to a lamb, and the massive eastern gate opened by itself in the middle of the night. Shortly afterwards all over the country before sunset chariots were seen in the sky and armed battalions hurtling through the clouds. Then at Pentecost the priests entering the inner Temple heard a great noise and commotion with the voice of a host crying, 'We are departing hence.'[2]

It is worth quoting the words of Dean Farrar in his famous work *The Early Days of Christianity*. 'Men seemed to be tormented and terrified with catastrophes and portents. "Besides the manifold changes and chances of human affairs," says Tacitus, "there were prodigies in heaven and on earth ... for never was it rendered certain by clearer indications, or by more deadly massacres of the Roman people, that the gods care nothing for our happiness, but do care for our retribution." In Rome a pestilence had carried

off tens of thousands of the citizens ... In Lydia an en-
croachment of the seas had wrought fearful havoc. In Asia
city after city had been shattered to the dust by earthquakes.
"The world itself is being shaken to pieces," says Seneca,
"and there is universal consternation." Comets, eclipses,
meteors, parhelions, terrified the ignorant, and were themselves the pretexts for imperial cruelties. Auroras tinged the
sky with blood. Volcanoes seemed, like Vesuvius, to be
waking to new fury ... The whole Empire was in a state of
agitation.'

The Christians insistently declared, 'The Day is at hand!'
Suddenly and unexpectedly it would be here, and no chance
would be left for repentance. Therefore every hour of the
brief interval before Christ's return was precious and must
be employed to the full, not in social activities but in
preaching the Gospel.

One of the chief witnesses, the letters of the Apostle Paul,
dwells continually on the shortness of remaining time. This
clearly establishes that the formulation of a new religion—
Christianity—was not contemplated. We should read these
letters through at one sitting, noting their white hot urgency
and sense of strain with so much that must be done so
quickly, in organization for rapid extension of work, in
admonishment of folly and crass stupidity in view of the
eleventh hour state of emergency. Soon, much sooner than
many might wish to believe, it would be too late.

Well, we may say, Paul and his fellow apostles were
wrong. Jesus and all his early followers were wrong. The
Day did not come. The calculations of the Messianists, like
those of all End of the World predictors, were hopelessly
mistaken. In due course the Church, discovering that the
life of the world was going on as of yore, seemingly indefinitely, extricated itself lamely enough from being impaled
on the horns of its dilemma, and adjusted its emphasis
accordingly. A new Christian religion was brought into
being with novel doctrines and largely an otherworldly
outlook. Christ would come to the believer at death, or he
would return after a very long time. The wording about the
climax was largely retained, but its import was spiritualized.

Of course we must assent that the protagonists of the Last
Days were the victims of their own wishful-thinking. No
casuistry can disguise the fact, and no reasonable person
could come to any other conclusion. And this tells heavily
against the peculiar Christian claim that once at the end of
the Ages God appeared among men to put away sin by the
sacrifice of himself.

This was not the grand finale, and the curtain was not
being dropped at the end of the drama and tragedy of
human waywardness. But we may be persuaded that the
quite extraordinary flare up of Messianism between approxi-
mately 150 B.C. and A.D. 150 can have been no idle and
purposeless phenomenon. The Christian Church from the
second century onwards offered its own explanation, but by
this time it had become so alien to the atmosphere of its
beginnings that its testimony was substantially perverted.

We may certainly think of the period as one which
demanded that there should be a great change, a fresh
impetus towards the transformation of human relationships.
Because Jesus appeared as the Messiah what he stood for
would be carried to the ends of the earth, and with remarkable rapidity. Nothing else than the electrifying Good News
that the Messiah had come would have produced such zeal
to brave every peril and hazard to convey and publicize it.
Had there been no Messianism, had Jesus been simply
prophet or religious teacher, no Jews would have gone forth
to proclaim the Gospel. And had Jesus declared himself to be
Divine only the heathen would have heeded him and he
would have had no following among his own people. The
story of Christian beginnings would have been quite
different. We do well to ponder this. The initial Gospel had
nothing to say about the Deity of Jesus. It had everything to
say about his Messiahship, and what this meant for humanity.

As it was, Jesus as Jewish Messiah set the seal on those
aspects of Jewish faith which insisted that the love of God was
to be made manifest in the treatment of all persons as beloved
of God. No one was to be regarded as objectionable on
grounds that he was an alien, a sinner, a heathen. Neither

in any circumstances was anyone to be treated with hostility. No people of God could function which lorded it over others. It could never be a curse to those whom it was designed to bless.

This was essential, since many who deemed themselves to be the Elect of Israel of the Last Times, like the authors of the Dead Sea Scrolls, had shown themselves by their narrow conservatism, their hostility towards compromising Jews as well as towards Gentiles, to be far removed from a general love of mankind. They might be saints by their own standards, but the spirit they exhibited brought to a dead end the whole concept of the holy nation. The chains had to be broken, and very quickly, if the Divine Plan was not to be defeated. There had to be an evolution which repudiated any question of a rigid nationalism.

The mission to mankind was Israel's, but there was nothing that prevented non-Jews from becoming Israelites. A substantial influx of Gentiles could make Israel far more positive in its outward-looking concerns in line with the purpose of its calling. It was not uncommon for Gentiles to be converted to Judaism, and there were very many who without becoming full proselytes accepted the God of Israel as the one true God and frequented the synagogues. The universal proclamation of Jesus as the Messiah considerably augmented the influx of those who abandoned their idolatry. Suddenly the Door of Faith was wide open, and the new development was seen to be prophetically demanded. It was written, 'I will say to them which were not my people, Thou art my people; and they shall say, Thou art my God.'[3]

The doctrine of the Remnant was emphasized in another respect. The children of Israel, according to the Scriptures, would be as the stars of heaven for number, and as the sand on the seashore, yet only a remnant would be saved.[4] The late *Clementine Recognitions* explains, 'Inasmuch as it was necessary that the Gentiles should be called into the room of those who remained unbelieving, so that the number might be filled up which had been shown by God to Abraham, the preaching of the blessed Kingdom of God is sent into all the world.' Thus the proclamation of Jesus would bring into

Israel a predestined number of believing Gentiles, who would turn from their idols and serve God and his anointed.

The development provoked a bitter conflict between Paul, selfstyled apostle to the Gentiles, and the other apostles. The issue was not whether Gentiles could become Israelites, but whether for this purpose faith in God and acceptance of Jesus as Messiah was sufficient. The apostles and elders at Jerusalem held that no one could be an Israelite who did not obey the Law of God given to Israel. If Gentiles were admitted on any other terms this would be a breach of the Divine covenant and the integrity of the People of God would be destroyed. Paul argued otherwise, that to be children of Abraham and heirs of the promises it was needful only to have the faith of Abraham; and since essentially the seed of Abraham was the Messiah, if one was united with the Messiah one was automatically a child of Abraham.[5] Neither side was contending that there was to be a new People of God other than Israel or in place of Israel. Paul in his letter to the Romans (ix–xi) emphatically repudiated any such notion. The burden of all his arguments (see for example Eph. ii. 11–13) is that those from the Gentiles who accepted Christ had by that acceptance become members of the Commonwealth of Israel. Such former Gentiles had been grafted onto the stock of the olive tree of Israel, and he warned these that if they lorded it over the temporarily severed branches they would find themselves cut off. The complexion and substantially the present composition of Israel had changed by a special dispensation that the purposes of God might be fulfilled, but never the reality. God had not gone back on his promises to Israel.

Since I have discussed Pauline thinking in *Those Incredible Christians* there is no need to elaborate here how Paul was led through this controversy to propound certain doctrines about the person of Christ, about the atonement, faith, grace, predestination, etc., which Christianity with no little misunderstanding subsequently adopted. But there was no justification for Christianity to go radically astray, as it did, in becoming a new religion which altered its whole character and sacrificed its identity with the Israel of history. For Paul and his supporters all followers of Jesus were in the direct line of descent from the Patriarchs and the people who had been brought out of Egypt and led through the wilderness. They were *our* fathers.[6]

The word Church in its original apostolic employment meant nothing else than the body politic of Israel. The Greek *ekklesia* was used as a translation of the Hebrew *kehillah*, the congregation of Israel, as it is used in the Greek version of the Old Testament.[7] It no more signified something different than the Greek *Christos* signified something other than the Messiah, the anointed one. The Church was no new institution, but a fresh development of the old one. The Messiah, as we noted in the *Psalms of Solomon*, was to gather to himself a people as the children of their God. This people would be Israel redeemed and purified. This much at least received some fulfilment. On the rock which was the Messiahship of Jesus the ruins of the house of Israel were rebuilt, the fallen tent of David was reerected.[8]

For the early Christians Israel was the People of God and they represented Israel. The Gentiles had never been part of Israel, but the Jews had been. Not all Jews, but a large part of them, had defected from Israel, and this had enabled believing Gentiles to change their status. Therefore it could be said to these, 'But you are a chosen race, a royal priesthood, a holy nation, a people for God's ownership, that you may recite the merits of him who has called you from darkness into his marvellous light, who once were "no people", but now are God's people, who once "had not obtained mercy", but now have received mercy.'[9]

The Church, then, was understood to be redeemed Israel, Israel under the New Covenant prophesied by Jeremiah, not another and different people. Continuity with the past had not been broken. For Paul, the Law in the heart—being under law to the Messiah—had broken the chains of a bondage to the Law of ordinances, and this liberty meant that now many more, namely previously excluded Gentiles, could acquire the status of Israelites. He quoted Isaiah liv, 1, 'Rejoice, thou barren that bearest not; break forth and cry, thou that travailest not: for the desolate hath many more

children than she which hath an husband.'[10] The same text
was later used by the Church Fathers to underline 'that the
Christians from among the Gentiles are both more numerous
and more true than those from among the Jews and
Samaritans,'[11] and to infer the rejection of the Jews as the
People of God in favour of the Christians consisting now
predominantly of Gentiles. The climax came when Christianity became the official religion of the Roman Empire,
and it could be declared by the Emperor Constantine, 'we
will have no dealings with this most hateful people, for the
Lord has marked out another way for us.' From that time
on anti-Jewish decrees were multiplied, and hatred of the
Jews as deicides was fostered by bigoted churchmen.

That God had exchanged his chosen people for another
people was emphatically repudiated by the Jews, and they
had the more justification as Christianity developed into a
Gentilized and quasi-idolatrous religion which exhibited no
marks of being the Israel of God, and as a People of God
showed no evidence of being better, but was rather worse,
than the supposedly rejected Jews.[12]

After a burst of militant Messianism, particularly in
A.D. 66 and in A.D. 133, stimulated by suffering, but which
only brought upon the Jews greater misery and disaster, the
Jewish people became largely quiescent. While praying
daily for restoration and the coming of God's Kingdom
among men, they betook themselves under their wise
teachers to the study and practice of the Torah, that they
might learn to know its secrets and conform to its obligations.
The pursuit was to save the Jews, and keep alive under every
kind of adversity the sense of a sacred calling. But it also
meant opting out of any corporate initiative until God
should be pleased to reveal his will.

There is more to be said on these matters presently. Here,
what it has been essential to point out is that the Church
according to its initial inspiration was to be the continuation
of Israel in an extended dimension, not a replacement of it.
Christians in the New Testament are never spoken of as
Gentiles, but as ex-Gentiles, called out of every nation,
kindred, people and tongue into the Commonwealth of

Israel. If the Church had continued to regard itself in this light, its whole attitude to the Jews, to the world, and to its own nature and function might have been different.

When eventually the general and direct reading of the Bible became possible, still the habit of thinking of the Church as a spiritual body with a heavenly future was paramount. Statements could be quoted from the New Testament to support this. The Church is the body of Christ, and Christ said that his kingdom was not of this world.[13] 'In my Father's house are many mansions . . . I go to prepare a place for you,' and 'our conversation is in heaven.'[14] But in both these texts there is reference not to believers going to heaven but to Christ returning from it to his people. Therefore some Christian groups began to reaffirm that the tenor of New Testament teaching, as it was originally understood, was that Christ would return to the world to reign there with his people in the millennial age.

But in this case what of the prophecies concerning the future of the Jews? Were they not to be redeemed and fulfil their mission to the nations as God's people? Either then, as Paul believed, the Christians and Jews were to be reunited as one people, and this implied an earthly mission for the Church, or two peoples of God would have to be recognized with different functions. Some who have jibbed at identity have accordingly had to propose a most extraordinary two-tier structure, and speak of God's heavenly people the Christians and God's earthly people the Jews.

In the whole of Messianic teaching it is a heavenly state that *comes down* and is reproduced on earth in conditions of peace and harmony. The New Jerusalem does not stay in the skies: it descends, 'and the nations of them which are saved shall walk in the light of it: and the kings of the earth do bring their glory and honour into it.'[15]

If the Church was Israel enlarged and reanimated through the coming of the Messiah it should have been ready to implement the task of Israel as a priestly nation distinct from all other nations and ministering to them as a nation. All Christians would have one and the same nationality and would be wholly independent of every sovereign state. There could be churches in different countries, but their members would not be citizens of those countries, only domiciled in them. This was recognized by the anonymous pre-Nicene author of the *Epistle to Diognetus*, when he wrote of the Christians, 'They dwell in their own countries, but only as sojourners . . . Every foreign country is a fatherland to them, and every fatherland is foreign.' We are to say this, not because Christians are heavenly citizens of a heavenly city, and are on earth as if they were visitors from another planet, but because identified as Israel they are subjects of the King of Israel, the Messiah (Christ), and therefore have the responsibilities of Israel as a priestly nation to serve, reconcile and unite all mankind.

In terms of the Divine Plan for humanity neither Christianity, Judaism nor any other *religion* can undertake this task.

NOTES AND REFERENCES

1. See Schonfield, *Those Incredible Christians*, chapters ii and iii.
2. Josephus, *Jewish War*, VI. v. 3.
3. Hosea i. 10, ii. 23.
4. Gen. xv. 5–6, and see Rom. ix–xi.
5. See Gal. iii and Rom. iv.
6. I. Cor. x.
7. See the Septuagint at Deut. xxxi. 30; Ps. xxii. 22; I. Kg. viii. 14, etc., and cp. Acts vii. 38; Heb. ii. 12.
8. Acts xv. 16–17.
9. I. Pet. ii. 9–10.
10. Gal. iv. 27.
11. Justin Martyr, *Apol.* liii.
12. Nicolas Berdyaev, *Christianity and Antisemitism*, 'It must be sadly confessed that the Christians have not risen to the heights of the revelation they have received, and have in general been considerably inferior to the Jews.'
13. Jno. xviii. 36. These words do not necessarily imply that Christ's kingdom is elsewhere than in this world. As Berdyaev, *op. cit.*, remarks, 'Christ's words may mean that the kingdom of God does not resemble earthly kingdoms, that its foundations are different, that its justice is diametrically opposed to the law obtaining here below. In this case the Christians would be wrong to submit to the prince of this world, wrong not to labour in promoting the justice of God's kingdom—not to take up

the task of transforming the world.' Thus what Jesus could be saying, according to John, is that his kingdom is of a different order of behaviour than is represented by the actions of the rulers in whose hands the world now is. His manner of government is not like theirs.

14. Jno. xiv. 2–3; Phil. iii. 20.
15. Rev. xxi. 2–3, 24.

8

The Times of the Gentiles

THE man chiefly responsible for proclaiming Christ among the Gentiles was a Jew of the Roman province of Asia, Paul of Tarsus. He was an intellectual and a mystic, and at the same time a man of great energy and administrative ability. But like a good many scholars he was so much in love with the virtues of his theories that he quite neglected to consider how they would work out in practice. The human factor did not sufficiently enter into his calculations. He had the right idea that Israel must be concerned with the salvation of mankind and that believers from among the Gentiles must be given opportunity to join the people of God. Where he failed was in not realizing that a Greek or barbarian did not automatically become an Israelite simply by faith in Christ. Dipping him in water did not eliminate his previous background, way of thinking and behaviour, and make him inwardly Jewish. There needed to be adequate prior training and instruction, and commitment to the responsibilities of Israelite status. This was provided for in the reception of Gentiles into the Jewish community, and Paul's fellow-apostles demanded the same thing in respect of his converts.

But Paul was so eager, so carried away by his thesis, that he swept all such considerations aside. He himself had been brought up with the strong moral sense of the Pharisees and in the atmosphere of Jewish monotheism. He could therefore remain under law to Christ when he ceased to observe as binding the observances of the Mosaic code. The Torah was in his heart, and his conduct guided by its spirit. He did not have to turn his back on his inherited Jewishness. He therefore thought of his converts by reason of their faith in God and his Messiah as almost effortlessly becoming as he was, and did not sufficiently allow for their profound difficulties in being required to adapt to a quite new way of life. It was easy to describe them as Israelites, but quite another thing to expect them to think, feel and behave as such.

It was a great shock to Paul to discover that in everything but name so many of his converts were unchanged. They brought into the churches their former factiousness, immorality and temperament. Indeed, some of them were worse than the Gentiles, since they interpreted freedom from the Law as freedom from all restraint and discipline. Drawn largely from the slave population of the Empire, they repudiated all authority. Washed in the blood of the Lamb, they were now whiter than snow. The merits of Christ covered them and rendered them guiltless whatever they might do. Thus Christians everywhere were looked at askance by decent people as evil and subversive.

The influx of Gentiles, which was to have created a more sentient outgoing Israel, was to give rise in fact to a gentilized religion having less and less in common with Israel. As an eighteenth century Unitarian expressed it, most of the converts from the Gentiles 'gave their bare names to Christ, but reserved their idolatrous hearts for their native superstitions.'[1] In the end the Church, when it dominated, took whole populations into fellowship. It was only needful to win over the heathen king to have all his subjects baptized as Christians without any regard for what they understood of their new faith or the requirement of any radical relinquishment of their native superstitions. The Church in its zeal was only too ready not only to Christianize the inhabitants of countries, but to facilitate the nominal change by retaining as far as possible heathen beliefs and practices by simply giving them a Christian expression and interpretation. How could there arise from such a process any real distinction between the holy nation and other nations? The new objective was Christendom, a Holy Roman Empire.

Lord Bryce has explained the philosophy of the new objective. 'As God, in the midst of his celestial hierarchy, ruled blessed spirits in paradise, so the Pope, His vicar, raised above priests, bishops, metropolitans, reigned over the souls of men below. But as God is Lord of earth as well as of heaven, so must he (the *Imperator coelestis*) be represented by a second earthly viceroy, the Emperor (*Imperator terrenus*), whose authority shall be of and for this present life . . . It is under the emblem of soul and body that the relation of the papal and imperial power is presented to us throughout the Middle Ages . . . Thus the Holy Roman Church and the Holy Roman Empire are one and the same thing, in two aspects; and Catholicism, the principle of the universal Christian society, is also Romanism; that is, it rests upon Rome as the origin and type of its universality; manifesting itself in a mystic dualism which corresponds to the two natures of its Founder. As divine and eternal, its head is the Pope, to whom souls have been entrusted; as human and temporal, the Emperor, commissioned to rule men's bodies and acts.'[2]

Manifestly, such a concept had nothing to do with the Divine Plan as expounded by the ancient Israelites. To the contrary, it represented a baptized Roman imperialism, which Messianism, Jewish and Christian, denounced as opposed to the Kingdom of God.

The Jews had been castigated by the Prophets for succumbing to the blandishments of heathenism, and their sufferings were held to be punishments for their folly and failure to live up to the ideal of a holy nation by wanting to be like all the other nations. But now the Christians, ostensibly loyal Israel, conforming to the will of God reflected in the teaching of Jesus, had fallen into the same errors. The Church declared the Jews to have been rejected for their waywardness and unbelief, but was quite unable to see that with less justification, because it claimed to have greater light, the Church had more grievously sinned and much more merited condign punishment and rejection. The admonition of Paul went unheeded, when he wrote, 'Do not be arrogant, but fear. For if God did not spare the natural branches, neither will he spare you. Mark, then, the kindness and severity of God, severity towards those branches which drooped, kindness to you, provided you continue to merit his kindness, otherwise, you too will be cut off.'[3]

The Roman Church, transparently, incorporates many pagan ideas and usages, and actually glories in the fact. Professor Karl Adam has stated, 'We Catholics acknowledge readily, without any shame, nay with pride, that Catholicism cannot be identified simply and wholly with primitive Christianity, nor even with the Gospel of Christ, in the same way that the great oak cannot be identified with the tiny acorn ... The Gospel of Christ would have been no living gospel, and the seed which He scattered no living seed, if it had remained ever the tiny seed of A.D. 33, and not struck root, and had not assimilated foreign matter, and had not by the help of this foreign matter grown up into a tree, so that the birds of the air dwell in its branches.'[4]

In another Roman Catholic work we read, 'One of the elements of the religious life ... without in any way modifying the intransigence of Christian Monotheism, attenuated, as we might say, that which its apparent severity might make it difficult to accept in the case of relatively primitive minds accustomed to all the religious varieties of polytheism. The cultus of the saints, which began with that of the martyrs, provided them with a satisfaction which they instinctively sought, and carried on the idea of a populous heaven such as they loved, and an earth in which many localities were as before consecrated by the memory of holy presences ... Christianity, which provided an answer to the highest aspirations of souls eager to find a truly divine God, adapted itself in this way to the instinctive human desire to find a religion near to mankind.'[5]

So much for the words of Paul, 'Do not be ill-matched with unbelievers. For what has rectitude in common with lawlessness? Or what fellowship has light with darkness? What harmony has Christ with Belial? Or what share has the faithful with the faithless? And what agreement has the temple of God with idols? For we are the temple of the living God, as God has said (Lev. xxvi. 11–12), "I will dwell

with them and walk with them, and I will be their God, and
they my people." "Therefore come out from among them,
and be separate, says the Lord (Isa. lii. 11). Have no contact
with the unclean."[6]

The creation of the Christian religion necessarily involved
a retreat from the teaching of Moses, the Prophets, and
Jesus, which more and more became a rout. The Jews quite
rightly resisted having anything to do with the new creed
once it had been fully formulated. As one Protestant Christian writer has observed, 'The great people of God's choice
were soon the least adequately represented in the Catholic
Church. That was a disaster to the Church itself. It meant
that the Church as a whole failed to understand the Old
Testament and that the Greek mind and the Roman mind
in turn, instead of the Hebrew mind, came to dominate its
outlook: from that disaster the Church has never recovered,
either in doctrine or in practice . . . If today another great
age of evangelization is to dawn, we need the Jews again.'[7]

But Christians would gravely delude themselves if they
were to imagine that Jews on any major scale could subscribe
to the tenets of the Christian religion, which owe so much
to the legacy of polytheism. Because Christians have not
become Israelites, but have remained essentially Gentiles,
their spiritual inclinations are towards doctrines for which
they have been prepared by inheritance from the pagan
past. It is natural for them to have certain religious needs
which the developed expression of Christianity was designed
to satisfy, and therefore they cannot readily see why Jews
should have other religious needs arising from their own
inheritance. It seems to them sheer obstinacy that the Jews
should be unable to appreciate not only the superior merits,
but the positive rightness of the Christian creed. For Christians their faith applies to the condition of all mankind, Jews
not excepted, and its central doctrines of the Incarnation
and Atonement, with God becoming man and suffering for
the sins of humanity, appear to be wholly proper and
consistent with what might be expected of God. They are
especially emphatic because they regard the Divine revelation to Israel as being behind their thinking and leading up

to it as demonstrated by the New Testament writings, and do not apprehend how much gentilization took place to produce Christianity as we know it.

'Christianity,' as T. E. Lawrence pointed out in *The Seven Pillars of Wisdom*, 'is a hybrid faith compounded of the Semitic as to its origin, and the non-Semitic as to its development. It therefore carries within itself a problem, which as yet it is unwilling to resolve, and of which indeed it is not correctly aware ... due to the extraordinary manner in which the Semitism in Christianity has been sublimated.'

This is what created a difficulty for the early Christian apologists. Because so much of what Christianity taught was akin to the contemporary pagan cults and mysteries, they were forced to accuse Satan of having diabolically imitated the Christian verities to the damnation of the heathen. It did not occur to them, having themselves come from the Gentiles, that Christianity had been impregnated with the notions of the Hellenic world, which incorporated Egyptian and oriental cults, since they saw it in relation to the Greek version of the Old Testament, reproducing Hebrew records which they claimed were much more ancient and authentic than pagan traditions.

There is no need for me to enlarge on the subject, as I have appreciably covered it in my previous work *Those Incredible Christians*. It does not present any problem to trace the various circumstances from Paul onwards to the Nicene and Athanasian creeds which caused the formulation and development of the Christian religion. The point I am making is that Christianity is not the spiritual successor of Judaism, but a synthesis of Judaism and paganism. As such, it is a corruption of as much significance as the ancient Israelite defection in blending their religion with the cults of the Canaanites. Therefore, it is not for the Jews to embrace orthodox Christianity, but for Christians, if they are to be Israelites indeed as the People of God, to review and purify their beliefs, and to recapture what basically they have in common with the Jews, the Messianic vision.

There is a trend in modern Christian exposition which indicates a growing up and away from the antique Christian mythology, induced by greater scientific knowledge and a more objective examination of the Christian Scriptures. But it has not gone far enough yet to require the abandonment of the central doctrines. The aim is still to preserve them to the extent that it is possible, to find in them some credible reflection of eternal truth, since if Christianity were destroyed millions would be religionless, and surely, at least the ethics are worth hanging on to and people must not be denied the benefits of prayer and corporate worship. But Jewish teaching offers everything that the Gentile can now feel to be needful, and, in fact, Christians are beginning to approach and study Judaism as they have not done since the parting of the ways nineteen centuries ago.

Of course Christians in bulk are no more likely to become orthodox Jews than Jews to become orthodox Christians. They could not be expected to adopt Jewish rites and ceremonies. But they could create a pure monotheistic religion suited to non-Jewish congregants, just as Liberal Judaism has modified rabbinical orthodoxy. The new Christianity would not be hard to devise, since in substance it would be a return to original Christianity.[8] Similarly, Liberal Judaism largely harks back to Prophetic Judaism. In this new Christianity the Messiahship of Jesus would replace his Deity. He would be held to be Son of God as obedient to the commands of God in representing God's will, and not in any supernatural sense. There would be emphasis of the Social Gospel, which in effect is the Messianic task, held in common with the Jews, of extablishing the Kingdom of God on earth. The Jews in these circumstances would have the possiblity of recognizing the Messianic quality of Jesus as the epitome of Jewish love and compassion in action,[9] and therefore as the instrument of the restoration of Israel to favour with God and man. The severed parts of the People of God would be relinked with dynamic effect on world affairs.

All this is possible; but whether it is probable is another question. A forward step like this is unlikely to be taken by both Christians and Jews unless they are impelled to it by others more ready to assume their responsibilities, unless they are moved to emulation because they are being replaced by those who are prepared to fulfil the tasks which the Divine Plan calls for in our time.

It would almost seem, though this is not really so, that since the destruction of Jerusalem in 70 A.D. the Divine Plan has been in suspension. The author of Luke-Acts speaks of Jerusalem being 'trodden down by the Gentiles, until the times of the Gentiles be fulfilled.'[10] What he meant by the Times of the Gentiles was doubtless Roman world domination; but he could not have expected that in one form or another this would persist for nineteen centuries or more. We continue to speak of imperialism because the spirit of Rome is still with us.

The essence of Romanism was the idea of a Common Superior, the antithesis of the Hebrew concept of a priestly servant-nation. The Roman Church endorsed Roman imperialism, but even with the rise of Protestantism the glamour of ancient Rome as lord of the world was still irresistible for ambitious Powers anxious to claim for their own glorification the heritage of the Caesars. The Biblical Doctrine of a Chosen People was perverted to imply a national title to authoritative office, where every fresh access of material prosperity became proof of a peculiar Divine favour and blessing. Those states which could assert some sort of legal claim based on descent proudly displayed their Eagle emblem; but others who could make no such claim were not thereby prevented from finding some other grounds, such as their way of life, for proposing their superiority.

'Of all the birds,' wrote Erasmus the Humanist, 'the eagle alone has seemed to wise men the type of royalty, not beautiful, not musical, not fit for food, but carniverous, greedy, hateful to all, the curse of all, and with its great powers of doing harm, surpassing them all in its desire of doing it.' Whether it is a Master-Race, Capitalism, or a Dictatorship of the Proletariat, it is still Romanism, and aided by Mars and Vulcan is capable of overthrowing in a single ghastly hour all the painful painstaking progress towards a better kind of civilization.

While the Times of the Gentiles prevailed the Jews were reduced to helplessness. The Torah endured, kept in the synagogues in a curtained cupboard. Continually it was brought out and read from. The minister of each congregation has stood with the scroll in his arms proclaiming, 'Hear, O Israel, the Lord your God is one Lord.' The pious Jew has made the same proclamation on his deathbed. The watchword has been 'remember.'

'Pride and humiliation hand in hand
    Walked with them through the world where'er they
        went;
Trampled and beaten were they as the sand,
    And yet unshaken as the continent.

'For in the background figures vague and vast
    Of patriarchs and prophets rose sublime,
And all the great traditions of the Past
    They saw reflected in the coming time.

'And thus forever with reverted look
    The mystic volume of the world they read,
Spelling it backward, like a Hebrew book,
    Till life became a Legend of the Dead.'[11]

'Ye are my witnesses.' But witnesses to whom? Does turning inward consitute a witnessing? The Jews have not proclaimed, 'Hear, O ye nations, the Lord is *your* God.' As one writer has put it, 'We Jews have done nothing for the world for centuries.' Yes, individuals have done much. Jews have been prominent in many fields of knowledge, in commerce, in philanthropy, and in movements for social reform. But collectively the accent has been on survival. Despite the persecutions, the pogroms, the death camps, we shall endure. God lives, and therefore Israel is indestructible. Is this a witness or an act of defiant faith?

In modern Zionism there has been a revival of corporateness; but this too has found its chief justification in a will to survive, and only faintly because of a sense of world mission and responsibility towards all nations. The state of Israel, once achieved, could not even see clearly how to be at peace with its neighbours. Its concept of regained nationhood has echoed the old folly of wanting to be like the other nations, not a peop.le dedicated to the service of mankind.

So as yet the Christians do not know what to do about the Jews, and the Jews do not know what to do about humanity. Both have turned away from their Messianic vocation. They have become strange bedfellows in opting out of commitment to change the world. To some extent their common problems have prompted dialogue. There are Councils and Societies of Christians and Jews. Christians are making a friendly study of Judaism, and Jews of Christianity. The Roman Church has retracted part of its attitude of hostility.

The Christians, too, are seeking to revive their own corporateness through Ecumenism and the work of the World Council of Churches. There has even been mooted a restored Christian nationhood.[12]

Neither Christians nor Jews have yet regained the vision splendid which could bring them together as the People of God, one Israel, capable of bringing world Romanism to an end. All that can be said of manifestations in this sphere is that we can detect some straws blowing in the winds of change; but the winds are by no means blowing at gale force. Prophetically speaking, there is demanded a shaking which will break down complacency, and clearly the terrible state of world affairs has not been able to administer it. If those who are the heirs of the prophets continue to make their excuses for refusing the Messianic invitation, then salvation must come to mankind from another quarter. The children of the Kingdom, Jews and Christians, will have missed their opportunity, and the Kingdom of God will be taken from them and given to a nation bringing forth the fruits thereof.[13]

We are living today in a new eschatological era. The old eschatology, of the time of Jesus, held that judgment was coming upon the world in blazing fire; and the saints were so busy with their predictions of woe, quite misunderstanding the ways of God, that they failed to see that their own love of humanity as a Messiah collective would change the world

for the better much more effectively than the incineration
of sinners. Unfortunately, there are similarly those today,
who again choose force instead of love, and who, provided
they can find a way to save their own skins, will willingly see
the kingdoms of this world go up in flames from a deluge of
nuclear bombs. Indeed, there are not a few, of differing
ideologies, who believe that a new peaceful and harmonious
world order can only be built on the smoking ruins of the
old. Only so can the enemies of capitalism be eradicated.
Only so can the enemies of communism be eliminated.
What is called peace-loving today is manoeuvring into a
position where *our* side has the whip hand.

Are these the circumstances in which the Divine purposes
for mankind can come to fruition? If the Times of the
Gentiles are to be fulfilled it means that Romanism, based on
might is right, on domination and power-seeking, even
given a religious or ideological sanction, must be shamed out
of business by love in action.

If we can go more carefully, more penetratingly, into the
history of the past nineteen centuries, with love and compassion in our hearts, we should be able to discern evidences
that despite appearances the world has not at any time been
abandoned to an arbitrary fate. And it is consistent with the
existence of a Divine Plan that around the world today there
should be sensitive and articulate people in a state of
expectancy, feeling almost instinctively that in this hour of
man's crisis there ought to be a contrasting 'happening'
which is electrifying and beneficial. Some give a name to it,
according to their persuasions, while others are without
imagination as to what form it may take. But the feeling is
there, and it has been growing with the years. Is it only a
psychological reaction?

At the end of the second world war L. P. Jacks expressed
the situation in this way. 'Who can doubt that the unimagin-
able sufferings and the heroic endeavours of the present time,
the depth of the one and the height of the other, the mingling
of shame and glory, the tension and distress of the war-agony
are the symptoms of a world in birth pangs? But the birth of
what? Perhaps of a great surprise.' And he explained: 'It

may be that just when confusion is at its height and about to break out into conflict, the clamour will be hushed by the sudden trumpet-call to a new enterprise for humanity ... I mean, by the unexpected emergence of some commanding aim, of an overarching purpose that would capture the imagination of multitudes, drown their quarrels, over-ride their disputes, make them ashamed of their former petty-mindedness, and carry them forward on a tidal wave of magnanimous resolve to an end worth attaining by man.'[14]

NOTES AND REFERENCES

1. John Toland, *Nazarenus*, 1718.
2. Lord Bryce, *The Holy Roman Empire*.
3. Rom. xi. 20–22 (ANT).
4. Prof. Karl Adam, *The Spirit of Catholicism*.
5. *The Triumph of Christianity*, Bk. IV of *A History of the Early Church*, by Jules Lebreton, S. J. and Jacques Zeiller.
6. II. Cor. vi. 14–17 (ANT).
7. *The Calling of the Jews*, by Canon H. Goudge in the collected essays on *Judaism and Christianity*. Similarly Dr. C. H. Dodd speaks of the Church as being able to gain from closer relations with the Jews, 'who have preserved, in living tradition, elements of the prophetic ideal which belonged to Christianity at the first, but were overlaid by Greek metaphysics and Roman law' to 'a real impoverishment of ethical ideals,' *The Epistle of Paul to the Romans*.
8. The Church 'must retrace her steps and find again the prophetic spirit of the revolutionary leaders of ancient Israel. She must be prepared to break with much that time has hallowed or privilege made dear. "Back to the first-century Church!" must be her slogan—which practically means "Back to Jewish Christianity,"' Olga Levertoff in *The Jews in a Christian Social Order*.
9. The Jews have chiefly had before them the manifestation of Christian antisemitism, and could only imagine that this behaviour was sanctioned by Jesus.
10. Lk. xxi. 24.
11. H. W. Longfellow, *The Jewish Cemetery at Newport*.
12. 'After long contemplation as to the mode of integration required by the Body of Christ at this particular period of historical development, I am convinced that nationhood alone is strong enough to fit it for its historic task in the Redemptive Purpose of God,' Alexander May, in *The Healing Nation*, 1946.
13. Mt. xxi. 43.
14. See *The Hibbert Journal*, July 1944.

9

What may be Gleaned

In the foregoing pages I have affirmed, and to an extent argued, that Godness is operative in the universe and thus in the affairs of our planet. I have claimed that a Divine Plan for mankind is in progress, and I have sought to illustrate this from Jewish-Christian history, because the Hebrews for three thousand years and more have been convinced of their special relationship to such a purpose, and therefore their experiences should offer some evidence in confirmation of their contention.

At the same time I have stressed that great circumspection is needed in approaching the subject of Divine revelation. Those who believed they were receiving and communicating God's will were not oracles, and we are not to suppose that what they foretold was bound to happen, or that a partial fulfilment must necessarily and more remotely have complete fulfilment. Prophecy is not history dictated by God in advance. The prophet is distinguished by certain qualities of mediumship, which work particularly in two ways: they enable him by absorbing a set of circumstances to correlate them and perceive their trend and inner significance, and they make him a suitable recipient of impressions which may derive from a human or non-human source. Communications may come in images, words or flashes of insight; but in whatever manner they are received they have to pass through the mind of the recipient and their expression can be coloured by his or her equipment and personality. But

what so often sets the prophet apart from other mediums or
sensitives is an awareness of being prepared for a special task
which may be contrary to his natural inclinations, or being
suddenly, and frequently inconveniently, called upon, even
conscripted into service. He is told to go and say this, or go
and do that. The experience of the prophet Amos is a case
in point. He insisted, 'I was no prophet, neither was I a
prophet's son; but I was an herdsman, and a gatherer of
sycomore fruit: and the Lord took me as I followed the flock,
and the Lord said unto me, Go, prophesy unto my people
Israel.'[1]

What, then, in the context of Hebrew tradition are we to
look for as evidential of a Divine Plan for mankind? First of
all, I would say, an awareness of being involved in a far-
reaching beneficial purpose of a character which made
demands of an exacting and in certain respects uncongenial
nature, a purpose which was not in line with the general
contemporary way of thinking. Second, there should be able
to be seen, despite all exigencies of human contrariness and
events resulting from unaware people following their own
desires, a movement developing and expanding in the direction of a progressive implementation of the discerned
purpose. Third, there should be an apparently fortuitous
arising of circumstances and conditions conducive to and
unwittingly facilitating its advancement.

As I have already pointed out, we have to make full
allowance for human interpretation and opposition. To say
that this or that did not happen does not, therefore, affect
the issue. We are not dealing with a programme the exact
times and terms of which have been specified and recorded.
No one at any period has been put in possession of comprehensive information, or could know the end from the
beginning. There could be glimpsed sufficient only to convey
that there was a high purpose of a nature that justified man's
creation and experiences, and to indicate to those having
this consciousness what was required of them to cooperate
in bringing it to fruition.

It is of great value that the evidences I have suggested—
and they are not the only ones—can be considered in

relation to a considerable space of time, the span of many generations, so that if the human mind alone was concerned it would be virtually impossible to maintain methodological progress for so long. It can be granted that once an idea has caught on and become accepted as of Divine origin there is an inducement to subscribe to it and to endeavour to go along with it in action. But it would take much more than human contrivance to enlist continually a great variety of unconnected events and factors in its service. All the more so, when there are differences of belief and opinion about precisely what has to be accomplished and by what means.

There are many who still maintain that human history is purposeless. Yet there is abundant proof that, at least, evolution and hierarchic order is present in it. All our sciences, our political and economic systems, our social patterns have evolved. Our geographical knowledge of our planet has grown and has had evolutionary consequences, and it has been the same with our means and methods of communication. Frequently, both new discoveries and catastrophes like war and pestilence have stimulated change and progress. It is purely an assumption, and not a very convincing one, that all this is purposeless. The assumption is made, not on the basis of evidence that the human story is without purpose, but because to postulate the contrary carries with it implications which are inconvenient to the atheist. It is not denied, as perhaps it should be, that human beings and whole societies of human beings have purposes. There is simply a stop in the mind when it comes to conceiving mankind as fulfiling the purposes of any higher mind. The very thought of mind itself is troublesome, since it involves the existence of an immaterial dimension of consciousness.

As there is no body of facts which establishes that there cannot be a Plan, we are fully entitled to study Jewish-Christian history, which affirms that there is one and submits itself as a test case, to learn what may be gleaned from it. Bearing in mind the criteria we have proposed, let us briefly look at the sequence and relationship of circumstances which appear to support that a purpose has been manifesting itself in human affairs, and which afford some understanding of what is intended. At the stage we have now reached, with so much behind us, it should be practicable to see things in clearer perspective.

We cannot go back very much earlier than 1000 B.C. because we cannot be sure how much that is related of the Patriarchs and Moses in the books of Genesis and Exodus is factual. We can accept that there were movements of the Hebrews into Palestine and later into Egypt culminating in a larger migration out of Egypt and a conquest of much of Palestine. There could well have been a belief that these movements were called for by Divine intimations and guidances. What is evident is that this belief had become definite by the time of the Hebrew monarchy, and consequently the chroniclers depicted past history in this sense. Thus we have the account of God's call to Abraham to journey to Canaan, and of the covenant made with him that the country would be given to his heirs as a Promised Land. The theme is continued through the narration of the story of the sojourn in Egypt, the exodus under Moses, the giving of the Law, and the wanderings in the wilderness.

We may say that the Israelites had to justify their occupation of Canaan; but they did it in a curious way. There was nothing exceptional in claiming that their God had instructed them to take over this country. But it was exceptional for the Israelites to see themselves as being requisitioned to be a priestly nation for the express purpose of being a blessing to other nations. This was not at all in line with contemporary motives for aggression, which unashamedly were concerned with self-interest, the levying of tribute and the increase of power and prestige. For the Israelites, they were a people chosen and set apart from others with a mission directed to the welfare of all mankind. And they could assert this while surrounded and sometimes overrun by hostile neighbours.

And why should Canaan specially be their Promised Land? Was it suited to an intention that things would happen here for the benefit of humanity, so that progressively it should be singled out as a Holy Land? Geographically it formed part of the Fertile Crescent, and was a meeting place for the continents of Europe, Asia and Africa. On this land impinged and converged many peoples and their cultures, Sumerians, Amorites, Hittites, Egyptians, the Peoples of the Sea, Philistines, Assyrians and Chaldeans, and later Medo-Persians, Greeks and Romans, Arabs, Franks and Turks. All and more were drawn here in their time.

In Israel was born the doctrine of a servant-nation ministering to all nations, and therefore the antithesis of power-politics and imperialism, which was to become the permanent feature in what was canvassed as the Divine Plan. For through the Hebrew Prophets there began to be awareness of a Plan. The servant-nation was not to enslave and must treat foreigners no differently from its own members, because they had known what it was to be slaves and aliens. The servant-nation must teach the ways of God and set an example; for God was one and the God of all mankind, and all peoples of the world were his children. The vision of the Prophets embraced a future in which all war and injustice would be brought to an end, and all idolatry would cease.

It is easy enough, because we have become familiar with these ideas, to treat them as natural sentiments. It is only in the context of the times and conditions when they were expressed that they stand out as so remarkable. But the Bible also informs us that the vision went unmatched by performance. The Hebrews chose statehood with all its snares and pitfalls, and were enticed by the polytheistic cults of their neighbours. If the vision was not mere utopianism statehood would have to be taken away to restore concentration on the singularity of Israel's mission. This happened very quickly. The kingdom of Israel was destroyed by the Assyrians, and that of Judah by the Chaldeans. This could have been the end; but it was not. The new Babylonian Empire smote the Assyrians, and was in turn smitten by the Medo-Persians. The penitent Jewish remnant of Israel was allowed to return from exile by decree of Cyrus the Mede, but not to revived statehood. Was this accidental?

The land to which the Jews returned had largely been purged of pagan cults, and they themselves instructed by scribes and prophets became a religious community more closely knit than before. The Bible emerged as a collection of sacred literature, and the doctrine of the Faithful Remnant came into prominence. Yet still there was insufficient devotion to the vision to inspire corporate action. The Jews were not a light to the Gentiles.[2] But one of the things which did come in with the Persians was the idea of a Cosmic Drama, an age to age contest between Light and Darkness, Good and Evil, which in the end would be crowned by the victory of Righteousness. This was to give rise to a developed Jewish eschatology, in which this idea was brought into relationship with the teaching of the Prophets with emphasis on a coming Day of the Lord and the appearance of Messianic personalities.[3] Was this accidental?

How could the Jews be stirred to spiritual action among the nations? We find the issue affected by two major circumstances. First the victories of Alexander the Great brought East and West together within the framework of a united world concept. The Jews were brought in closer contact with Greek culture, and became much more widely distributed by increasing settlement in other lands. Second, the attempt by one of the heirs to part of Alexander's empire, the Syrian king Antiochus Epiphanes, to compel the Jews to adopt the Greek religion made them take their faith and its universal implications much more seriously. Both the wider contacts and the revivalist fervour caused the Jews to engage in missionary work as never before. The intensity of effort was closely linked with a reading of the Signs of the Times, which now insisted that the Last Days were at hand. As a result the knowledge of God and of a distinction between Jews and all other nations became widespread.[4] But the Jewish impact was made very little in a spirit of love and service, as their propaganda literature indicates, and therefore was still far removed from the objects of a servant-nation. Consequently, there was encountered a good deal of resistance and antisemitic feeling.

The time was ripe for a substantial new development, and

circumstances were conducive to it. Jewish belief that the
End of the Age was approaching was now very strong. The
Messiah was eagerly awaited, the holy king who would put
down evil and inaugurate the era of the Kingdom of God on
earth. This also meant for the eschatologists the destruction
of the Roman Empire, which was seen as the final expression
of ruthless pagan power. But if Israel was to fulfil its mission
to mankind the accent must be on love towards all, even
enemies. Hostility could never promote peace and justice.
Accordingly, when Jesus appeared as the Messiah he
laboured to explain to the people what qualities were
demanded of the servant-nation. He finally submitted
himself to cruel suffering at the hands of the Romans to
demonstrate his contentions. By his teaching and actions he
epitomised what was called for from Israel as God's son and
servant, and he thus qualified to be the mainspring of a
fresh initiative.

Like so many of his generation, Jesus expected speedy
results, and in this he was mistaken. But had he not expected
them, and his followers likewise, there would have been no
impetus, no desperate haste, to carry the Messianic news far
and wide. The conditions assisted the process. There were
now Jewish communities throughout what was described
as the habitable world, and the Roman Empire itself, which
the Kingdom of God was to supersede, had made the task of
evangelization much easier. Travel was more safe and rapid
because of the Roman Peace. Territories had been linked by
great trunk roads, and piracy at sea had largely been
suppressed. The extensive use of Greek considerably overcame the language barrier.

A new recruit to the Messianic cause, the Hellenic Jew
Saul of Tarsus, threw himself ardently into an all out effort
to gain converts from the Gentiles to make up for the loss of
adequate Jewish support. As Saul, better known as Paul,
saw it, God was giving Gentiles the opportunity to join the
ranks of Israel by faith in the Messiah. The servant-nation
would thus experience an enlargement which would
facilitate the universal impact of the proclamation of the
Kingdom of God in line with its function and true character.

Israel must move outward from self-centredness. The necessity was underlined when the Jewish Zealots plunged into war with the Romans, and victory for the Romans destroyed the Temple at Jerusalem and terminated the long history of the Levitical priestly office. Henceforward the Jews would have a more spiritual nationhood operating through the synagogues and built around the prescriptions of the Torah, as interpreted by the Rabbis.

It was indeed a change of era, presenting a marvellous fresh opportunity for progress towards the coming of the Kingdom of God. Unfortunately human wilfulness once again retarded its advent. The new Israelites, who had been former pagan Gentiles, coloured their faith with Gentile notions and created the religion of Christianity in which Jesus was worshipped as God incarnate instead of being followed as Messiah. There was a blending of semitism and heathenism, and in due course the development of rites and ceremonies and a quasi-heathen priesthood associated with their performance. The People of God was effectively rent in two, with the new religion persecuting and villifying the old. But the Jews did not perish. While Christianity became more other-worldly they remained as a living reminder of a purer faith, which also insisted on the earthly fulfilment of the ancient vision of a Messianic age of world peace and justice.

Could there be any gain in this sorry state of affairs? Only in the context of a Divine purpose. Christianity became the official religion of the Roman Empire, and as such it was able to promote powerfully a widespread acknowledgment of God and a relinquishment by many nations of a cruder idolatry to an extent that the Jews had been incapable of achieving. As a result a very important halfway step was being taken towards the ideal, and Jewish ethical teaching through Christianity was accepted as the standard of conduct by which society, individuals and kingdoms, should be guided. This eventually would make it more practicable to advance towards principles held in common.

Peoples, however, were being Christianized on the whole superficially. The objective of the Church was not to call out

of the nations a ministering servant-nation, but to bring as
many peoples as possible under its sway. It was in fact aiming
at a new Romanism, the concept of a Holy Roman Empire.
The Roman Church has never surrendered this concept,
though it was frustrated in its medieval expression. What was
left of the idea of a separate priestly people was considered
to be satisfied by the corporate functioning of an ordained
priesthood headed by the Vicar of Christ, the Pope.

We have now, for some time, passed beyond Biblical
history, and have to note that later developments were not
less significant. What in particular we have to observe, in
spite of a number of setbacks, is a progressive resistance to
Romanism, the doctrine of a self-appointed Common
Superior, and the growth of a universalistic humanitarianism.

Already in medieval times with the development of
commerce there was a movement which brought into being
a number of small-scale self-governing communities.[5] There
were the trade guilds and ship guilds and town charters.
These stressed the brotherly relations subsisting between the
members or citizens, and laid down regulations to deal with
quarrels and injuries. One town would also send to another
for a ruling in law on some particular issue, or act as
arbitrator in inter-city disputes. Within the town the
neutrality of the market-place had long been a recognized
institution, and no feud could be prosecuted at the place
where people came to trade, nor within a certain radius
from it. These fellowships with their mercantile expansion,
though still recognizing the ruler as common superior,
steadily undermined Romanism and laid the foundations for
democracy. They also helped, when the modern nation-state
was born, to create a groundwork for international law.[6]

Such a law of nations was essential, which regarded each
nation-state as an individual entity in a world society or
community. The very same considerations which had
produced the small-scale fraternities might be held to
operate more potently—because of the horrors of war—to
establish an international fraternity. Such a consequence
seemed to follow from the Tragedy of the Thirty Years' War
(1618–1648), which stimulated Hugo Grotius to compose

De Jure Belli ac Pacis. He set up the Natural Law, which is the Divine Law, as the basis for the Law of Nations and the substitute for a Common Superior. The conduct of nations must be founded on the principles and sentiments of an enlightened humanity. So 'wise kings regard themselves as entrusted with the care of not one nation only but of all mankind.' He proposed the holding of congresses of Christian Powers, where international disputes could be settled by the disinterested Powers. 'Means might be devised, indeed, to compel conflicting States to accept a peace on reasonable terms.'[7]

This was advanced thinking, which took a long while to bear fruit. But it speaks for a new pattern of relationships which was emerging as the outcome of a variety of circumstances. There had been the challenge of Islam, the terrible experience of the Black Death, the decline of the Papacy, the Reformation, all contributing to developing popular participation in government. Gunpowder had shattered baronialism and printing had increased literacy. The Bible began to come into the hands of the people and the Old Testament teaching to exercise a new influence. Travels and voyages made contact with a greater world. The Earth was demonstrated to be a globe and part of a heliocentric system.

The Age of Reason dawned. Rousseau, to quote Winwood Reade, 'taught men to yearn for an ideal state which they with their own efforts might attain; he inspired them with the sentiment of Liberty, and with a reverence for the Law of Right. Virtuous principles, abstract ideas, the future deities of men, were now for the first time lifted up to be adored. A thousand hearts palpitated with excitement; a thousand pens were drawn; the people that slumbered in sorrow and captivity heard a voice bidding them arise; they strained, they struggled, and they burst their bonds. Jacques Bonhomme, who had hitherto gone on all fours, discovered to his surprise that he also was a biped; the world became more light; the horizon widened; a new epoch opened for the human race.'[8] The Gospel of Liberty, Equality and Fraternity, was proclaimed with a fanaticism that could only achieve such violent apostleship from men's consciousness of

something of tremendous import which hitherto had been
missing in their associations. Crowns! Mitres! What did these
matter when the humblest was awed by the amazing
revelation, 'I am a Man. I belong to the Brotherhood of
Man'?

With the industrial revolution and the growth of nonconformist religion the people became more insistent on their
human rights. There began to flow a steady stream of
legislation along the channels of social service and social
justice. The common man reached out to his brothers in
other lands, forging fresh international relationships, and in
the aims of socialist communism expressing in an extreme
form a solidarity which cut right across state boundaries.
Marx and Engels were the fiery prophets. 'All previous
historical movements,' they declared, 'were movements of
minorities. The proletarian movement is the self-conscious,
independent movement of the immense majority. The
proletariat, the lowest stratum of our present society, cannot
stir, cannot raise itself up, without the whole superincumbent
strata of official society being sprung into the air ... The
working men have no country. We cannot take from them
what they have not got ... They openly declare that their
ends can be attained only by the forcible overthrow of all
existing social conditions. Let the ruling classes tremble at
a Communistic revolution. The proletarians have nothing
to lose but their chains. They have a world to win. Working
men of all countries unite!'[9]

The extension of consciousness did not, as it transpired,
spell the end of Romanism. In Communism and Capitalism
it produced additional varieties of imperialism. But on the
other hand the principle of mutual service was receiving
ever wider application, softening rigidities and cutting
across divisions, allying itself with the beneficent aspects of
scientific discovery in combating disease, raising standards
of living and education, speeding up communications, and
promoting numerous cooperative enterprises. What was
most notable in the nineteenth century was that more and
more people, countries, races, creeds and classes were being
included-in as active participants in social and political life.

The extension of the franchise, anti-slavery legislation, emancipation of negroes and Jews, the trades unions, the care of the aged and destitute, the more humane treatment of criminals and the insane, serve as only a few examples of the developing sense of social responsibility.

There was also the burgeoning of knowledge of the world and of nature. Exploration filled in blank areas on the global map, geology and archaeology retrieved the mysterious past of the planet, ethnology studied the varieties of the human species. The internal combustion engine and telegraphy brought mankind closer together. Electricity added a new dimension to living conditions. The mind of man was awakening to a wholeness of things as never before in human history, and with this awakening it began also to dawn on a meditating minority that 'all war is civil war.' The century which had seen so much change ended on a hopeful note with the convening in 1899 of the International Peace Conference at the Hague.

The story continues into the twentieth century still more dramatically and significantly, as we are well aware. Once more, but in a wider and more intense context, we find ourselves in a Last Days atmosphere, and many are trying to read the Signs of the Times. An age of rich promise is also one of deep despondency. Has all the striving, so much of it noble, been all in vain? Or will another more comprehensive Messianic activity come to our rescue?

If our brief outline appears meaningful, then we shall have an assurance of what we are to expect. Whatever may help to save us will have an identification with the character of the Plan as it has manifested itself previously in the past three thousand years. There will have to be a fresh application of the methodology of the servant-nation. There has never been any alteration of the designated means of deliverance. It is only its component structure which has varied as called for by the changes in man's situation and the lack of dedicated resolve on the part of those who had been chosen.

We have the clue to history clearly presenting itself in the Jewish-Christian story, and this is why it is so important. To bring out its purport more explicitly I have selected only a few features, and these not always the most prominent in the history books. But it would not have affected the issue if I had been much more comprehensive. It would have only imposed a greater strain on the reader's attention. I could also, of course, have gone outside Jewish-Christian matters and offered a world conspectus; but again the result would have been the same. It is not to belittle or disparage the place of other cultures and faiths in the scheme of things that they have been omitted from survey. And I believe that in the next phase of world affairs a major part will be played by Asia, Africa and South America.

Evolution does not imply an unimpeded progress devoid of setbacks and dead ends. It represents an ascending complexity with ever greater attendant risks and potentialities, where real advances are procured by adaptations capable of surmounting obstacles and retarding factors. It is in the inherent will to survive and overcome that purpose is suggested, and as higher levels of capacity and consciousness are reached by so much more is purpose brought out of the abstract into the concrete. The power both to discern and to cooperate with an overall purpose becomes the distinguishing mark of those who are in line with the evolutionary process. However knowledgeable people may be, because we are now somewhat ahead of the primitive, if they are not sentient as regards the operation of Godness in the human sphere they are identifying themselves with an aspect of development that will terminate when its contribution is completed, and which will have no place as evolution proceeds.

The ancients depicted what was going on as if it were a continual struggle between opposing divine forces of good and evil, light and darkness. Their faith made them prepared to bet on the ultimate victory of the Good Power. The dualistic interpretation survived in Christianity as a contest between God and the Devil. Naturally, in the end God must win. No one would want to deny that positive and negative are phenomena of nature. We should not, therefore, altogether dismiss the antique symbolism as an absurdity. But in the context of the human drama we may rather think of the clash, which has constructive value, as between God's will and man's will, and not between relatively equal divinities competing for the human soul.

It is God who has given to man for his benefit an increasing degree of autonomy, and evolution requires that he should exercise it in learning that his best interests are served in discovering and conforming himself to God's will by making it his own will. The outcome, as some have proposed, will not be the destruction of the Devil, but his conversion. There will be a marriage of heaven and earth, and harmony will reign.

But our concern here is not with ultimates. We are seeking enlightenment on what must have been provided for to enable us to correct our present grievous errors and extricate ourselves from the perils we have brought upon ourselves. If we will go with God the solution must be revealed to us. Everything will then depend on the diligence and sense of responsibility of those who are instructed.

The reading of events which we have furnished has emphasized two contrasting principles, those of domination and service, the one tending to slavery and the other to liberation. Significantly it is service which makes men really free because it illuminates the inward personality by its outgoing embrace of the meaningfulness of everything and everyone outside itself to which it becomes positively related. The spirit of service thus manifests itself as a Godlike quality. God is accepted as Lord by reason that he is understood to be serving and to be at the service of all his creatures.

The old idea of the Two Principles gave the impression of a kind of chess game played out through the ages in which successive moves by one side were countered by those of the other. Such a notion makes God to be governed by the conditions of our humanity, and reflects a low level of intelligence. Godness operative in our sphere does not mean that according to how things are shaping God makes up his mind what to do next. We have rather to think of our world as in some manner programmed for self-development with at higher stages an increasing measure of capacity to exercise free will, and with built-in corrective factors functioning when a wrong choice has been made. This can be, of course, only a rough and ready assumption deriving from our own creative powers in the domain of mechanics, and what we are able to observe in physics and biological chemistry. We cannot expect to have more than a modicum of insight into the mechanics of spiritual chemistry.

At our present stage of development we should now be able to detect that what we have termed Romanism is a wrong employment of Godness qualities, and Messianism a right one. If we choose Romanism, even for what appear to be good ends, what we construct and aim at will not work out. If we choose Messianism, which may seem to be weak and ineffective, the result will none the less be beneficial. We have, therefore, standards by which we can test the validity of any course of action. If it calls for force or domination, sooner or later it will fail. If it calls for love and service, even if it involves temporary suffering, it will succeed. The fulfilment of the purposes of God can be postponed under our Time conditions if we do not meet their requirements; and they can be speeded up by our will to work with them.

Thus, when we reflect on all our yesterdays with an earnest desire to learn their lesson, we can contemplate today and tomorrow with assurance, provided that we are prepared to implement what we have gleaned. 'In quietness and confidence shall be your strength.'[10] The time is ripe for a further expression of Messianism in keeping with past indications to manifest itself to meet our desperate need. We can profit by it or reject it for our generation, either totally or partially, and our decision will govern what we have to endure. But if we fail it will still crop up again and again, if need be, for ages unborn. In the end the Divine Plan will be our plan.

NOTES AND REFERENCES

1. Amos vii. 14–15.
2. Ezek. xxxvi. 20–22.
3. Cp. the concept of Beliar in the Jewish Pseudepigrapha and the doctrine of the Two Spirits in the Dead Sea Scrolls. At the same time we

have the presentation of the Two Messiahs, from Levi and Judah, and accent on the coming Wrath. A modern interpretation of the Cosmic Drama, the battle between Eros (the Life Force) and Thanatos (the Death Force) has been offered by Herbert Marcuse. See *Eros and Civilization* (Boston, 1966).

4. See Schonfield, *Those Incredible Christians*, chs. ii and iii.

5. See Kropotkin, *Mutual Aid*.

6. See George B. Davis, *The Elements of International Law*.

7. Grotius, *The Law of War and Peace*, quoted in the translation of extracts by W. S. M. Knight, Peace Classics Series.

8. Winwood Reade, *The Martyrdom of Man*.

9. See the *Communist Manifesto* (1848).

10. Isa. xxx. 15.

Part Two

I

Twentieth Century Man

In no previous century of which we have record have there been so many indications of a change of times as the one which, as I write, is approaching its closing phase. Chiefly it has signalled the beginning of the Space Age, and this in a great variety of connections. Man has been able to take to the air as a new environment of his movement and activities, both to travel around his planet with increasing speed and facility, and to eject himself beyond its pull to start to explore the solar system. He has landed on the alien surface of the moon, and his controlled instruments have reached Venus and Mars. His devices are revealing more and more of the universe, while in his own world he can transmit information about events so that they can be seen and heard almost instantaneously in any part of it. His penetration is extending to the beds of the seas and deep into the crust of the earth. He is probing into the basic stuff of life and into his own unconscious.

This has been a century of so many remarkable advances in science, technology and medicine, that the conditions of existence have been altering with extraordinary rapidity. Had there been an inner wisdom commensurate with these other achievements this could have been one of the most fruitful centuries in promoting the general good of mankind. Much good has in fact been done in many ways. There has been a substantial enrichment and improvement of the human lot. But also there has been great loss in lessening

human dignity and justification of being. For so many, as
G. K. A. Bell expressed it, 'life, which they ought to be
making, seems made for them, and made in spite of them,
and, too often, made wrong. There is no centre, no plan, no
sense of a whole to which or for which they are, themselves,
in some way responsible,'[1] and he quoted the old engineer of
Kipling's poem *M'Andrew's Hymn.*

> 'What I ha' seen since ocean-steam began
> Leaves me no doot for the machine: but what about the
>   man?
> The man that counts, wi' all his runs, one million mile
>   o' sea:
> Four times the span from earth to moon ... How far,
>   O Lord, from Thee?'

As it is, this century of such vast promise and performance,
hailed as that of the Common Man, has proved to be one of
increasing doubt and uncertainty, frustration and sense of
impotence, and worst of all the century of the Great Fear.

The eruption of Romanism, in various guises, has been
widespread and on an unprecedented scale. The lust for
power and domination has been intensified with multiplication of means of mass propaganda and mass destruction.
Systems have become insatiable gods demanding human
sacrifice, with politicians and military men as their hierophants. The state has acquired an artificial status as a lord
of creation, coercing and controlling those over whom it
wields authority in a grim struggle for self-assertion, and
where possible the mastery of lesser lords. Democracy has
become a convenient euphemism to disguise oligarchy.

The growing complexity of corporate life with its profound
dependence on the specialist has served to encourage subservience to authority and to accentuate nationalism.
Emphasis of the state ego could more readily be contrived
where there was popular inclination to evade governmental
involvement, and acquiescence became the most comfortable
policy for the individual who found his immediate concerns
quite enough of a problem. The personification of the state,

the system, the group mind, took away correspondingly the desire for personal commitment, and fostered an insidious and subtle invasion of human liberty.

Fortunately the human spirit is not easily quelled, and tyranny whether blatant or elaborately concealed has never been able to have things all its own way. Revolt can be suppressed, but not eliminated.

'And after this let Caesar seat him sure;
For we will shake him, or worse days endure.'

As one study report has declared, 'The modern world is not like that which was unified by the legions of Rome; the peoples composing it are neither barbarians nor representatives of effete civilizations, though many must still be schooled in liberty and in the essentials of human dignity. These enduring needs of mankind can never be satisfied by a philosophy based on human inequality and asserting that a race of masters should organize a subservient world.'[2]

Individuals and minority groups have never ceased to be aware that the power-structure of society is contrary to their real interests and well-being, and has given rise to a world order in which conflict predominates with the consequent threat that political folly may go too far and bring upon mankind such ruin and disaster that a substantial part of the population will be extinguished and the survivors reduced to almost insupportable misery. They protest and demonstrate and break out into violence, the young especially; but they are like sheep without a shepherd who can do little more than bleat their unhappiness in ineffective and superficial slogans. The will has largely been taken from them to devise and create a better order. They do not know or want to know all the intricacies that such an order would represent, because this would entail involvement and acceptance of responsibility. They still expect that their clamour will force the powers-that-be to think and act differently, thus relieving themselves of the obligation to harness their own energies to the drudgery of methodical reconstruction. The road to hell today is not so much paved with good intentions, as with

ideals unsupported by any intention patiently and persist-
ently to bring them to fruition.

It is in the political domain, because this is the most
difficult, that dearth of new imagination and enterprise has
been most in evidence, though some valuable work has been
done by scientific study groups and conferences.[3] As a rule,
however, their findings do not go beyond saying what is
desirable: they remain an academic exercise, useful but not
inspiring to action.

I have stressed certain negative aspects of the situation;
but the positive things which have been happening must be
accorded due weight and a fuller treatment. These may be
embraced by the word Community, community in the
major sense affecting relations between states, and community in the minor sense concerned with the relationship
between small *ad hoc* groups of individuals. In both contexts
there have been gains and losses.

As I have already made reference to minority groups, and
as these have an important microcosmic significance, I shall
confine myself for the rest of this chapter to developments in
this sphere, leaving the subject of the World Community for
later treatment. There is, of course, a correspondence
between the two expressions of community, since the small-
scale groups are in effect both a condemnation of things as
they are in the world at large, and an endeavour to offer an
experimental representation of what sensitive people feel
they ought to be. We can, therefore, learn much from them
which should inform our consideration of the wider issues.
Essentially they mark a decline of faith, not only in politics,
but in the teachings and practice of organized religion.

Religion has seemed so much a part of the existing
Romanist world order, whose policies it has so often supported or come to terms with, that in its traditional formulations it is viewed with the same kind of disenchantment.
But while, as a consequence, millions are now in a spiritual
vacuum, many have received a fresh impulse towards
soul-experiences, including the psychedelic, which they are
trying to acquire outside the churches, chapels, synagogues,
temples and mosques. In many ways the search is very like

that of the Thibetan priests for a new Dalai Lama. People
are questing for an earthly incarnation of the free spirit of
man in individuals, but also in groups. It is the higher
certainty, the wider comprehension, the fuller self-development, and the consciousness of the fundamental oneness of
all things at which they aim, and by which they are invested
with that dignity of which the enslaving spirit that now
prevails would seek to deprive them.

It is a brave effort, and in part a genuine contribution to
a psychological adjustment to changed conditions, but to
avoid self-centredness it requires a counter-balancing activity
in social service, and this it very often achieves. But just as
often the mind is turned inward. Here the spiritual disciplines of the orient are frequently called on for the rescue of
the confused occidental. To many, India stands for detachment and disinterestedness. 'Of course, the snag is,' as Dean
Inge once put it, 'that we may fancy we are disinterested
when we are only uninterested.'

The inclination to step aside from the turmoil and the
evils of society is a very ancient one, and the organization of
small select communities has always owed much to oriental
inspiration. Patterns have changed very little through the
centuries. The worthiest endeavours have been those which
have sought to test whether it is practicable in a selfish and
competitive world to live up to those principles which all
religions have proclaimed to be fundamental for a right
relationship between man and man. One of the pioneers of
modern community activities has defined this aim.

'Community experiment is an open-eyes attempt to make
practice square more nearly with principle; to bridge the
gulf between thinking and doing; to reduce human problems
to a compass in which they can be grappled and not simply
theorized over; to put conviction to the test of living; to
submit ideals to the test of working experience; to let action
speak louder than words. To these ends it mobilizes spiritually
dedicated people into a positive and dynamic fellowship of
faith and service.'[4]

There has been a proliferation of community enterprises
in the twentieth century because of the unnatural character

and conditions of modern life, its false values, its emphasis of
the artificial, its estrangements and conflicts. The community
group sees itself not only as a protest, but as a rectification,
a return to the grass roots of living, a reassertion of the true
basis on which a harmonious and peaceful world order must
be erected. It is a condemnation of the state, recognizing
that there is no possibility of any real world community, or
even national community, under predominantly centralized
governmental control. It stresses that where organization
becomes too comprehensive and remote, essential fellowship,
the sense of belonging, the self-fulfilment of personal participation, is destroyed. Men are not to be treated as ciphers, as
cogs in a vast machine, who can be directed, coerced, and
regarded as expendable: they have rights which are much
more than rights in law, and chiefly the right to be persons
who matter, who count for something, who have a say in
things, who form relationships, and who are accorded a
consideration which justifies their existence, to themselves
and to their fellows.

The unity of such groups, to quote Macmurray, 'rests
upon the feeling in each member that they all "belong
together." This is the type of union which exists between
friends, and its original locus in human society is the family
or the kinship group. Such groups cooperate, of course, but
their cooperation is not based on a calculation of interest.
It has a "sacramental" character, because it expresses the
sense of "fellowship" or "brotherhood"; the consciousness
of inner, emotional unity. Such a group is not unified
because it cooperates. It cooperates because it is already
unified."[5]

Sociologists are well aware of the problems arising from
the multiplication of faceless and soulless masses, which while
normally dully conforming and quiescent can readily be
made hysterical and violent. The population explosion
aggravates the dangers in the more densely packed areas.[6]
If men are not allowed to be whole persons in small adjusted
and largely autonomous groups, then there must be Romanism, the harnessing of the population to a state cult or an
ideology which claims to be acting in its best interests. There

will be rigid controls to suppress all subversive tendencies and the definition of an external or internal enemy, country, race, class or system, to direct hostility away from the ruling authority. Engaging in war will be regarded as one of the means of maintaining peace at home.

Under Communist governments, mostly in countries where a feudal system had previously existed, the endeavour has been to unite oligarchic rule with the satisfaction of group expression, by creating worker and peasant communities and cooperatives with a common allegiance to state-socialism. This has created a form of democracy in which the people seemed to themselves to be governing, though they were not in fact doing so, except within rigidly prescribed limits. The system has illustrated one way of coordinating parts within the whole, but only on terms of a strict allegiance and the designation of the state's enemies as the enemies of the people. It does not, therefore, contribute to the development of a free society, and does not remove the necessity for free group experimentation.

Such experimentation certainly has something to teach about a way of life, which somehow will have to be translated into universal practice if there is to be a more ideal world order. How this may be done will enter into the presentation of the Divine Plan for our time. But one aspect we must touch on here, and this is the question of kinship.

Religion in the past had as one of its functions the extension of the principle of community beyond the limits of natural relationship through some ceremony of adoption. It was not enough for a group to accept a stranger as a member. He had to be felt and believed to be kin, reborn into the inner unity of the group.[7] Modern liberal teaching has tended to reject this ancient wisdom. It has sought to make men conscious of brotherhood without the spiritual sanction, and this has proved to be a very uphill task. Naturally there are some who have managed to do this, but they have chiefly been those whose humanism is so intense as to acquire a religious quality. Apart from the religions, it is still mainly within relatively small groups that the conversion of the stranger into a brother takes effect, frequently by some ceremony.

The Brotherhood of Man might be realizable if all men sincerely believed that they were the children of one Father and acted accordingly. But this is not so. Therefore it is a fundamental problem, which small-scale community may help to solve, how to create an inner spiritual unity that is non-exclusive and universal? Can there be found a comprehensive ideology to unite mankind, which permits and welcomes diversity within the kinship, and does not have to act coercively?

The young are especially concerned about this, because their lives and futures are at stake. They want war abolished, and they are sick of shams, double-think and double-talk, political posturings and equivocations. They are still starry-eyed and do not see the problems as complex, only those responsible for the 'system' as being wilfully obtuse and perverse. Don't talk about difficulties, they insist. Make it happen! Make it real! The young are simple literalists, and they move into group formation to demonstrate their contentions. Since it is said, 'Love one another,' this they will do frankly and without inhibitions. 'Share what you have,' and gladly they will do it. Their naivety may be extreme, but it is necessary to counteract the deviousness of so much sophisticated thinking. 'Except ye be converted, and become as little children, ye shall not enter into the Kingdom of Heaven.'[8]

We cannot hope to solve our problems if we are so entangled in a thicket of 'ifs' and 'buts' that it becomes impossible to take self-liberating action. We need, therefore, the initiatives of the young and of the young in heart to enable us to break away from the 'system' which crushes the soul and regiments individuals for its own selfish and frequently unjust ends. We must have Messianism to overcome Romanism, and this involves, as a point of departure, a corrective simplification. We have to have the Flower Children of all ages, the Davids who will face up to the mailed Goliaths, if we are to achieve a capacity to remedy our situation.

Mahatma Gandhi has been in this century one of the older 'children of the kingdom,' proclaiming a gospel of

Ahimsa (positive love) realized through *Satyagraha* (soul-force). '*Satyagraha*,' he stated, 'differs from passive resistance as the North Pole from the South. The latter has been conceived as a weapon of the weak . . . whereas the former has been conceived as a weapon of the strongest, and excludes the use of violence in any shape or form . . . All well-constructed societies are based on the law of non-violence. I have found that life persists in the midst of destruction, and therefore there must be a higher law than destruction. Only under that law would a well-ordered society be intelligible and life worth living. And if that is the law of life we have to work it out in daily life. Wherever there are jars, wherever you are confronted with an opponent, conquer him with love—in this crude manner I have worked it out in my life. This does not mean that all my difficulties are solved. Only I have found that this law of love answered as the law of destruction has never done.'[9]

Pacifism has endeavoured to implement this creed. To think of it in the negative sense as merely a conscientious objection to military service is to miss its true significance completely. It is an objection to war and military service, of course, but it is that because of a spiritual perception of the worth of the individual, which makes the taking of life for any cause a blasphemy, and regards the resolution of hatreds and enmities as the most important requisite for the building of a better world order. Pacifism (peace-making) is a positive as well as a blessed business, which calls men to come out and be separate from the dictates of any authority which finds it necessary to resort to force and coercion either for its own preservation or the domination of others.

One of the protagonists of this faith expressed it thus. 'In accordance with individual interpretations of War, pacifists have, in varying degrees, foresworn the use of bad means. In place of these they can only substitute good means to the extent to which they can realize imaginatively the implications of a universal outlook. "Liberation from prevailing conventions of thought, feeling and behaviour," says Aldous Huxley (*Ends and Means*), "is accomplished most effectively by the practice of disinterested virtues and through insight into the real nature of ultimate reality. Such insight is a gift, inherent in the individual; but, though inherent, it cannot manifest itself completely except where certain conditions are fulfilled. The principal precondition of insight is, precisely, the practice of disinterested virtues." The wide outlook, then, is seen to be dependent upon insight, and the first duty of pacifists is not to preach pacifism or war-resistance, but to practice disinterested virtues.'[10]

Non-violent groups, therefore, are seeking, ostensibly, to carry out a new way of living as a nucleus of a new world order. Their self-training in the technique of non-violence is designed to foster and forward a universalist outlook by achieving an inner unity and community without which any outward unification cannot long endure. As Vera Brittain has pointed out, 'The movement that seeks to create this community which knows neither force nor frontiers is inevitably a revolutionary movement. It is a society within society, a living force which depends neither on economic systems nor political machinery—though it may work through both—but upon the power of the spirit.'[11]

While this is true, experience has shown that except on a very small scale it is virtually impossible to contract-out of either the political or economic system. Geography does not now offer any Isles of the Blest where the disinterested virtues can be practised without compromise and accomodation.

It is perfectly feasible to create a society within society, but the existing groups, unfortunately, have shown no disposition to think out the implications. Their amateurism has been quite pathetic. They have not visualized in detail or agreed upon the character and structure of the new world order of which their own order will be the exemplification and a kind of halfway house towards the goal. To drop out is not to create, and the world is never going to return to the simple life of a primitive tribalism, however idyllic in imagination. Consequently, the better society cannot exist until those who desire to promote it have worked out in terms of modern technology, politics and economics how it is to function, while still conforming to its principles.

There are plenty who offer panaceas for the various world problems; but this is not what is required, since there is no universal will to accept them or try them out. The only possibility for the success of any of these propositions is that they should first pass the test of a sufficiently organized society within society which agrees to conduct the experiment. Most of the panacea-pedlars turn away from this. For them it is all or nothing. Much cerebration is therefore wasted in futile efforts to persuade the wrong people to do the right things.

To establish its validity the exemplary society has to become integrated and planned out with reference to every aspect of its corporate existence. It has to recognize itself in such a manner as will commend it and secure for it recognition by the authorities now in command. It has to win for itself a place in the scheme of things which permits it a high degree of autonomy. This it is not going to accomplish as long as there is a refusal by its own constituents to take into account and find a home for every facet of a world order which is scientific, highly mechanized and industrialized, highly diversified, and continually expanding in coverage and resources.

World Community is imperative, but it is nonsensical to suppose that it can be reached in one jump. We have to act with decision, but not in panic. We have to be urgent, and yet proceed as if we had ample time at our disposal, comprehensively and systematically. One of the more hopeful signs of movement in the right direction has been the great increase of agencies for international voluntary service, the greater acknowledgment of responsibility towards the underprivileged, the new links forged by trade, improved communications, and the international conference of individuals and bodies engaged in many professions and occupations. The study of common needs has advanced further than in any previous century. The more intractable problems are not being shelved and totally neglected. Those in power and authority may often be fools, but they are not as a rule damned fools, or necessarily arrant knaves.

Twentieth century man is in dire trouble, partly because

of his unprecedented progress in so many fields; but in the
light of the spirit which he has shown himself able to manifest
there is nothing to suggest that he is doomed.

NOTES AND REFERENCES

1. G. K. A. Bell (Bishop of Chichester), *Christianity and World Order.*
2. *Preliminary Report of the Commission to Study the Organization of Peace*
(International Conciliation, No. 369).
3. For example, the Pugwash Conferences.
4. Leslie Stubbings in *The World Citizen*, December, 1941.
5. John Macmurray, *Challenge to the Churches.*
6. See Konrad Lorenz, *On Aggression.*
7. Macmurray, *op. cit.*
8. Mt. xviii. 3.
9. Gandhi, *Satyagraha.*
10. Walter Griffith, *Pacifism for To-day and To-morrow.*
11. Vera Brittain, *Humiliation with Honour.*

2

War and Law

THE political map of the globe in the twentieth century has had as its components an ever increasing number of sovereign states as one piece of territory after another has achieved independence. At the dawn of the century there were no less than eight declared empires, of which only two at this juncture still nominally remain. In addition several other countries were imperial in that they had colonies and dependencies, out of which again in many cases new states have been created. The trend has been progressively towards a greater fragmentation by nationalist self-assertion, while at the same time there have been new groupings of states in the form of commonwealth, federation, blocs and alliances.

The proliferation of states, like that of communities, has been a healthy sign, since it has conferred on many more peoples the capacity of self-expression and permitted them to have a say in world affairs. But it has also demanded a more universalist approach to the problems of world order, since without it a high percentage of the new states could have no possibility of survival either politically or economically. Their existence also added to the risks of minor wars being blown up into large scale wars, and even global wars.

War is a horrible thing in any circumstances, but in the present century it has finally been stripped of any glamour attaching to it in becoming total and mass-destructive. Never previously has it constituted a threat to all humanity.

The fiendish weapons of modern science, as already employed and as known to be available, have put paid to any ignorance of what could be unleashed if those in control should make a false move or miscalculation. There has therefore had to be a movement on the part of states towards regulating their relationships. Unfortunately, nationalistic and ideological interests have been so prominent, and governmental cunning so much in evidence, that organization for peace has continually been handicapped. The bewildered and brainwashed populace has been deprived of the possibility of taking concerted action to assert a right to life and unimpeded fellowship. The protestations of the few have been quite inadequate, because they have neither thought out nor committed themselves to any remedial plan which did not require state assent for its implementation. Such ideas as have emerged in this direction have virtually been nullified by lack of political sagacity and spiritual inspiration.

The century opened promisingly enough with a serious endeavour to put into effect the thinking of Grotius, nearly three hundred years previously, at the Hague Conferences of 1899 and 1907. But even before these there had been the Geneva Conventions of 1864 and the establishment of the International Red Cross.

The inspiration behind the Red Cross, that of Henri Dunant, aimed at mitigating the horrors of the battlefield by creating a category of non-combatants to minister to the wounded. Hospitals, ambulances, and personnel would be protected from attack by display of the neutralizing symbol, a red cross on a white ground. The International Red Cross subsequently grew into an organization providing a variety of relief services not confined to war conditions. The establishment of this agency was a remarkable humanitarian achievement, by which states for the first time accorded recognition to a category of neutralized persons.

The Hague Conferences sought to go further in attempting to reduce the possibility of war between civilized states. Before resorting to arms the signatory powers were to use the good offices of one or more friendly powers as mediators, and

uninvolved states would have the right to offer themselves as
mediators in any international dispute. In questions of a
judicial character the principle of arbitration was to be
acknowledged, and the Conferences set up a Permanent
Court of Arbitration whose seat would be at the Hague.
Respect for law was to replace belligerency. Here again there
was recognition of a special role, this time to be played by
states. The Convention laid down (Art. III), 'The right of
tendering good offices, or mediation, belongs to the powers
who are strangers to the dispute, even during the progress
of hostilities. The exercise of this right can never be considered, by either of the litigant parties, as an unfriendly act.'

The setback to these enlightened policies occasioned by
the Great War of 1914–1918 was very real and very shocking.
That performance should lag so far behind precept was
widely felt to be flouting the growing moral sense of mankind. To many war itself, no matter how caused or justified,
was now intolerable. Not only was there considerable vocal
opposition, but a new assertion of a human right to refuse
engagment in the slaughter of fellow human beings. There
was a higher law than that of states to be obeyed, and not a
few had the courage at the cost of personal suffering and
insult to proclaim themselves Conscientious Objectors.

But the terrible and prolonged slaughter of the flower of
youth increasingly produced a general consent that this
sacrifice must not be in vain. This must be the 'war to end
war'. Woodrow Wilson, President of the United States,
became the mouthpiece of this clear reaction of the ordinary
man and woman.

'It is a peculiarity of this great war,' he said, 'that while
statesmen have seemed to cast about for definitions of their
purpose and have sometimes seemed to shift their ground
and their point of view, the thought of the mass of men,
whom statesmen are supposed to instruct and lead, has
grown more and more unclouded, more and more certain of
what it is they are fighting for. National purposes have
fallen more and more into the background and the common
purpose of enlightened mankind has taken their place. The
counsels of plain men have become on all hands more simple

and straightforward and more unified than the counsels of sophisticated men of affairs, who still retain the impression that they are playing a game of power and playing for high stakes.'[1]

Wilson insisted that nations must be as much governed by law as the private citizen of any state, and that to this end there must be established an effective organization of peace. 'What we seek,' he declared, 'is the reign of law, based upon the consent of the governed and sustained by the organized opinion of mankind.'[2]

The tragic fact, however, was and has remained that an organized opinion of mankind has never existed. By his reiteration that it was a Peoples' War, and must be followed by a Peoples' Peace, Wilson may have had a premonition that statesmen would bungle the business if left to their own devices. And this, of course, is what happened. The Covenant of the new League of Nations was an adjunct to the Versailles Treaty of Peace, instead of being an entirely separate instrument. The peoples of the world knew very little of what was really going on at the Peace Conferences, and all the high promises of future submission to international institutions were inextricably mixed up with reparations, frontier demarcations, constitutions of new states, plebiscites, etc.

In spite of these grave failings, which in the end wrecked the peace through national timidity and self-seeking, the League did represent a further advance in the direction of world community. While its membership was not universal, and its provisions made success dependent on concerted action which it was impossible to achieve, it did make it a matter of common concern to deal on an international basis with questions of health and labour, the treatment of subject peoples, world communications, and the control of arma-ments. None of the member states was prepared to take the risk of investing the League with independent and superior power; but there was a willingness to create a new machinery having some of the attributes of state organization divorced as far as possible from individual state interests. In this respect progress was significant. For the first time there was

brought into being a Secretariat of International Civil
Servants, whose functions in office called for an allegiance
higher than that of the state and which was representative
of an embryonic world citizenship.

The League proved to be a totally inadequate instrument
for averting another general war. It had neither the inner
strength nor the coercive power to meet and overcome the
challenges of fresh imperialistic designs. As a consequence,
in the circumstances of the second Great War of 1939–1945,
a group of four of the principal Powers on one side of the
struggle proposed to establish a development of the League
which would 'have teeth in it' by means of a Collective
Security system. The so-called United Nations would
become guarantors of 'international peace and security
pending the re-establishment of law and order and the
inauguration of a system of general security.'[3]

The second great war of the century was no more a world
war than the first had been, since there were still states
which were either neutral or non-belligerent. Countries like
Sweden and Switzerland, which could act as intermediaries
and interest-protecting powers, continued to be required by
both sides in the struggle. But the war was more total, in that
civilian losses were greater than those of the military and
destruction was much more directed to non-military targets.
It created new war crimes, attempted genocide in the wilful
extermination of six million Jews, and the horrors of the
release of atomic bombs on Hiroshima and Nagasaki.

When the war ended hostilities did not end, and twenty-
five years later a peace settlement has not yet been reached.
The United Nations Organization was brought into being,
but under conditions which were no more promising for
world order than those of the League had been. The principal
change was the creation of a Security Council with five
permanent members, representative of East and West, each
having a power of veto. The arrangement tacitly acknowledged that there was no general willingness for a serious
diminution of sovereign rights and obedience to any world
law or authority. Quite apart from the conflicting interests
of the members of what was simply a new kind of coalition,

the system made it clear that the United Nations was not to be regarded as any superior power in its own right. It could not function at all to coerce the great Powers themselves, and the United Nations could only contribute to the maintenance of peace between the small Powers to the extent that it had the common backing of those who wielded the real power. And, even so, small countries could flout United Nations decisions, because they realized how much reluctance there was for decisive intervention, in case by some mischance war might be extended and become uncontrollable or because a settlement might seem to favour one or other of the chiefly competing interests.

Increasingly, settlements and understandings when arrived at have been by negotiations conducted independently of the U.N. There has been a brave showing that the United Nations is worth its keep, but it has suffered a progressive loss of influence and prestige. Conceivably, it might have fared better if its function had been one of peace-making rather than peace-keeping, and if the member states had been willing to give more authority to the activities of the organization's Specialized Agencies. Its principal value now, with a greatly expanded membership, is that it affords a meeting-place for the ventilation of views and facilities for behind the scenes diplomacy. What has also been manifested in recent years is that at the U.N. the big boys are no longer in command under a constitution which gives each member one vote. The balance of power has been altered by the grouping of small states, like the Afro-Asian bloc, which can operate against either the Western alliance or the Communist bloc.

To public alarm, as ever more horrific weapons are conceived and manufactured, even the semblance of world order has vanished at the time when it is most sorely needed. The concept of 'World Peace under World Law' has irretrievably gone down the drain.

When we say this, we are speaking of what St. Paul called 'the law of commandments contained in ordinances.' We are not ruling out the higher law of the spirit of life and of love. Paul, a Roman citizen, was inclined to think too much of

Jewish law in a Roman sense, though it was vastly different. He understood law as specifying certain sins or crimes for the infringement of which there were laid down appropriate punishments. All law, Jewish included, has this character. The judges administer it as it appears on the statute books, whether in fact it may be just or unjust. But Jewish law was rapidly moving away from this kind of judgment. The judge must judge justly, and not strictly according to the letter. To do this he must be concerned not merely with the crime, but with the personality and motives of the individual who is on trial. He must see into the heart. Modern law in enlightened countries has therefore progressively introduced certain modifications to distinguish between degrees of culpability and to give judges greater latitude in the punishment they determine for the guilty. Jewish law, however, went considerably further. It had the avowed aim of seeking to discover circumstances which would permit the accused to be declared innocent. It was not only the defence which had to present such circumstances: it was the responsibility of the judges also to quest for them. And there could never be a single judge, since he could be biassed against the prisoner.

International law has never been of the same order as state law, and has never been occupied with punitive legislation. Even the Permanent Court of International Justice could only make recommendations and awards in the area of international disputes which had no binding force other than the consent of the parties concerned. The War Crimes Tribunal, for all that it signified of revulsion against inhumanity, was a bad business, both in the absence of any world legislation and because the proceedings were conducted by the victors of the war, however impartial and unprejudiced those responsible might endeavour to be.

The Romans had built up a *jus gentium*, a law of nations, on the basis of the usages of the various nations over whom they ruled. But since nowadays there is no Common Superior of men and nations, World Law is strictly out of the question in the proper legal sense without the constitution of a World Government comparable to state government.

There has been no disposition to create such a government, and it is a vain movement which advocates it on the ground that if world peace is to be achieved it has to be enforced. This would be harking back to Romanism. There have been many proposals to convert the United Nations into such a government, and even in advance to give it control of dangerous situations by having at its disposal a so-called International Police Force. What could happen was sufficiently seen in the Korean War, when there was a pretence that South Korea was being defended in the name of the U.N.

It has to be underlined that there is no requirement of enforceable world law to create world peace. The concept is Romanist, not Messianist. Messianism uses the Hebrew word *Torah* in an educative sense, not in the sense of the Greek *Nomos* or the Roman *Lex*. In the world context we need to think of law educationally and not punitively. Many well-intentioned people are quite naive on this subject. A typical over-simplification is the following: 'An area of government is an area of peace. You are familiar with the keeping of peace in the areas of your city, your state and your nation. A world government is obviously the path to world peace—if government is somehow possible over so great an area.'[4]

In this case the argument from the particular to the general is not a sound one, and even in the particular calls for qualification. The writer was obviously not thinking of lands—and these are numerous—in which the police are the agents of the controlling political authority, exercising ruthless power; but even in countries where this is not so police brutality has become all too familiar. Peace which is secured by violence is not true peace: it is merely the crushing of rebellious opposition to real or fancied wrongs. It is highly desirable that the police should be not at all an arm of the state, and be responsible to an independent and popularly elected judiciary, which also frames the civil and criminal code applicable to social behaviour.

However this may be, the evidences are that if power corrupts, so does violence tend to brutalize. The way to

peace cannot be by putting a big stick into the hands of
authority, national or international.

In our time a distinction has been made between Cold
War and Hot War. This alone is sufficient to indicate that
war is not confined to clashes between armed forces. War is
also conducted on the spiritual plane, and by no means
invariably for selfish ends. Wherever men believe passionately that there is injustice they will fight; and the fighting
moves into the area of violence when men are goaded beyond
endurance by persistent denial of remedy for their grievances.

The setting up of any system of law cannot in itself be the
means of abolishing war. However good it may be, if its
expression is one of 'commandments contained in ordinances'
it cannot successfully subdue aggressive tendencies or make
provision for the impartial rectification of all wrongs. The
attempts have been made in the stipulations of the Hague
Conferences and in the Charter of the United Nations, and
in the various Declarations of Human Rights, and they have
all failed. These experiences have afforded no encouragement
of belief that the according of coercive powers to a World
Authority constituted on a basis of law could do more than
prove what has already been apprehended in principle, that
'all war is civil war.'

There is therefore no short-cut to the solution of the
problem of war, unsatisfying as this admission must be to
those who realize the gravity of our present perils, and want
to do something urgent and decisive to remove them. We
are forced to tackle initially the causes of war, not one major
cause, but all the causes; and this will demand of us not only
intelligence and a judicial detachment, but total commitment
to a higher law of love which sublimates violence.

'There is a reasonable hope,' says Konrad Lorenz, 'that
our moral responsibility may gain control over the primeval
drive, but our only hope of its ever doing so rests on the
humble recognition of the fact that militant enthusiasm is an
instinctive response with a phylogenetically determined
release mechanism, and that the only point at which
intelligent and responsible supervision can get control is in
the conditioning of the response to an object which proves

to be a genuine value under the scrutiny of the categorical question . . . The first prerequisite for rational control of an instinctive behaviour pattern is the knowledge of the stimulus situation which releases it.'[5]

What object can man choose as a genuine value to enable him to achieve control over his destructive militant propensities? I believe it to be one for which man is qualified more than any other creature, that of mutual disinterested service. The spirit of service can accomplish what neither aggression nor coercion can achieve. Service binds, while force rends asunder. Service heals, while force wounds and destroys. Service knows no enemies, entertains no jealousies, accepts no distinctions. Service melts where force hardens. Service convinces where force threatens. Service is the only quality which can make authority endurable and endure. It puts into action what Paul in a famous passage said of love (the Greek *agape* and Latin *caritas*).[6]

To quote Lorenz again. 'We know that, in the evolution of vertebrates, the bond of personal love and friendship was the epoch-making invention created by the great constructors when it became necessary for two or more individuals of an aggressive species to live peacefully together and to work for a common end. We know that human society is built on the foundation of this bond, but we have to recognize the fact that the bond has become too limited to encompass all that it should: it prevents aggression only between those who know each other as friends, while obviously it is all active hostility between all men of all nations or ideologies that must be stopped. The obvious conclusion is that love and friendship should embrace all humanity, that we should love all our brothers indiscriminately. This commandment is not new. Our reason is quite able to understand its necessity as our feeling is able to appreciate its beauty, but nevertheless, made as we are, we are unable to obey it.'[7] But Lorenz believes that one day we will be able to obey it, because 'reason can and will exert a selection pressure in the right direction' and this in the not too distant future.

In many connections, which include the Specialized Agencies of the United Nations, we already see the begin-

nings of a selection of certain common human needs as the
area in which a spirit of service can operate disinterestedly
to a substantial extent. Whatever can be taken out of the
arena of strife, and transferred to the domain of mutual aid,
advances the prospect of abolishing war and the violation of
human rights.

Even if self-interest remains a factor in such engagements,
the very activity of working in association tends to smooth
the rough edges of hostility. The discovery is made that
enmity is skin deep, largely induced by false notions and
lying propaganda, and that we are all brothers under the
skin. All direct contact, and for a protracted period, is
therefore important, far more important than any legislation.
We are in a world which is rapidly becoming too small for
segregation and power-rivalry. There are dangers which
threaten our common abode. We have to unite to overcome
them.

It is true that there are many individuals, sections and
states, who are isolationists, who still think the aim must be
to gain something at the expense of others. We cannot
change them by animosity or control them by laws. From
the bottom of our hearts we must pity them, and rehabilitate
them by love and friendship. Fear puts up barriers. Only
service can break them down.

One fruitful way has been wisely stated. We cannot reach
the goal of world unity at one jump, but progressively we
can 'put on a world basis everything that will work on a
world basis.' To this end it is of real consequence not only
to create all the international ties and institutions that are
practicable, but also to build up a body of opinion and
activity which is essentially universal in its thinking and
behaviour and which cuts across all divisions. Some of the
steps in this direction we have considered in this and the
previous chapter, and in the next we shall look at others.
From this viewpoint the United Nations in one particular
represents remarkable and encouraging progress. A non-
governmental organization—for that is what the U.N. is—
has been accorded certain privileges previously only granted
to a sovereign body. It has ambassadors accredited to it, its

buildings are extraterritorialized, its officials enjoy diplomatic privileges, and their loyalty is not primarily to the state of which they are citizens but to the whole body of member states. A *de facto* world citizenship is in evidence, even without the *de jure* existence of a World Government.

Precedents in international relationships have been created, which are forward-looking and significant. One of the most difficult obstacles to World Community has already been surmounted.

NOTES AND REFERENCES

1. Woodrow Wilson, Address at a Public Meeting in New York, Opening the Fourth Liberty Loan, Sept. 27, 1918.

2. Woodrow Wilson, Address at Mount Vernon, July 4, 1918.

3. Moscow Declaration of October, 1943, of the Governments of the United States, the United Kingdom, the Soviet Union, and China.

4. Stewart Boal, President of the Conference upon Research and Education in World Government (CURE), *Preface to Freedom in a Federal World by Everett Lee Millard*, 1959. The argument is effectively countered by Sir Herbert Read, 'All the plans for a World Government that I have seen make provision for an international police force, to which would be entrusted the final task of "enforcing" the decisions of an international (or supernational) tribunal. Force does not become sanctified by being denationalized—indeed, such a rootless (and ruthless) universal force would lose some of the inhibitions that still restrain a national force. Nations (and races) are organic; a World Government, or International Police Force, is an inhuman fabrication.' (See *Gandalf's Garden*, Issue 6, 1969).

5. Konrad Lorenz, *On Aggression*, 1966.

6. I. Cor. xiii. The lines on service were penned by the present author in a Memorandum published in 1941.

7. Lorenz, *op. cit.*

3
One World

THE ancient Jewish-Christian vision of ultimate world unity
has in the circumstances of the modern world been regarded
as calling for a concrete political expression. What form a
World Government should take, and how it could be
brought into existence, has engaged the thought of many
minds and given rise to many movements. The chief incentive has been the urgent need to devise a practical method to
assure perpetual peace. There has by no means been absent
the ideal of world community and harmony; but world
government advocates as a rule have considered this to be a
long term objective. They insist that a world political
structure must be created without delay, for unless this is
done civilized life may be extinguished by scientific warfare
and ideals would be of little avail to the remnant of survivors
on a tortured and ruined planet.

It cannot be said that as yet world political unification has
the support of humanity in general. The promoters of world
government schemes are prone to exaggerate greatly the
extent of popular assent, and also the desire of the sovereign
states to effect a radical change in their relationships. The
schemes have predominantly, though not exclusively,
originated in the West in countries which have inherited
the Jewish-Christian tradition, and bear the stamp of
Western concepts of democracy. The East on the whole
rates ideology higher than political organization. Oriental
philosophy is primarily concerned with individual behaviour,

and Lenin's Communism foresaw the disappearance of the state.

In the present phase of intensified nationalism the idea of a Common Superior is now very little canvassed in the extreme form of a Master Power, because due to the fear of recurring Romanism the accent is on the equality of sovereign states. But big Powers have not wholly abandoned a role of hegemony, acting as the greatest among equals. So the world government planners have a difficulty in setting in motion the process which will attain their goal. In their zeal and haste they incline to turn a blind eye to the obstacles in their path, and to be impatient with any suggestion that involves inching forward methodically over a protracted period. For them there is only time for a quick jump, and they will yield to no persuasion, in spite of experience, that such a jump is out of the question.

The principal proposals envisage some form of World Federation, because this permits the continued existence of sovereign states. A Commission Report I have several times quoted has this to say on the subject.

'We have come to regard the nation-state as the primary unit in international society, in the same way that we have come to regard the individual as the primary unit in domestic society. The nation sums up much of political history for five hundred years. No one can predict when this concentration upon the nation-state shall have run its course . . . We must continue to assume that the nation-state is the unit of world society. Any federation of such states must be flexible and capable of adjusting itself to continually changing conditions. Clearly the organization of international society with the greatest chance of success will be that one which will assure a dynamic peace with the minimum of sacrifice of national sovereignty . . . Federation organizes consent on the international scale while empire organizes coercion on that scale. Though coercion of the part by the whole is the essence of government, in the system of federalism that coercion can only be in accord with law, to which those bound have directly or indirectly consented. World federation balancing the autonomy of the

nation-state with the authority of the family of nations was
the system implied by the founders of modern international
law after the break-up of the medieval empire.'[1]

Initially, world federation was seen, for instance, by
Immanuel Kant in 1795,[2] as a pacific alliance (*foedus
pacificum*) between states, though of a peculiar kind, by
which they submitted themselves to be bound permanently
by mutually coercive laws, so that for the future they could
not make war on one another. He apprehended, though he
did not develop the thesis, that this could imply a federal
authority with legislative, executive and judiciary powers,
as in a Republic.

Federalists naturally present their solution of the world's
problems as eminently reasonable, just as Communists
present theirs. In either case we have nothing to lose but our
chains.

What freedom does absolute sovereignty confer? asks
W. B. Curry. 'It compels us to do without things we want in
order to spend vast sums on armaments that we don't want.
It causes us to throttle each other's trade and to impede
each other's travel. From time to time it causes us all to be
conscripted and thus lose our freedom altogether. Finally it
gives rise to periodic outbreaks of mass mutual homocide
during which millions lose not merely their freedom but
their lives. Is it possible to conceive of anything much more
bound than this freedom of sovereign states?'[3] Surely the
inestimable gains which a world federation would confer far
outweigh the loss only of the martial elements in our national
pride!

The price to be paid for the infinite good that would be
accomplished is no more than the transfer of minimal
sovereign rights by the nation-states to a government
representative of them all, not to an alien Power, but one
which arises out of themselves and their peoples. State
autonomy for domestic affairs, national languages and
cultures, even a preference for monarchical instead of
republican government for the individual states—it is
claimed—all are safeguarded by a world federation. Ultimately it must come about. Why not now?

There are very cogent reasons why it should not be now, and very good reasons why it should never come about at all.

A United States of the World is totally unpracticable while ideological conflict exists. The principal ideologies are poles apart in their thinking about the character and structure of society, and consequently about the manner in which world government should function. This is why some federalists opt for a beginning to be made with an Atlantic Union or a European Union (meaning Western Europe). But even with Regional Federation there are very great difficulties, as already experienced with the Common Market, when the States to be federated consist of different nations with different languages and cultures.

Facing realities, the life of man, socially and politically, has been too compartmentalized for him to be capable as yet of adequate comprehension of the larger unity required of him. In his faith, his dreams and visions, in his highest thoughts, and even ambitions, he may sometimes get there; but in his practice he is only at ease within the limited spheres to which he has become habituated. The intensified nationalism of today derives its strength from this innate conservatism, which psychologically, is in revolt against that technological progress which has both amplified and complicated man's existence. From an impersonal viewpoint the world becomes much smaller, but from the viewpoint of the average individual it has become infinitely larger. There is so much more of it that he has to take in, with resultant spiritual indigestion. To tell such an individual, struggling to assimilate the variety of ideas and processes which in such a brief space of time have been thrust upon him, that he has now to regard himself as a world citizen and give his allegiance to a world government, is to load on the last straw that breaks the camel's back. The more you try to draw him on into that wider association, the more he will resist and pull back. He will assert his right to independence, to live his own life, which means to stay in the little world which he can just about cope with, and in which he feels comfortable.

Nation-states, and similarly, racial, religious and social groups, in this connection, only reflect the attitude of the individual, and the stress they lay on sovereign equality and independence is substantially dictated by the same primitive fear of loss of identity. What is urged upon states is as repugnant and frightening as was for the Church the change of concept from a geocentric to a heliocentric system. Our own state and environment is the centre round which the rest of mankind revolves. We refuse to contemplate that mixed up with a lot of foreigners we should revolve around a central world authority. So the very considerations which bid us become part of a new unified system make us shy away from it. The federalists have quite failed to take account of these psychological difficulties. The formula for transition which they offer is mechanical not spiritual. They take for granted that their definition of the goal already commands assent, and therefore the only matter for discussion is the method to be employed.

There are plenty of thinkers, however, who have other ideas of federalism than a Federation of States. They have been described as Functional Federalists. One of these was H. G. Wells, who insisted, 'It is totally unnecessary to think of any world government or world "Super-state" in a reconstructed world. There will never be a Parliament of Man; a President of the Earth. The sovereign-government pattern does not apply to a unified world at peace.' In his opinion, 'the legal form in which the new world order will arise will be as a system of federally co-operative world authorities with powers *delegated to them by the existing governments*. The governments can go on existing, giving their consent and benediction to the new administrations they have authorized ... As the new methods get into working order the national governments will vanish, softly and unobtrusively, from the lay-out of the world.'[4]

This is stating the case for Functional Federalism in an extreme form. The basic idea is that there should not be one world authority, but a number, each charged with responsibilities in some particuliar sphere of human needs and activities, the air and the oceans, energy, transport and communications, health, food and agriculture, finance, conservation of wild life, and so on. It would be like converting the Specialized Agencies of the U.N. into governmental bodies, with powers delegated to them by sovereign states. Eventually, as Wells saw it, the nation-states would become obsolete and disappear.

Most functional federalists do not contemplate the final extinction of political government. But they do apprehend that as yet there does not exist a developed world consciousness, and that there is no general will towards political federation. On the other hand, if the minds of governments could be directed away from issues of political sovereignty, and concentrated instead on matters where self-interest does not run directly counter to the common interest, then many of the causes of war would steadily be overcome. So many non-political problems having been settled amicably to the general benefit; the obstacles to political federation would be found in due course to have gone too, and world federation would have become both natural and practicable.

The functional approach has the merit that certain precedents for what it visualizes have already been created, and it would operate through practical services to the world community which would be non-militant. In the atmosphere engendered by a system of federally co-operative functional world authorities there would be opportunity for a greater sense of world unity to develop in the citizens of every state, so that increasingly they would feel that they were world citizens benefitting from world institutions.

Citizens of a federation like the United States naturally tend to think of a world system as something like their own expanded to world proportions. But such thinking exhibits very little understanding of the world at large, and is even arrogant. Americans are entitled to believe, in spite of unsolved racial problems, that their system is the best for themselves. But there is no justification for regarding it either as ideal or suited to universal needs. The British have had much the same belief in their own parliamentary system. It appears that in many parts of the world both these systems are rejected as inapplicable and undesirable.

It is folly, therefore, to propose that any existing system of government can serve as a model for World Government. The circumstances are quite different to begin with. A World Government will have no equals and no rivals. It will have no foreign affairs, for all its affairs will be domestic. There will be no frontiers to be guarded, and all seas and lands will be within its jurisdiction. But also it will embrace a great diversity of races and cultures, and social and political systems. This is assuming that nation-states are retained as components, which is a very questionable assumption. They may prove to be quite unnecessary, an obstacle which will have to be eliminated.

Reason suggests that initially there may have to be some kind of compromise and some quite new ideas, but there has been very little recognition of this in the World Federalist constitutions so far devised. Functional Federalism has done rather better in working for the creation of functional world institutions in the area of the common needs of all mankind. Such engagement can help to remove the risks of inter-state belligerency by substituting inter-state co-operation. The thing that must not be attempted is to set up any system of peace enforcement on a coercive basis. This would be Romanism.

It has been very difficult to impress this on World Federalists, though there is now made a distinction between maximalist and minimalist proposals, and the latter are receiving more attention than previously.

One of the effects of the continuing risk of world war, which we have to note, is that a good many individuals are now entirely out of patience with the state governments and believe that the people for their own preservation must take the law into their own hands. These individuals are seeking by popular elections to bring into being a Peoples' Congress or Convention with sufficient strength and support to demand action by governments in favour of World Federation. These movements have not got very far because they have grossly underestimated popular inertia, and because the promoters on the whole are more blessed with zeal than sagacity. Nevertheless, their efforts have been of value in emphasizing at the level of the ordinary individual the concept of a realized world citizenship.

As in other evolutionary developments, a sentient minority is revealing itself as ahead of the time, committing itself to the acceptance of responsibility towards and on behalf of mankind as a whole. With some world citizenship is associated with World Federation, while with others it is identified more broadly with the Brotherhood of Man. But in all cases it reflects the recognition of the world as a unity and the need for a higher allegiance to all humanity without distinction or discrimination. 'The world community,' it has been said, 'is in need of its own form of loyalty. Without this the world can never become a governed body.'[5] Another writer similarly has stated, 'National life has succeeded because out of loyalty to the nation its members have worked together for their common benefit, with the common resources. So it must be in the international community. We must have a loyalty to it as citizens and as nations and our common effort with the common resources will rehabilitate the world.'[6]

These views are typical of many, and they signify that world citizenship is being emphasized in the present century to an unprecedented extent. The concept is anti-Romanist and therefore Nazism opposed it and ascribed it—not without historical justification—to the Jews. Gerhard Kittel, professedly a Christian theologian, siding with the Master Race, declared, 'The internationalism of Jewry is dangerous also from another angle. At the cradle of modern Judaism stands the idea of humanity as superior to the concept of race. Therefore it was natural that the Labour question became internationalized by the Jew, Karl Marx . . . For a Jew of this species, all cultural activities are not activities of the race, but of humanity. To him, racial culture is but a preparation for a culture embracing all humanity.'[7] Curiously, modern Communism, professing to follow Karl Marx, also opposes Jewish cosmopolitanism.

So the ideal of the Brotherhood of Man is a Jewish criminal invention! Certainly Jews have been prominent in the World Government movement, and at the end of the

1939–1945 War one of them, the American ex-bomber
pilot, Garry Davis, became a focal figure whose testimony
and adventures in crossing frontiers without a passport gave
rise to the Paris-based International Registry of World
Citizens. He told his story later in a book entitled *My
Country is the World*.[8] A somewhat similar figure working in the
cause of peace is Abe Nathan of Israel. Another activity led
to cities in many parts of the world adopting a charter of
mundialization, by which they proclaimed their adherence to
the World Community.

Since Jesus was a Jew, Christians could be expected to be
bitten by the same Messianist bug. At the beginning of the
1914–1918 War there was a Persian Christian, Yervant H.
Iskender, resident in Scotland, who had founded a movement
called Citizens of the World. This movement, he said, 'is
based on the natural Law of Unity . . . If men were to become
all members of one world-wide family,[9] there would no
longer be any pretext for war . . . An all-embracing unity is
thus the solution of the problem of putting an end to war for
ever . . . The world's inhabitants must, under one inspiring
name—"The Citizens of the World"—unite to put an end
to war.'

Corporate action was planned. 'As soon as the "Citizens
of the World" think the time is at hand they shall say, in the
spirit of the Great Teacher, and of His great Apostle, Saint
John the Divine, with one voice, echoing from one end of the
world to the other: We are all brethren, and we refuse to kill
one another for any pretext. God gave us dominion over all
the Earth and, therefore, we refuse to maintain the artificial
and conventional barriers which have separated the nations
for so long, and with results so disastrous.'[10] Iskender
devised a kind of universal passport, and claimed in 1914 to
have 10,000 members and supporters.

I must pay tribute at greater length to another Christian
pioneer Jewishly inspired, whom most people today have
never heard of. At the time of the Conference on Christian
Politics, Economics and Citizenship (COPEC), in 1924, a
paper was presented written by George Cyril Armstrong
entitled *The Holy Nation*. The paper was not then pub-

lished, but extracts from it appeared fourteen years later in
The Plough, July, 1938. This did not come into my hands
until 1942, but I was able to communicate with the author
in his old age and advise him of what was then taking place,
and obtain his permission to reprint his material.

So far as I am aware, Armstrong was the first in modern
times to reassert in concrete terms that Christianity could
aid mankind through regained nationhood, according to the
original intention. He summed up his thesis in the following
words.

'The time is ripe for us Christians to assert again that
sacred Nationality founded by God when he called Abram
out of Chaldea, and refounded at Jerusalem on the Pentecost
following Christ's ascension into Heaven. It had been God's
will to work through the leaven of a chosen Community. But
the leaven must be pure and strong and uncorrupted if it is
to do His work.

'The Christian Nation must claim full independence both
politically and economically. This is essential not merely
because the biddings of secular governments clash with the
biddings of Christ, but because the military and commercial
fabric of secular civilization ensnares and fetters at every
turn the Christian who wishes to follow his conscience and
to do the thing that is just and right and brotherly. The call
is for a living and growing *nucleus* of men and women who
will put loyalty to Christ before all else, and will work and
pray for the rebuilding of Jerusalem here on earth.

'One of our first steps to be taken to secure our economic
independence is the foundation of a Christian City with
enough land around it to supply the physical needs of its
citizens. Frugality and simplicity of life, and the sacrifice of
many comforts, will be required of the pioneers. Industry,
education, law—in a word, the whole social life of the
Community—will be based on Christian principles for
Christian people . . .

'From such a concentration of Christian life and thought,
embodied in a world-wide Nationality transcending in
practice as well as in theory all distinctions of race and
culture, the profoundest results may be expected . . . We

often suppose that our task is to Christianize the nations. So, in a sense, it is. But we must begin by renationalizing Christianity, so that we may speak to them as nation to nation. We are told that the peculiar culture of each race and language is a precious inheritance which Christianity must preserve and sanctify. So it is. But there is a culture more precious still; the social and intellectual life which springs from our common faith, but cramped by many a secular band remains as yet in undeveloped infancy. Not till the Christians of India and China converse with those in Britain and France as fellow-citizens may the treasures of the races be duly mingled, or Christian civilization expand in unfettered growth.

'The scheme now submitted to the Churches is the outcome of many years' observation and reflection. If it runs counter to some of the most powerful currents of the time, the Gospel on its first proclamation was at a like disadvantage. The Gospel was of God, and drew to it the children of God. If the ideas here set forth are of God, and the time is ripe for their realization, they will draw to them the men and women who shall build and rule the restored Commonwealth of Christ upon earth.'

A third contribution to One World thinking on particular lines was made in the early Twenties with the proposal put forward by a body called World-Conscience: An International Society for the Creation of World Peace by the Establishment of a World Centre City of Communication.' The proposal emanated from the Villa Helene, Rome, and embodied a scheme conceived by a Norwegian sculptor Hendrik Christian Andersen and 'worked out by him in all its details during the many years in which he studied it in Paris, Washington and Rome, while, for the actual planning of the buildings he had the professional assistance of some forty architects and engineers.'[11]

The essentials of the scheme were stated in these terms. 'The most efficacious and perhaps the only means of ensuring world-co-operation in all branches of human activity is the establishment of an *International City* which—materially, intellectually and spiritually—would fulfil the function of a

universal clearing-house. Sooner or later it will be recognized that the world needs a city belonging to no one nation
but to every nation; a city existing by general consent for the
welfare of mankind at large and, above all, entirely beyond
the sphere of political interests. Such a city . . . would be of
incalculable benefit in promoting a spirit of mutual friendship and appreciation between the various races of the earth.'

More recently a comparable scheme has taken shape in
India in the design for *Auroville*, commemorating the life and
thought of the sage Sri Aurobindo, who died in 1950. The
chosen site is the Coromandel Coast north of the former
French colonial city of Pondicherry. Auroville is visualized
as 'a city for the golden age' and 'India's contribution to a
planetary society.' The literature states, 'Now for the first
time we shall have a total city, one in which each house
expresses a common realization, a common will.' The
whole town is to be dedicated in all its aspects 'to the One in
Man.'[12]

Again it is to be noted that the World City concept is of
Jewish-Christian origin, and can be traced back to the
visions of the New Jerusalem of the Prophet Ezekiel 2,500
years ago, echoed by the author of the Book of Revelation
in the New Testament.

It would be easy to devote a volume to the variety of ideas
and projects which testify to the emerging emphasis of World
Unity. Some of these, as we have seen, are quite specific.
Others are more identified with promoting international
fellowship, understanding and reconciliation, and engagement in service to humanity. World citizenship is being
increasingly affirmed spiritually and politically. It is a much
more serious business than the old cosmopolitanism. The
cosmopolite was at home everywhere, and obligated to
nowhere. He was more worldly than world-minded. The
world citizen of today, however, is the man who, being fully
conscious of the responsibilities of citizenship, has elected to
begin to discharge those responsibilities in relation to
humanity as a whole.

The task is no easy one where so much is formless and
vague, where there is no unifying symbol, much less a

comprehensive structure, where the rights of citizenship do not exist and its responsibilities therefore are difficult to define, and where a total world loyalty can still be regarded as state treason.

Many thoughtful individuals and groups have been doing what they can to make good these deficiences. They have been stressing the cultivation of a world outlook and an education for world citizenship by teaching the history of man in his cultural, social and political development alongside national history. They have been devising world auxiliary languages, like the Polish Jew Zamenhof's *Esperanto*. They have been fostering in many connections closer international relations and the setting up of world institutions.

All such activities have been creating important precedents or in some way laying foundations for the future. They are beginning to bridge spiritually the gulfs which science and technology have overstepped materially. It has remained, however, to bring world citizenship to birth in a manner which could enable it to be recognized and acknowledged as a real status available to those who are spiritually ready for it. A new category of human beings has to appear, representative of a prior and overriding right of loyalty to mankind. Without this, since states and peoples are still a long way from preparedness for a development which would embrace them all, there can be no substantive advance towards world unity.[13]

Thus a factor in world affairs has to manifest itself, which has not been entertained by people in general and has not entered into the careful calculations of statesmen, one which makes world citizenship visible and tangible.

NOTES AND REFERENCES

1. *Preliminary Report of the Commission to Study the Organization of Peace* (International Conciliation, No. 369).
2. Immanuel Kant, Essay on *Perpetual Peace*.
3. W. B. Curry, *The Case for Federal Union* (Penguin Special).
4. H. G. Wells, *Phoenix*.

5. Professor G. M. Stratton, *International Delusions*.

6. Karlin Capper-Johnson, *Looking Towards Peace*.

7. Professor Gerhard Kittel, *Die Judenfrage* (The Jewish Question), 1933.

8. The writer has known Garry Davis for a great many years, and on occasion rendered him some service when in difficulties with authorities as a result of his escapades.

9. The concept of world citizenship was enlisted in the cause of the abolition of slavery. An early example was a tract by Granville Sharp published in 1776 in which he declared, 'Under the glorious dispensation of the Gospel we are absolutely bound to consider ourselves as Citizens of the World.' Later the English abolitionist Joseph Sturge and the American Elihu Burritt 'sponsored a series of international peace conventions around 1850; and for a time during the 1850s the latter published a journal appropriately entitled *Burritt's Citizen of the World*.' See Staughton Lynd, *Intellectual Origins of American Radicalism*, chapter 5 (Pantheon Books; Random House, 1968). I am indebted to Mr. Carroll Richardson for drawing my attention to this work.

10. My knowledge of Iskender's movement derives from a booklet and circular he issued in September 1914, and I have a copy of his World Citizen Passport. The movement does not seem to have outlasted the war.

11. I was given, I believe in 1943, a booklet about the proposal, from which I have quoted, and also a plan of the *International City*, including a detailed guide to its features.

12. My information comes from a booklet about Auroville sponsored by an organization called *World Goodwill*. The centre of activity is an Ashram at Pondicherry, which has had as a presiding figure a French lady known as The Mother. I have also been in contact with another proposal for an International city-zone in Morocco.

13. I may refer here to *The World in Union*, by John S. Hoyland, in which he said, 'In the first Christian generation men saw the vision of the Heavenly City coming down upon earth. We need the same vision, but expressed in accordance with the problems of our time . . . It is a vision of sovereignty realized through the attainment of a world-union which will make possible the control of all the relations of mankind by God's method of freedom and goodwill . . . We must learn to live already in the world-union of the future. We are to be a "colony of heaven" in this sense, pioneers and outposts of the world-order we are trying to build.' See also Robert Shaull in *Containment and Change*: 'The essential thing is for those who have adopted a revolutionary position to preserve a certain degree of group identity. Thus they may be able to run the risks of being "in" but not "of" the structure, and live as "exiles" within the society to which they belong.'

4

The Brink or the Eve?

F o r those who have eyes to see and ears to hear the happenings of the past two hundred years convey the message that a major period of trials and tribulations has been coming upon mankind even more crucial than what was experienced in the second and first century B.C. Opinion has alternated, as it did then, between a pessimism which held that the world was on the brink of doom and an optimism convinced that it was on the eve of a tremendous beneficial change.

As regards the previous eschatological age I have described its features in this and my two preceding books, and the similarities should therefore be readily observable. Characteristic of that earlier age was its apocalypticism, of which the Messianic was the key expression among the Jews, the people immersed in the significance of prophecy and psychically attuned to what was going forward. The modern inheritors of the Jewish-Christian tradition, brought up on the Bible and nurtured in its imagery and expectations, have correspondingly sensed the purport of the signs of their own times.

The former age was initiated by the seductions of Hellenism, which were countered by Messianic Judaism with its proliferation of eclectic sects and an explosion of missionary zeal. In the same way the new eschatological period was heralded by the Age of Reason, which evoked the Christian response of like sects and missionary activity. The evangelical revival strongly emphasized the Second Advent of Christ

163

and encouraged the fresh interpretation of the prophetic records in relation to the contemporary scene. Again there was a busy engagement in calculating the dates of the Last Times.

When the first Great War came the *Four Horsemen of the Apocalypse* were seen to be riding again, and on many lips there was the dread word *Armageddon*. Inevitably the students of prophecy had their eyes on what was going forward among the Jews. It was written that they would return to their homeland. The genesis of Zionism was therefore seen as a portent, and developments were avidly followed from the Balfour Declaration of 1917, favouring a Jewish national home in Palestine (which had then been wrested from the Turks), to the establishment in 1948 of the state of Israel. The pogroms and the Nazi onslaught on the Jews demonstrated the beginning of the 'time of Jacob's trouble,' while Czarist and Communist ambitions in the Middle East, latterly associated with the Arab combinations against Israel, were held to be connected with the ancient vision of the hostile confederacy of Gog and Magog.[1]

There were so many Signs of the Times for the faithful to note. Had not Jesus foretold that there would be 'wars and rumours of wars', nation roused against nation, and that there would be famines, plagues and earthquakes?[2] Was it not true that, as predicted, there had come great apostasy and men's hearts failing them for fear of what was coming on the earth? Did not the unleashing of the atom bomb portend a future fiery destruction?[3]

While sensitive Christians have been reacting in their way, they have not been the only ones to be affected. A new avatar of Krishna has been anticipated in the East, and there too, and elsewhere, seers and sages have been making startling predictions. Spiritual communications have been multiplied, emanating variously, as alleged, from Great Masters, the White Brotherhood, Lords of the Planets, and great souls from the past. Abundant warnings and admonitions have been 'coming through' of catastrophes and changes, but also promising help and protection which would enable man to survive and enter the new more enlightened

Aquarian Age. There have been visitations, the sighting of UFOs (unidentified flying objects), and reports of many other strange phenomena.

The spirit of aggression so much in evidence, mob violence and hysteria, the hot fires of revolt in the young, the increase of criminal activity and sexual passions, the growth of mental illness, all suggest a major psychic disturbance, the causes of which appear greater than what can be attributed to the effects of inventions and new discoveries. It is as if some mysterious force was making an impact upon us, or as if our planet was passing through the invisible and undetected cloud of an unknown gas.

The mind can try to rationalize, but all in all the circumstances do seem to betoken that in this age man is being subjected to some essential push or pull to get him over a hump at a particularly critical stage in his affairs. The operation of a boosting factor has been called for to counteract the dangers of human folly and suicidal tendencies, and to energize man for a further step forward along the road of evolutionary development. Multitudes who are without discernment are experiencing a heightened tension and emotionalism, while others more perceptive—but limited in their terms of reference—are getting images and ideas consistent with their disposition and affiliations. Only a comparative few are able to take cognizance of a wider range of factors, so that they apprehend their import and can lend their conscious co-operation to what is indicated.

The last great eschatological explosion occurred in a fairly well recorded historical period. This should make it rather easier for us, if we are genuinely concerned, to be more objective about our own time. We are in a position to compare, as regards the previous age, what was imagined and proclaimed would happen with what actually transpired. In so doing we must also take account of the patterns of belief, which readily inclined towards an assumption that magic and miracle was the true explanation of the unusual and unexpected, and even insisted that there must be appropriate phenomena to mark the intrusion of the Divine into human affairs. Where such patterns of belief are still endorsed by religious conservatism they are bound to influence interpretation. There is little one can do about this beyond explaining why the ancients supposed what they did. We do not have to exclude the supernatural, but it should never be for us the most likely explanation of anything extraordinary.

Looking back with informed judgment, it is very clear that much that was expected to happen did not materialize. Many of the prognostications were wildly fantastic. Others, while they could be said to have some correspondence to events, resembled very little the terms of the original prophecies on which they were based. Frequently what was most significant was missed altogether. The prevailing feeling was not wrong that consequential things for humanity were in train; but the excited and exuberant expression of their nature was quite unrealistic. There was a natural desire to view occurrences in heaven and on earth as portents, but in most respects the times were not specially abnormal. On the whole it is still true that we are impressed by the extravagant, and are prone to ignore or neglect what should more profitably be engaging our attention.

Taking the previous eschatological epoch as our guide, we can see how fallacious were the doom anticipations. There was no Day of Wrath poured out upon the world. Equally mistaken was the notion that the Kingdom of God was about to be established on earth. Despite understandable Christian contentions to the contrary, we must also say that no Divine incarnation took place, attended by angelic appearances and prodigies. The records of such demonstrations were largely human intensifications and overstatements of the realities. These were just as cogent, but would have been considered at the time too long-term and even too prosaic. Yet we can also see that without this boiling over and larger-than-life imagination vital things would not have come about, as they had to do. There had to be all kinds of circumstances, many of them not discerned to be relevant, as Preparations for the Gospel, and there had to be a dramatization of certain instrumental agencies and ideas.

There was assuredly taking place a far-reaching process

of change governing the future. Apocalyptic imagery caught hold of it sensitively, but portrayed it sensationally. The clash of principles was there between Romanism and Messianism. Romanism was in the ascendant, and to counter it a Messiah had to appear to embody a liberating spirit. Only through a demonstration of love and service could the minds of men be freed from subservience to the enslaving forces of power and domination.

The brief unspectacular career of an obscure Jewish village carpenter, who gave trouble to the authorities and was duly executed, was no world-shaking event. It was only because this same carpenter was the focus of an ancient dream of world peace and harmony, and was seen as the David who would overcome the mailed Goliath of Rome, that his name and fame and electrifying words got through to the peoples of the Empire, to whom he was revealed as their predestined saviour. The might of Rome did not seem to be seriously affected. Rome could hit at the followers of this man, and at the Jews, whose ideals and insights had produced him. Jerusalem, the home of Messianism, could be destroyed, but not its transcendental influence. Romanism would continue for as long as men chose to worship the Beast; but now there was a means of remedy, which made nonsense of Caesar's pride and arrogance, and certified that one day, sooner or later, free men would laugh it out of existence.

But where did the remedy really lie? Not in putting Jesus on Caesar's throne as a better God-man. The world of nations could only be saved by a nation, which disregarded territory and abjured force, and which corporately embodied the Messianic principles of love and service. The role of such a nation had been revealed long before to the Hebrews. The coming of Jesus gave it a new lease of life and a wider composition. This was the heart of the matter, the fresh disclosure which signalized, however events might seem to contradict it century after century, that essentially the Age of Imperialism had ended and the Messianic Age had begun.

In perceiving this, we are led back to the thinking contained in Part One. If a Divine Plan for mankind was in

progress in Biblical times it must be continuing to operate.
And since we are living in another crucial period for humanity, much more dangerous and complex than the beginning
of the Christian era, the appropriate expression of Messianism
for our time must manifest itself. The nature of it will
necessarily be in line with the tenor of the previous indications, but representing a new expansion and a more
sophisticated development.

With the story of the past eschatological period in our
minds we can eliminate as out of the question that our world
is on the brink of some overwhelming catastrophe, whether
through war or the activities of nature. This is not to say that
there will be no more major wars, upheavals and afflictions;
but the most gloomy forecasts of the pessimists and prognosti-
cators will again fail to materialize. There will be strange
happenings to alert the spiritually-minded; but the way
prophecies are fulfilled will not be exactly as imagined, any
more than they were in days of old. There will be a second
coming of Christ, but not as anciently depicted, just as the
circumstances of the previous advent were not at all as many
students of prophecy had anticipated. What we should
expect is that through better knowledge an understanding
of the real Jesus and his Messianic message will be given
back to us, thus restoring him to us as he has not been seen
for nearly two thousand years, so that the right actions can
follow. This time it may be offended Christians who reject
the revelation, and Jews who welcome it. But all who are
ready of all faiths and persuasions will be drawn into participation in the Politics of God as once more clarified and
coming to the rescue of mankind.

If we genuinely have the welfare of humanity at heart we
must avoid all enticement to jettison sober judgment.
Marvels naturally attract us, and the disposition to entertain
them is all the greater at a time when we feel that nothing
less than higher aid can save the situation. That feeling is
right and proper; but it still has to be true that the aid will
not come *to* us but *through* us. It is we ourselves, selflessly
animated, who will have to do what must be done. This is
the law of our being, and the freedom with which we have

been endowed. We cannot wish the job on to anyone else, any superman or superhuman agency. What we have a title to is spiritual help, to guide and strengthen us for the purposes which only we can accomplish. The great error of the previous eschatological age was that people were gazing up into the skies or seeking some abnormal leadership instead of enlisting the resources which would illumine and fortify their own resolve. Faith that is divorced from deeds is not faith at all, but superstition. Faith is what causes a man to say, I will open myself that deeds may be done through me. We have the power to open ourselves either for good or evil. The salvation of humanity will come when some part of humanity has done this unfeignedly for the good of all others.

Not long ago I felt the need to say this very simply, and found I could express it aptly in the words 'Me for Mankind'. These words signify what I understand to be implied by world citizenship.

Here I would like to pause for some further reflections before I unfold what I have been enabled to learn of the Divine Plan for our time. I have covered a great deal of preliminary ground, and the reader may already have judged where the argument is leading. In what has been surveyed in Part Two there is one thing we have still to consider, how all the circumstances described appear when they are viewed as Preparations for a Gospel. But before this it is needful to bring about, if I can, a closer community of thought, because it is so important to see eye to eye where the issues are of such tremendous consequence. I have tried to furnish material that is deserving of meditation; but perhaps I can put forward something additional, which even if it does not convince will convey more clearly what is at the back of the action to which I am committed. I may still hope that this will command assent as desirable and practicable, no matter how much at fault the reasoning in its favour may be.

In speaking of Godness at work in the universe and in our planetary history, there has to be—as it seems to me—a reference both to what so far has been experienced and to what has been scientifically ascertained. I have been particularly concerned to get away from notions which would imprison God in creation and apply our limited terms of reference to questions of his existence and nature. We should try to rid our minds completely of the idea that God is governed by any concepts of time and space.

We must not cheapen God, which it is so easy to do when contending about him. It is not implied at all by a Divine Plan for mankind that in any sphere or dimension God is moving through time on a course parallel with ours, attending to daily business of our prayers, petitions and problems, taking decisions on how he will act according to how things are shaping here. What we describe as the interventions of God in our affairs could be due to factors belonging to the make-up of the universe which act as a stimulus and corrective as may be required. We are aware that we can draw on certain spiritual resources from within, and also that others are acting upon us. It is by no means determined that we live only in a material universe, and we have to allow for the possibility that our total environment embraces an unseen or etheric universe. It is a very old teaching that everything material has a spiritual counterpart, persons, nations and even places.[4] Many psychic experiences point to there being some truth in such doctrine. What has been called heaven spiritually may simply be the etheric universe linked with and interpenetrating the material. Science is still trying to puzzle out, for example, what is a mind in relation to a brain. This is why I have preferred to speak of God only in the aspect of a Godness which is affecting us, by which both planning becomes evident to us and the realization that there is all needful provision for implementation.

It would be folly to restrict the function of Godness to creation of a material universe. But even in that universe it is revealed that there is provision for the maintenance and servicing of what has been created. The more we know about the constituents and mechanics of the universe which is more apparent to us the more amazed we are at the comprehensiveness of the provisions it exhibits, which include the capacity for evolutionary development. It is a perfectly tenable inference that there is a quality of Mind in such

activity associated with intention, and that accordingly
provision extends to the immaterial which is able to furnish
a spiritual boost and promote purposiveness. We are fully
aware that this is what happens with our whole selves, and
that in man a stage of development has been reached which
enables him to employ the non-material purposefully to an
increasing extent—ideas and images—with effect on the
material. It is built-in that we should strive to attain ends,
and that in pursuing them we have something which
instructs us that they are right or wrong, noble or ignoble.
I find it just as irrational and unintelligent to reject the
existence of spiritual agencies and means of grace as to
subscribe to any theological system.

'Means of grace' is a useful phrase in the context of the
Divine Plan. Grace is both a quality which renders the
possessor endearing, and an outgoing of benevolence which
endears what may not present itself as inviting endearment.
Beauty, it has been said, is in the eye of the beholder. It is
something spiritual, by which the sensation of being good
and pleasant is communicated. Grace implies that we have
to see with a special insight, and that there is a characteristic
which calls for that vision and invests what is seen with
lovability.

It is by grace that worth is apprehended, with the con-
comitant that what is found worthy is preserved and
cherished. The theme of grace entranced the Apostle Paul,
who employed it to demonstrate that we who—to his way of
thinking—would be repugnant to a righteous God because
of our sins can be rendered sin-free in God's sight through
the merits of the sinlessness of Christ. Transfigured by those
merits we are 'accepted in the Beloved' and his grace is
imparted to us. Similar Jewish thinking suggested that to
find grace in God's sight the merits of the Patriarchs could
be pleaded, and even the infinite worth of God's holy name
as guarantor of his promise to forgive. The idea of grace in
the Bible harks back to creation itself, where in the first
chapter of Genesis it is said that God saw all that he had
made as good. Professor Mollegen has expressed it that
'Creation as well as redemption is by grace. All contingent

existence is supported by the grace of God. We literally move and have our being in God's grace,' and by the same token, 'The grace-filled man is the free man who does what he desires and wills to do since he desires and wills the purpose of God which has become his own purpose.'[5] The purpose of God for man is what God has designed for him in grace, in that God sees man not just as he is, but as he must be by reason of the Godness in him, which endears man even in his imperfections. It is like when we say, 'Whatever you have done I still love you.'

Grace must therefore also cover what we humans design for our fellows. No one may be treated as an enemy or as inferior in dignity. Law, which is Romanist as it is administered, has to be overruled by grace, which is Messianist. This was what Olaf Stapledon was driving at when he wrote, that we must feel the identity of spirit in all human beings, 'its identity underlying its manifold, lovely, particular, personal idiosyncracy in each man and woman.'[6]

Through the Spirit of God all creation must find grace in our sight, for the spirit that is more than us, and is in all of us, we inescapably share. The Eastern has affirmed this when with hands brought together in adoration he greets us by bowing to the god in us. We all have a part in God, a fundamental family relationship, which constitutes an irrevocable basis of fellowship. In the ultimate it is upon that alone, the grace that sees us all as kin, that we have to build and plan more difficult and complex relationships, and which gives us a title and incentive to do so. Whatever, therefore, upholds the Spirit, and makes us perceptively conscious of the Spirit, is an indispensable well-spring of right action towards our fellows. Reverence for God is still the beginning of wisdom, for by it we learn to revere all life.

Out of grace comes purpose: it must involve for us an expanding fellowship, planning in communion for community. The grace of God towards us assures us that we shall be sustained and helped, that illumination will be given us as and when required out of the provision which has been made. But to reap all the benefits of that grace we too must have grace towards God and man. It is in this way that

God's purpose will become our purpose, when we love him with our heart, our soul, and our mind, and our neighbours as ourselves.

These reflections are very pertinent to the problems we are facing today. By grace we shall be enabled to drop and discard from our ideas of policy and conduct whatever in them may have refused room and accommodation for otherness in individuals and communities. We shall wish more and more to revolt against every limitation of fellowship. Whatever is narrow and sectarian in our programme will be relegated to second place in our esteem and allegiance—we are as yet too conditioned to get rid of it altogether—and what is comprehensive and universal will be advanced to first place. This does not mean, of course, a denial of the right of criticism and judgment; but it does mean setting ever wider bounds to the considerations which inform our judgment.

To be moving, however haltingly, in this Way of the Spirit must make a material change in our outlook and relationships, increasing sensitiveness, awareness, tolerance and desire for service. It must make us review and revise much that we may have thought it right to propose and propagate. We shall not blind ourselves to evil, but determine to overcome it with good. We cannot achieve good ends by evil means.

For all its evil, the antithetic force of Romanism, which means claiming the right to dominate by reason of asserted superiority or from motives of self-interest, is an instrument of the Divine Plan. Again and again it has had to come into play to counter apathy, challenge complacency and provoke to creative initiative, whenever men were inclined to opt out of responsibility, hug their chains, and generally to accept subservience and be reconciled to the 'inevitable'. It is part of nature's prodding device, and in human history has been most in evidence when a fresh forward surge was essential. The lesson surely is that the free spirit in man, however temporarily suppressed, will always break out of bondage. This is why the story of the People of God begins with the exodus from Egypt. So it has been down the ages, and so we can know with certainty that the great eruption of Romanist trends and inhuman behaviour in our time portends a new awakening and a resurgence of Messianism.

It is vital that we should realize this, so that we do not fall into confusion and despondency. It is Romanist false thinking which entertains the possibility of world peace under world law backed by force, or through the Communist dictatorship in the name of the proletariat. These conflicting ideologies are in fact on the same side. Messianism proclaims to the contrary that mankind can only achieve harmony through grace made manifest in mutual love and service.

We can apprehend that we are in another tremendous transitional period because Romanism has become intensified. In so many spheres, political, social and economic the striving for mastery has become acute. Lust for power and prestige has become obsessive. It is exhibited in racialism, nationalism, antisemitism, totalitarian regimes, military dictatorships, ideological and industrial imperialism, party politics and class war. The aim is to control, whether it be markets and resources or the bodies and souls of men.

In this aggressive age the old children's game is being played in deadly earnest:

'I'm the king of the castle.
Go down you dirty rascal!'

The boast again is made, 'Is not this Great Babylon, that I have built by the might of my power, and for the honour of my majesty?'[7] But also again the Spirit of God prophetically announces, 'Great Babylon is fallen, is fallen!'[8] There is no future for Romanism in any form. Its expression belongs always and at all times to an order that must pass away. The evolutionary process, the Divine Plan which calls for life made free and more abundant, inevitably dooms it to extinction. The future is for those who are born of the Spirit which blows where it will, and can be cramped and confined by no frontiers, no walls and iron curtains, no labour and detention camps, no defensive armaments, no restrictions of movement, utterance and association.

Among the signs of the new era at a lower level of consciousness are various manifestations, the accentuation of individual and national independence, revolts against authority and discipline, eccentricities of garb and conduct, demonstrations and resistance movements. At a higher level is the quest for new spiritual understanding and wider fellowship, the abjuration of violence, the pursuit of peace and harmonious relationships, activities in the service of the needy, the suffering, the under-privileged and oppressed, the growth of a community spirit reaching out to embrace all mankind. As Stringfellow Barr put it, 'Let's join the human race.'

It is plainly intimated that what is in travail to be born is the first whole-world age, the first era in which man can become united, the first actual achievement of world citizenship. This could not have begun to happen before the developments of the past two centuries and more. We were only starting to be emancipated. We had not sufficiently explored our planet geographically and recovered enough of our world's history. We had not the means of speedy travel and communication. We did not possess the knowledge, equipment and resources to bring the whole earth into occupation and productivity, and make food, goods and services universally available. We could not adequately educate people and improve physical and social conditions. We were not compelled by mass-destructive weapons and the exigencies of the conquest of Space to organize for global integration.

We still have far to go and many obstacles to surmount, physically and mentally, but it must be a very dull individual who cannot read the signs and recognize them as Preparations for a Gospel. It does not take great insight to determine that this Gospel will be concerned with world unity, and that its terms must acquaint us with the means by which it is to be achieved. On the basis of a Divine Plan a further manifestation of Messianism *has* to appear in a manner appropriate to our time, but arising from the previous expressions of it.

We are not on the brink of doom, but on the eve of regeneration.

NOTES AND REFERENCES

1. Ezek. xxxviii.
2. Mt. xxiv.
3. II. Pet. iii. 10.
4. In the Bible Jesus spoke of the angels of children and the book of Daniel refers to the angelic representatives of peoples (Dan. x). It was believed that Jerusalem and the Sanctuary had heavenly counterparts. 'As above so below' was the old idea, but we may preferably say 'As within so without'.
5. See Professor A. T. Mollegen on 'Grace' in *A Handbook of Christian Theology*, edited by Marvin Halverson and Arthur Cohen (Fontana Books).
6. Olaf Stapledon, *Beyond the 'Isms*.
7. Dan. iv. 30.
8. Rev. xviii. 2.

5

A Time of Testing

WHEN the seers of two thousand years ago proclaimed the impending Messianic judgment they described it as a Time of Testing which is coming upon all the world.[1] We ourselves are now in such a time. Former convictions, values and beliefs are in the melting pot. In almost every connection they are being challenged and tested to determine their worth and validity. There is a growing unwillingness to take anything for granted, and things once regarded as fixed and settled are now being ruthlessly scrutinized and frequently rejected. Those who are sentient, whether intelligently or instinctively, realize that we have to adjust to very great changes, and therefore we have to free ourselves from hidebound positions and examine every proposition afresh. There is nothing that is now sacred and immune.

Naturally, the traditionalists are alarmed and denounce the liberties that are being taken with their cherished ideas. Those who throw off the yoke will come to no good. Defiantly they cry out against new ways and new thinking, and raise the flag to rally the forces of conservatism and conformity. There are the moderates, of course, who agree that we have to go forward, but insist that we must do so slowly and cautiously, feeling our way with careful deliberation. They tend to get the worst of it, being swept aside and scorned by the more impulsive and attacked by the old guard as traitors to the cause.

There is no escape from the Time of Testing, however,

and out of it will emerge fresh patterns to shape the destinies
of the race in the coming era.

But it is not to be pretended that the immediate experience
can be a pleasant one. In a period so trying and uncertain
there is great emotional disturbance. Nerves are frayed,
tempers are aroused, tensions are heightened. When the
whole world seems out of joint and terrible things are
happening or threatened, when people are doubtful,
dismayed and frightened, the disposition to blame and
criticize is vastly increased. It is felt deeply that things should
never have been allowed to get into such an evil state, and
therefore fault is found with 'the system' and with every kind
of authority for failure in the exercise of responsibility, for
rigidity and instransigence, and unwillingness to provide a
remedy. The hunt is on for suitable scapegoats.

We meet with the same kind of circumstances in the
former Messianic period. Tacitus wrote of the reign of
Tiberius, 'Among the calamities of that black period the most
trying grievance was the degenerate spirit, with which the
first men in the senate submitted to the drudgery of becoming
common informers; some without a blush, in the face of day;
and others by clandestine artifices. The contagion was
epidemic. Near relations, aliens in blood, friends and
strangers, known and unknown, were, without distinction,
all involved in one common danger. The act recently
committed, and the tale revived, were equally destructive.
Words alone were sufficient; whether spoken in the forum,
or amidst the pleasures of the table . . . Informers struggled,
as it were in a race, who should be first to ruin his man; some
to secure themselves; the greater part infected by the general
corruption of the times.'[2]

In Palestine, as we know, not only did spies and informers
abound, listening for any word of antagonism to the authorities, whether secular or religious, but fault-finding and
witch-hunting was a commonplace. Brother was looking on
brother with a jaundiced eye, and with many the search for
error in others amounted almost to a mania. Rabbinical
tradition reports that it was 'a generation that judged its
judges.'[3] Jesus was faced with this situation when he said,

'Judge not, and ye shall not be judged.
Condemn not, and ye shall not be condemned.
For with what judgment ye judge, ye shall be judged;
And with what measure ye mete, it shall be measured
  to you again.'[4]

He also quoted the popular proverb about seeing the speck
in your brother's eye, but not seeing the beam in your own
eye. Nevertheless, he himself attacked the shortcomings of
those who joined issue with him. It is never easy to distinguish between healthy and unhealthy criticism; and those
who believe themselves to be in the right usually find it most
difficult to acknowledge that they could be wrong. There is
nothing more galling to professionalism than the disclosure
by an outsider of professional falsifications and inconsisten-
cies. Let the statements and the criticisms be never so valid,
they are none the less bitterly resented.

Manifestly, adverse criticism must often be merited, but
when one is at the receiving end it is hard to bear and still
harder to admit that the revelation of errors has justification.
There are two sides to every question, and it takes a deal of
grace when one is passionately committed to one side to see
the virtues of the other side. Especially is this so when the
clash is between an order which is passing away and another
which is coming to birth. The tendency is to take extremist
positions, with all that these entail of venom, hostility and
recrimination.

I have had to refer to these matters, not only because they
are pertinent to the problems of our time, but also because
of what I must conscientiously say in affirmation of the fresh
phase of the Divine Plan which is coming into operation.
This will inevitably affect Jews and Christians as custodians
of the Design of a Servant-Nation, and in general introduce
a factor in world affairs alien to much current political
thinking. So much is going to be changed and superseded
that I am very sensible of what certain reactions will be. The
'offence' of which Jesus spoke cannot be avoided, and again,
blessed are those who are not offended. The aim is not to
destroy, but to fulfil.

We may discern a necessity not generally contemplated, and envisage a structure for which there is no exact precedent; but whatever it is should arise naturally out of what has gone before, should be in keeping with the spirit of the times, and should represent a logical next step along the evolutionary path. We do not have to be afraid of novelty; but the newness should lie in the application, in the particular turn and direction which is given to what has already been revealed. It might be startling, and speciously attractive, to come out with some idea that ignores completely the historical developments, but such a radical departure could have little prospect of implementation.

It may help if we consider the world as an organism, because the issues are not merely those of better organization. At the human level the essential of a world order is a world conscience, and the modern quest for a disinterested international authority is in effect the quest for a world conscience. It has already been determined that it cannot manifest itself through any ideological power structure, since a comprehensive sensitivity is lacking. Neither can it do so adequately through any artificial or synthetic agency like the United Nations. The agency must be a natural one, and the promise of it is found in fact in the concept of a People of God, a Holy Nation. The components of world society are nations, and this is likely to be the case for centuries to come. We cannot yet know what form world unity will ultimately take; but we can look so far ahead as a co-operating association of nations, not dominated by any Herrenvolk, but guided by a conscience-nation, as free, interpenetrative and lacking in location as the soul is in the body.

The consensus of intelligent opinion holds that the spiritual aspect of the world problem is the most vital one; for unless action arises from compelling inner moral convictions the consequences are bound to be disastrous. In seeking our salvation we have perhaps been looking in the wrong place, the abodes of politicians and prelates. With our power-mindedness we have gone automatically to these quarters; but once again it may hold good that like the story of the wise men of old the quest should really be taking us to

the symbolic wayside inn where is not the home of those of
fixed abode. Like the Son of Man, the People of Man is not
likely to have any secure and enduring resting place. The
Priestly Nation of the ancient prophetic vision was not to be a
state. We cannot, therefore, hope to solve our problems
through a federation of states or religions. But there is
hopeful evidence, as we have seen, in the progressive growth
of a world-minded minority which has surmounted the
limiting factors of race, creed and territory. This minority,
which has recreated the Elect Remnant, bears all the marks
of ability to make the world conscience articulate and
effective.

In some respects the state is to the nation what the machine
is to man. The machine may reproduce many of the capacities inherent in man, and even extend them, but it is nevertheless artificial and soulless. It is one of the unhappy aspects
of our modern civilization that we have become so obsessed
with technological progress that we tend to set the machine
above man and even begin to describe man in mechanistic
terms. To think of human beings in this way is to regard
them as objects which are expendable and to be manipulated
at will. Humanity becomes artificialized, regarded like the
robots conceived by that perceptive Czech dramatist Karel
Capek in his play R.U.R.

So it is with the state and the nation. The nation is a
natural product of evolution, a soul-kinship of the human
group in succession to the older tribal groupings. But the
state is an artificial structure, a forcing-house into which
humans are herded. It is states that have frontiers, not
nations: hence the difficulty in drawing boundary lines
demographically. Frontiers change with political circumstances. Some nations today are cut in two by state boundaries, while various states contain several nations or parts of
nations within their borders.

It is of prime importance to be clear about this distinction
between nation and state. The state can reproduce many of
the characteristics of the nation, like the machine does of
man, but it is not the nation. And we perceive that the same
tendency is at work to glorify the state and to think of the

nation in state terms. Thus the expression nation-state is comparable to mass-man: it robotizes nationhood. Most nations have lands as most men have homes, but they are not irrevocably bound to them. Nations like men can be free and vagrant. There are still nations which have no territory of their own. So that the idea of a conscience-nation, interpenetrative and not identified with a state, is by no means far-fetched. The words of Jesus that the Son of Man 'hath not where to lay his head' may emphasize a truth for the salvation of nations. The release of nationhood from state and territorial bonds, in the first instance by the voluntary action of a Christ-nation, could be the first great step to be taken towards ultimate world community.

This is wholly in line with the Divine Plan. We have traced this plan in its earlier stages. Consistent with it the Jews have never lost their nationhood, though today they are citizens of many states with less than one fifth citizens of the state of Israel. Similarly, as we have noted, Christian thinkers like Armstrong and May have been rediscovering Christian nationhood. A former Bishop of Plymouth, Dr. Howard Masterman, has declared, 'It is only in view of the idea of nation as a unit of service that Christianity can co-exist with a world of nations.'[5]

The Gospel for our time has to be Messianic if mankind is to surmount the greatest crisis in its history; and this calls for a new expression of nationhood charged with spiritual qualities, one which is divorced from the power-structure of the state and concerned solely with the service of all humanity, its peoples and nations. But this nationhood has to be as real, as definite and as visible as any other. Only so can it make an effective impact on world affairs and international relations. The role of the Priestly People was anciently revealed to the Hebrews from whom the Jews are descended, and its composition was expanded to include multitudes of non-Jews as a result of the Messianic work of Jesus. In both cases the mission of the Servant-Nation was betrayed, the first time by the enticement to create a sovereign state, and the second time by the enticement to create a sovereign religion. The Jews and the Christians failed corporately in seeking simultaneously to be both Romanist and Messianist. This danger has to be avoided in the third development which has now been reached, when the Servant-Nation has to be reconstituted and further expanded. The lessons of the past have to be learned, so that neither a state nor a religion is the outcome.

The lessons of the past also teach that neither to states nor to religions should men look for remedy, for neither can provide it. It is vain, therefore, to repose confidence in a United States of the World or in a United Religions of the World, just as the state of Israel cannot save the Jews or the Ecumenical Movement the Christians. We can rule out that any Romanist structure claiming power and authority, whether political or religious, can possibly succeed; and it cannot serve the best interests of mankind to advocate or pursue policies which human experience has tested and found wanting.

It is most difficult to wean human imagination from reliance on power as the means by which effective things are done. The urge to dominate has now been magnified greatly by new instruments of power. But it cannot be pretended that they have made for peace and harmony. To the contrary, they have greatly increased conflict. How it is supposed that fresh concentrations of power can be salutary seems a kind of madness. It is as if Romanism was mustering all its pretentious forces for a last-ditch stand against further evolution.

And what is it that all the wielders of power fear? If we can answer that we are well on the way to a solution of our problems. In fact the most uncompromising power groups have given us the answer. They have told us that what they are mortally afraid of is what they call Cosmopolitanism, and they have identified the chief purveyors of it as the Jews. The Jews, taken as a whole, are liberal, undogmatic and free from class-consciousness, too much attached to universals to offer sacrifice on the altar of any human lordship, able to live anywhere under any conditions, too much in love with peace for aggressive partisanship, too idealistic to be harmful, moving in and through life with benevolent sympathy yet cherishing an independent entity deriving from an inner vision which the world at large has not yet been able to see and enter into.

What is described as cosmopolitanism thus answers to what we are now beginning to understand by world citizenship. Power groups flourish by designating others as enemies. They are, in fact, intrinsically weak, having to brag and to bully to sustain their ego, continually call attention to their virtues, possessions and achievements, maintain security by self-defensive measures. World citizenship does not bow down to the idols of Chauvinistic patriotism, cannot be exclusive, or passionately attached to some sectional cause, and will not be anti-anyone of any race, class or creed. No world citizen is good material for any state or religious system. He cannot be counted upon to toe any party or ecclesiastical line. His affections, sympathies and understandings are much too broad. The Jews are singled out for attack because they are found to typify the tolerance which all power groups find intolerable.

We have the paradox that states and religions (which include ideologies) subscribe to the aim of world peace, but their policies are directed tenaciously to prevent it coming about. They know full well that under conditions of peace the whole character of world society would be changed. There would be no more bogey men to frighten people into obedience, no more enemies of the Faith, whether racial, social, spiritual or political, to keep power-lovers in power. All justification for any kind of Romanism would have disappeared; and so every power-structured edifice resting on the pillars of authority and superiority would collapse.

Through the Prince of Peace, as the Apostle Paul saw, down goes the partition wall, down goes the law of commandments contained in ordinances, down goes enmity! The erstwhile foes and aliens are welded into one new man.[6] The Jewish Messiah, the Son of Man, is revealed as the type and forerunner of the modern world citizen, the New Man now beginning to appear. He is the true representative nowadays of the Israel of God.

What the upholders of power are seeking is not the advent

of world community, but the means of retaining the hostile attitudes which keep them in office without being pushed to the point where hostility would result in mutual self-destruction. This is called brinkmanship. While declaiming violently against each other in public, circulating false and malicious propaganda, and working against one another when an opportunity presents itself to gain an advantage, privately it is accepted that power groups have a vested interest in keeping opponents in business. A total victory would be as dangerous as a total peace for those in the seats of power. Euphemistically the desired state of affairs is termed Peaceful-Coexistence. It applies equally, of course, to party politics and interfaith relationships, and indeed to all power structures, social and racial, which would be completely undermined if their justification was removed by the disappearance of the opposition. It is power-thinking, not spirituality, which attaches men to God out of fear of the Devil, and offers the alternatives of salvation or damnation.

It is inherent in nature that there should be struggle. But as we rise in the scale of values we shall increasingly treat obstacles as challenges to display our best rather than as enemies to bring out our worst. We shall cease to accept that the right ends can be achieved by the wrong means. This is where, as regards the ideals of world peace and community, we may not entertain that any power-structure will take us to our goal. It is this delusion which has hampered real progress. There is no future in the idea of a Dictatorship of the Proletariat, or of a World Authority with teeth in it. Romanism universalized is no solution of the problem of war.

The true way lies in disinterested and comprehensive World Service, and it is for this reason that the world citizen as world servant is making his appearance on the stage of history. He is the individual who is possessed of a new spiritual world-embracing functional consciousness, who has begun to win free of all sectional loyalties which are to the detriment of others, who can no longer engage in war with his fellows or in any kind of partisan pressure. He does not only love his enemies: he acknowledges no one and no part of humanity as an enemy. What is beginning to take place in a minority is a kind of mutation, which heralds for the peoples of the world and commences to make evident the pattern of the age to come. The world citizen of this type is the embodiment, the incarnation, of the Politics of God, the Adam of the new era.

H. G. Wells, realistic visionary that he was, glimpsed something of what would have to happen. In many books he postulated the emergence of a new élite who would engage in an *Open Conspiracy* on behalf of mankind. Those involved would find each other round the world, and would be drawn together by their common purpose and convictions. He insisted that the élite would have to have minds which were crystal clear. 'A man's mind must be liberated before he can conceive the idea of setting men free.'[7] There must be nothing wishy-washy about the Open Conspirators. Wells once took Noah's Ark as a parable, and made his modern Noah say, 'We who must be at the heart of it all, must plainly achieve such a devotion as mankind has never known before, because plainly such devotion as righteous men have displayed in times past has not been enough to save us from this present disaster. Not only such a devotion, but such a clear-headedness. There's the rub. We must give ourselves, mind, body and soul ... The men of the new Ark must be of the utmost clearheadedness; of one mind ... The new age has to be an age of liberal opinion, but not of loose opinion.'[8]

We should beware, however, of imagining, as Wells did, that the stature of the distant future will be immediately attainable, and the first true world citizens will often be unlikely looking fledglings, with no apparent beauty that we should desire them, uncertain in their movements, and exhibiting only very slowly and gradually their distinctive qualities. The first generations of world citizens will make many mistakes, continually disappointing both themselves and humanity; and unless they themselves realize and understand this they will often despair. The new road will be no easier to travel than those which have preceded it.

Creative life has entered into our conditions and limitations on earth. While reaching upwards, man will always

remain a little lower than the angels; and every higher
manifestation of life in our world must still be of our world,
bearing the impress of its inheritance, and relatively varying
only by a shade from the kind which gave it opportunity for
emergence.

Even so, there is a tendency to set upon, persecute, drive
away or destroy, every manifestation that appears strange or
freakish to its contemporaries; and if the new type is genuine
and not a sport it will have to find a footing in an inhospitable
climate, and commend itself as the fulfilment of an existing
aspiration and not as the inimical and destructive annulment
of the old order. The world citizen must make his appeal
through service and example, so that he can increasingly be
accepted as an inspiration and incentive to others to make a
comparable advance. The sense of his integral kinship must
triumph over his unlikeness to the generality.

All this should be patent to spiritual thinkers. For example,
it was a belief of the early Christians that Christhood could
be acquired by a spiritual reproductive process, and so there
would arise out of mankind a type of new man in Christ as
the exemplification of an attainable higher order of manhood. The standard was set, but after nineteen centuries
that ennoblement of the individual is still a comparative
rarity. We need to apprehend that the creative energy
blooms suddenly at an appropriate time in each fresh phase
of development, that it manifests as the crowning achievement of the previous phase, and that it does not rapidly
multiply its kind.

The earlier impulsions to produce a Messianic nation did
not make the grade for reasons which we have considered.
Those concerned relapsed into conformity with the prevailing pattern. The pressure to be like others proved too
great, and they partially but not completely succumbed.
Their vestigial remains are still with us. The Servant-Nation
composed entirely of world citizens which is taking shape
today will have to stand up to an exacting test. It would be a
fatal blunder not to heed the warnings of the past. The *gens
sapiens*, like *homo sapiens*, can only achieve complete self-
fulfilment through identification with the eternal *Sapientia*:

and we are taught that 'the wisdom that is from above is first pure, then peaceable, gentle and easy to be entreated full of mercy and good fruits, without partiality, and without hypocrisy.'[9]

We can see, then, out of what substance the new world order will be evolved. In our errant anarchic condition a Christ-Nation is called for, to take away the curse of disobedience, of abuse of our national selves, to show us a pattern of national godliness, full of grace and truth.

The utopian dreams of political thinkers are but a prophetic voicing of a longing for such an ideal of nationhood, becoming ever more insistent with each graver crisis. It is really a holy nation that their vision seeks to embrace, the advent of a Messianic nation to be the servant and deliverer of the world of nations.

When we speak of a nation being holy we have to redefine the term because it has been brought into contempt. Holiness does not imply any superiority of status but the conscious direction of our powers and capacities to the performance of their pure and proper function. The most exact machine cannot be holy, for it is not in conscious control of its purpose. A holy nation, therefore, is one in which not only are all the parts knit together through the cultivation of the group soul, but in which every activity of nationhood is consciously employed for its true end.

Some of my contemporaries, like Malcolm Muggeridge, have abandoned hope of this world's redemption, and resignedly set their hopes on the ecstasies of heaven. But such defeatism has lost all contact with Jesus as Messiah, and with the promise of a redemptive people. It is the Divine Plan that there should be such a nation, introducing a quite unexpected factor into world affairs at this juncture, the People of Man and the People of Tomorrow, in which at first on a small scale those who are called out of all races and climes, peoples, tongues and nations, will mingle their blood and manifest a common love of humanity. The vision has had a long history of partial fulfilment, but the time has now come when full realization begins to be practicable.

For its peculiar mission the Messianic nation has to

separate itself from territory, because the whole earth is its homeland, and through its members to subordinate all lesser allegiances in order to associate freely with all nations, and become the Son of Man collective. The concept of such a free nation, free in spirit but also free from restrictive pressures, here unites with the concept of world citizenship, so producing a salutary microcosm as the evidence and assurance of the ultimate realized brotherhood of man.

If the concept still appears somewhat nebulous we can obtain some clarification from the speeches of President Woodrow Wilson, for it was as this kind of nation that he saw the United States of America. What he did not apprehend was that the United States, because of its territorial and commercial interests, could not match up to the requirements. Like the rich young ruler in the Gospel story it failed the test because of its great possessions. But Wilson's Messianic vision was right, and I cannot conclude this chapter better than by quoting certain things he said.

'We are the mediating nation of the world ... We are compounded of the nations of the world; we mediate their blood, we mediate their traditions, we mediate their sentiments, their tastes, their passions, we are ourselves compounded of those things. We are, therefore, able to understand all nations. We are able to understand them in the compound, not separately, as partisans, but unitedly as knowing and comprehending and embodying them all.'

And again, 'See, my friends, what this means. It means that Americans have a consciousness different from the consciousness of every other nation in the world. I am not saying this with even the slightest thought of criticism of other nations. You know how it is with a family. A family gets centred on itself if it is not careful and is less interested in its neighbours than in its own members. So a nation that is not constantly renewed out of new sources is apt to have the narrowness and prejudice of a family; whereas America must have this consciousness, that on all sides it touches elbows and touches hearts with all the nations of mankind. The example of America must be a special example. The example of America must be the example not merely of peace because it will not fight, but of peace because peace is the healing and elevating influence of the world and strife is not. There is such a thing as a man being too proud to fight. There is such a thing as a nation being so right that it does not need to convince others by force that it is right.'

'I thank God,' Wilson said, 'that those who believe in America, who try to serve her people, are likely to be also what America herself from the first hoped and meant to be—the servant of mankind.'[10]

The Americans rejected their prophet, and the European statesmen betrayed him; but his soul goes marching on. There are few now who remember, or who have read his words, but there was that in them which was more profound than the shallow and platitudinous utterances of most men of affairs.

NOTES AND REFERENCES

1. The *Time of Testing* is referred to in the Dead Sea Scrolls, commentaries on Psalms ii and xxxvii. It is also mentioned in the Revelation, iii. 10: 'Because thou hast kept the word of my patience, I also will keep thee from the Time of Testing which is coming upon all the world, to try them that dwell upon the earth.'

2. Tacitus, *Annals*, Bk. VI. vii.

3. The Talmud, *Baba Bathra*, fol. 15b.

4. Mt. vii. 1–2; Lk. vi. 37.

5. Howard Masterman, Bishop of Plymouth, in the Symposium, *Christianity and the Crisis*.

6. See Eph. ii. 13–15.

7. H. G. Wells, *Phoenix*.

8. H. G. Wells, *All Aboard for Ararat*.

9. Jas. iii. 17.

10. The quotations from Wilson's Addresses are taken from Schonfield, *This Man was Right*. Wilson's thinking owed not a little to American millennialism, the product of the nonconformist inheritance. See *Redeemer Nation* by Ernest Tuveson (Chicago, 1968).

6

The Third Phase

IT HAS been the affirmation of this book that Messianism is the expression of the Politics of God. There can be no serious Jew or Christian who does not endorse this. While there has been much to keep them apart, on which it is now incumbent that they should earnestly reflect, both have subscribed to the conviction of a coming time in which Messianism would have its crowning fulfilment. Both have also seen that a Chosen People has to play an essential part in such fulfilment, and have recognized a covenant relationship between God and his people to this end.

But the Jews and Christians, by their waywardness, broke the compact, and as a consequence the Plan, which demanded effective human cooperation, was prevented from coming to fruition. One of the errors of those who had been entrusted with the Plan's promotion was to emphasize summary Divine intervention to accomplish by supernatural happenings what it was the business of the designated human agency to achieve. This representation provided a selfsatisfying excuse for inadequacy of commitment. God could do everything, and therefore he should do it all. Jews and Christians still take comfort in leaving it to God. He will act decisively in his own good time. Truly, he *will* act, because his will must be fulfilled, but only by the means he has revealed, a Servant-Nation whose will is aligned with his. The failure in turn of Jewish and Christian Israel now appears providential in the light of history, since mankind's

perilous situation has become so much graver that a further
unfolding of the character of the Divine Plan in a fresh phase
of expression is imperative. But this does not lessen or
extenuate the failure of those on whom responsibility had
been conferred. Both have rejected their Messianic obligations and turned aside to follow their own desires.

Of course condemnation must be tempered with understanding. Undoubtedly there has been a great deal that is
good and worthy in Jewish and Christian life and faith. Had
this not been so they would hardly have survived with so
much vitality. But they have also been preserved as the Two
Witnesses, whose testimony offers convincing evidence of the
Divine Plan and what it has portended. Modern knowledge
is now beginning to lead Judaism and Christianity to
reconsider their teaching, especially in those matters which
have estranged them and put enmity between them. It is
being revealed that it is their independent fallacies which
have kept them apart, and one of the hopeful Signs of the
Times is the better relationships between them.

It still remains that Messianism, the common bond, has
to be reaffirmed, and Jewish and Christian positions revised
accordingly. Only thus can amends be made for the past.
The tasks of the Kingdom of God call insistently, and they
have to be heeded. Multitudes have been turning away from
Church and Synagogue because their antiquated formulations of doctrine are no longer credible, and because it
does not appear that religions can now meet the corporate
need of mankind. The records have to be kept and valued
as instructive relics of the infancy and childhood of the race,
but the mistakes of immaturity do not have to be perpetu-
ated. This was the conclusion of the Apostle Paul when he
wrote, 'When I was a child, I spoke as a child, I understood
as a child, I reasoned as a child: but when I became a
man, I put away childish things.'[1]

Comprehension of the Divine Plan has come a long way,
as our investigation has shown. In essence it is the same, but
the application has evolved. It could be grasped and
expressed only in the context of contemporary capacity.
This is still the case. It is what can be discerned as its

present requirements that matters, and being faithful to
what is discerned. Revelation can apply precisely only to
what is currently relevant. For what is to come long after it
can use only the inadequate language of present thinking,
interpretation and imagination. Our foresight may have
some likeness to the reality, and to some extent govern the
future as the child is father of the man; but it will not be the
reality, because what belongs to the mind and accomplish-
ments of a future age cannot exactly be matched in our own
consciousness.

It is useless, therefore, to suppose that prophets of old
could foretell circumstantially what would happen hundreds
and thousands of years later. Their vision could not compass
the details, and it would be foolish to believe otherwise. We
are in no way bound to former prognostications of the
Messianic Age, as people anciently believed themselves to be,
and many still believe to this day. But we should pay
tribute to the insight which recognized the operation of the
Politics of God in human affairs, and from what was conveyed to those of old contributed the impetus to move in the
right direction. It has always been possible to go on from
where past effort left off, but emotionally it takes a time of
great crisis to furnish sufficient incentive to make us receptive. The provision was always there of the means to be
employed. It was on tap, ready for our use when conditions
prodded us into opening ourselves to take it in. It is thus that
'man's emergency is God's opportunity.'

But in seeking enlightenment we have to cast aside all the
encumbrances which block perception. We obstruct our
vision, at our peril, if we interpose our preconceptions and
presuppositions. This is why H. G. Wells quite rightly
warned against muddle-headedness. Because we have a prior
discontent with organized religion this should not encourage
us to indulge in all kinds of pseudo-cultism.

The Divine Plan, since it is for the improvement of human
conditions, is not escapist. It brings us down to earth with a
bump, jolting us out of all scatter-brained fancies, and
requiring us to undertake a coherent very concrete job with
all our wits about us and that much extra of penetrating

clearsighted competence. We have to stop dreaming about
the New Age and Kingdom Come, and get down to building
it from the ground upwards.

Where the religions have failed is in offering ivory-tower
security, an inducement to get away from the hurly-burly of
involvement or to endure with piously folded hands. We are
not in this world to prepare for the next. We are in this world
to make it better. By evading the issue of what a Messianic
Age demands the repositories of the Messianic vision have
been driving away the virile in disgust. Instead of being good
shepherds, they leave it to the lost sheep to find their own
way into the fold, and what is worse connive at their
slaughter by wild beasts. God's anger is kindled against the
shepherds, cried the prophet.[2]

Thus a Third Phase in the unfolding of the Divine Plan
has had to become manifest, for a great cry has gone up
which could not fail of response. The Servant-Nation is
being reconstituted from the sentient minority which is ready
and willing to undertake the responsibilities of world
citizenship for the sake of all humanity. Jews and Christians
should be the first to sign on for service. But this time the
door is open to people of all religions and of none, who hear
the call and are prepared to accept the principles by which
the new nation is governed and the conditions of its citizenship.[3] Certainly the task is to be approached spiritually,
because otherwise there can be no reaching out in love to the
spirits of all mankind; but no religion can be the means of
accomplishment.

It is an old issue, with which this book began, whether and
to what extent religion should interfere in politics. It has
been a question here of two different authorities, each
claiming dominion over men, and frequently contending
with one another as a consequence. The issue is still a live one,
and is felt particularly by Christians—though it affects
adherents of all religions—because they are troubled by the
problem of divided loyalties. We have to face this problem,
since the Divine Plan is as much political as it is spiritual.

The Christian problem arises naturally out of the errors
and confusions to which Christianity lent itself. Let us take

first the position of Roman Catholics, because it is claimed
for the Pope that he is the Vicar of Christ on earth. In the
Middle Ages Pope Boniface VIII could assert grandiosely in
a well-known Bull, that 'all Kings, Emperors, and other
sovereigns, whoever they may be, are subject, like all other
men, to be summoned before the Apostolic Courts, for every
sort of cause; for we, by the permission of God, command
the whole Universe.'[4] That claim may seem ridiculous now,
but Roman Catholics are concerned to this day about how
far the Pope's authority extends.

The situation has been further complicated since, by the
signing of the Lateran Treaty of 1929, the Pope became
again a temporal sovereign. In the Treaty it is stated, 'The
Holy See declares, with reference to the sovereignty it
enjoys in international matters, that it wishes to remain, and
will remain, outside all temporal rivalries between the other
States and international meetings convoked concerning
them, unless the contending parties should unanimously
appeal to its peace mission; reserving however in each case
the right to assert its moral and spiritual power. The Vatican
City will consequently and in every case be considered a
neutral and inviolable territory.' The activities of the
present Pope, Paul VI, who has addressed the United
Nations and visited every continent, seem designed to
reassert Papal power and stage a revived spiritual Romanism
wearing the trappings of the Messianic but antithetic to its
true nature.

Protestantism, on the other hand, and also the Russian
Orthodox Church, has on the whole taken up a temporizing
Vicar of Bray attitude. But many socially and politically-
minded clergy are not at all happy about it. Not only is there
the World Council of Churches, but many a 'turbulent
priest' not always of the best type, who believes he has to
speak out boldly. This kind of dissatisfaction has become
increasingly vocal, and two clerical statements can illustrate
its trend. 'The Christian community,' said one, 'has a responsibility for economic change. Its task is not only that of
proclaiming an ideal. It exercises its functions rightly in
examining the reality and effectiveness of those policies

which control the material life of man, and it has been
raised up that it may so order human relationships that the
principles of Christ may be built into the life of the world.'[5]
Said another, 'To those who are afraid of putting the
Kingdom of God through the political order, we answer
that there is no alternative. For if we do not control the
political life with the Kingdom-of-God programme, then
either Communism or Fascism will take it over.'[6] Neither
writer is Messianist in spirit, for they speak of 'ordering' and
'controlling' which is Romanist.

The Christian dilemma is that while Christians believe
they are adherents of a religion they cannot get away from
Romanism, and have to act correspondingly inside states
which have quite other aims and methods than the Messianic.
'To a Christian man, his duty to his nation can never be the
first claim on his allegiance,' declared one British bishop.[7]
But this is where Christianity has gone wrong, because the
Christian's own nation is not in fact the state to which he
happens to belong: it is the Messianic nationhood of which
the Church has deprived him by converting itself into a
religion.

This is why Cyril Armstrong was prophetically right when
he announced nearly fifty years ago, 'The time is ripe for us
Christians to assert again that sacred Nationality founded
by God when he called Abram out of Chaldea ... The
Christian Nation must claim full independence both
politically and economically. This is essential, not merely
because the biddings of secular governments clash with the
biddings of Christ, but because the military and commercial
fabric of secular civilization ensnares and fetters at every
turn the Christian who wishes to follow his conscience and
to do the thing that is just and right and brotherly.'[8]

God's nation is not a Power dominating and controlling
the nations, but a nation among the nations, serving them
and setting them a national example. It is what I have called
a Christ-Nation. We have to get right out of our minds that
the Politics of God call for coercive authority, whether
religious or secular. We can find many evidences, and in all
the ground we have covered I have cited a number of them,

that a movement of thought is proceeding which is pointing towards what our time requires and making it possible for it to come into being. But we are so enveloped in a smog of our own creation that solutions get distorted by power notions and we are unable to perceive that there can be an answer which dispenses with the idea of mastery.

We see the nation-states as power units. And so we imagine that for world peace we have to build them into bigger units with greater power, federations, blocs, the United Nations, right up to a World Authority. Whereas what we aim at cannot at all be achieved by such means. What can achieve it would in the natural way never occur to us; and when revelation presents it our natural inclination could well be to scoff at it. We would ask the same questions as they asked the Messiah, 'Where is your authority? Who of consequence has acknowledged you? What resources have you? How many followers have you got?' If the answers are unimpressive to our power-consciousness, we, the practical people, will shake our heads and turn away muttering, 'He's quite mad. The whole thing is impossible.'

But dare we today be so confident in our rejection? Look to what an extremity the practical people have brought us! Why should we be seeking a remedy, why should we be living in fear, if the Powers-that-be knew all the answers? Almost every word and move of the political pundits gets reported and speculated upon in the Press and on radio and television, but the voice of sanity does not readily get a hearing. The chief reason why an obscure village carpenter in Galilee got himself talked about was a power reason, because he was superstitiously credited with working miracles. No miracles, no Messiah! Such is the verdict of men. Would it not be wiser to review this judgment, so that we do not make another silly mistake which we can ill-afford? The Christ-nation, the Servant-Nation, is not going to work any miracles. Its work will be slow and arduous, and very largely unspectacular, quite unattractive and unconvincing to those in a hurry, who will continue to busy themselves as of yore with the speciously authoritative.

None the less, those of us who have a truer insight are

going ahead with the building of this new nation. But we are not going to create another state, another aggregation of power. We shall not live in a separate country which we have to defend against our fellows; but we shall have our own appropriate polity. All our people will be world citizens, and they will be real citizens of our republic or commonwealth, having a status identified with the interests of all mankind. They will be drawn from men and women in all lands, in all walks of life, with different skills and aptitudes, who have accepted a prior loyalty to humanity and have elected to serve humanity. They will have a secondary citizenship of sovereign states in which they are domiciled, and work for the good of the people among whom they live, as they will work for the good of all men. But they will not be subject to any state laws or enactments which are contrary to their proclaimed principles. They will not engage in war, or in preparation for war, or in any activity of a subversive or partisan character, which would be to the hurt or detriment of others. They will meet periodically in community groups to determine the works of service to be done at all levels, and for the conduct of their affairs in common with the whole body-politic of the Servant-Nation. They will aim, like the Society of Friends, to win respect for their activities and way of life.

All this will be difficult, but not impracticable. Every aspect of the enterprise has already been thoroughly investigated. The Servant-Nation of today reflects in many respects the position of Jews and Christians in the last Messianic period. Many of the official Roman edicts are on record relating to the measure of internal autonomy granted to the Jewish communities throughout the Empire. These communities had exemption from military service and from labouring on the sabbaths, a right of assembly, resort to their own courts of law, the remission of funds abroad, and so forth.[9] The communities were held together by cultural. religious and national bonds, and linked by visiting apostles, They had their own chosen officers who acted as their representatives. The Christian communities were organized on a somewhat similar pattern, on a basis both spiritual and national. Passages in the New Testament define their relationship with the state and with local authorities.

It is pertinent to recall here the *Epistle to Diognetus*, where it is said of the Christians, 'But while they dwell in cities of Greeks and Barbarians as the lot of each is cast, and follow the native customs in dress and food and the other arrangements of life, yet the constitution of their own citizenship, which they set forth, is marvellous, and confessedly contradicts expectation. They dwell in their own countries, but only as sojourners; they bear their share in all things as citizens, and they endure all hardships as strangers. Every foreign country is a fatherland to them, and every fatherland is foreign.'

'It is evident,' writes the fourth century Christian historian Eusebius, 'that but a short time after the appearance of our Saviour Jesus Christ had been made known to all men, a new nation suddenly came into existence; a nation confessedly neither small nor weak, nor situated in a remote corner of the earth, but the most populous and religious of all, and so much the more indestructible and invincible as it has always had the power of God as its support. This nation, appearing at the time appointed by inscrutable wisdom, is that which among all is honoured with the name of Christ.'[10]

Thus in the Jewish and Christian polity of the past we have a prototype of the Servant-Nation of today. To build such a nation no permission is required. Those who see their duty clearly will do what they must manfully and nothing will deter them. And what they do will be to the real advantage of every state. The conditions now are actually much more favourable, partly because most states are genuinely seeking ways of international cooperation and the outlawing of war, and partly because certain important precedents have been created.

The precedents are found in a variety of connections. Among them may be instanced degrees of internal autonomy accorded to certain racial and religious minorities, the functioning of several small states and principalities within the framework of larger state units, like Monaco, Andorra, Lichtenstein, San Marino, the Vatican, and the sovereign

status of the Religious Order of the Knights of Malta. There
are the conventions regarding protected and neutralized
personnel applying to the International Red Cross, and
diplomatic immunities and privileges accorded to categories
of officials of the United Nations and to the organization
itself under Article 105 of the Charter. There is the neutrali-
zation of the Secretary-General of the U.N. and his staff
under Article 100 of the Charter. By permission of a host
state the government of any foreign Power may exercise
soverign functions on its soil and jurisdiction over the
nationals of the Power domiciled in the country concerned.
Any building or plot of ground may temporarily or permanently be internationalized or extra-territorialized, and
not merely embassies and legations. In fact there are no
obstacles whatever in international law, custom or usage, to
the functioning of a world people like the Servant-Nation in
the manner which its new expression requires.

As regards citizenship, this in any case is no longer a
fixed star in the political firmament. Citizenship is not now
universally recognized as a natural right, automatically
conferred by birth and enjoyed until death, unless voluntarily exchanged for another citizenship by naturalization.
In some countries a person can lose or be deprived of his
citizenship or citizen rights, and we are now fully familiar
with the terrible condition of statelessness.

Neither is there any universal agreement that a change of
citizenship has automatically to be conceded. States have
refused to relinquish citizens even when they have validly
acquired another citizenship. There are circumstances
which permit an individual to hold two citizenships and use
two passports, employing whichever may be convenient.
Two kinds of citizenship may also be recognized, such as
existed with British and British Commonwealth citizenship.
The terms and conditions of citizenship are therefore what
any state chooses to make them, and it is fully within the
competence of every state to allow a citizen to hold a valid
world citizenship additionally. This indeed would be the
rule if there existed a World Federation of States.

The position of the Servant-Nation must in certain respects

be exceptional, since it is not a state technically and its members will be universally distributed. While it has to have autonomy it is not a foreign Power. It is a cross-section of our common humanity, the voice of Everyman hitherto unheard and unrepresented in the councils of the nations. It holds before every people that part of its image which is united in brotherhood with all mankind. World citizens are not required to divorce themselves from their background and ordinary civic obligations. It is only stipulated in their case that the responsibilities of state citizenship shall be restricted to those which do not do violence to world responsibilities. The areas of state obedience cover everything conducive to good neighbourliness; and it should be held that such persons are the most satisfactory kind of citizens. They make a positive contribution to the welfare of the community. They also assist actively in promoting peaceful international relations and economic wellbeing, thus increasing state security from external aggression and internal subversion. Even without a specific higher citizenship it is customary for states to recognize a limitation of obligations where a special vocation is concerned, as in the case of priests and ministers of religion and members of the medical profession. This also now applies to citizens released for duties with the United Nations.

The existence of the Servant-Nation does not give rise to a problem of dual allegiance, for the allegiances are not equal. There is a primary allegiance to mankind, and a secondary allegiance to the state. These allegiances should not be imagined to be opposed, since the good of the whole benefits every part. This is understood in all states of a federal or unionist character. The Servant-Nation is itself in a sense a federation, not of states but of individuals, and it is because of its world vocational character that its members claim universal respect as servants of humanity. No state has to fear that any high percentage of its citizens will embrace this world citizenship, and certainly not as a means of opting out of civic responsibilities. Those who want an easy time of it do not undertake the strenuous and exacting responsibilities of being world servants. This is readily illustrated by the comparative paucity of numbers of voluntary workers in human welfare societies and agencies.

The creation of the Servant-Nation is of the greatest possible advantage to mankind. Some of the reasons should be obvious. State machinery is rather ponderous and slow-moving, and the human mind inevitably runs ahead of it, and must do so, if there is to be adequate progress and improvement. If the machine is called upon for a spurt it is liable to break down or crack up. Then with states there is war or bloody revolution. A new machine has hurriedly to be built or improvised from parts of other machines. After the Hague Conferences we had the League of Nations only because of the first world war, and we had the United Nations only because of the second world war. Must we have world unity only because of a third world war?

This is not necessary. As state machinery cannot move fast enough to keep pace with the accelerated rate of change in human needs and conditions, there can be constructed a lightly built mobile machine not bedded in the concrete of territory, which can scout ahead and explore and report back. We can employ an agency that is not a state, and yet sufficiently statelike, to experiment in world unity and fresh forms of social and political life. In this way inevitable progress will be robbed of its terrors, since it will first be tested out on the harmless proving-ground of the Servant-Nation.[11]

But the Servant-Nation has many other valuable and essential functions to perform. During the world wars there was need for neutrals as intermediaries and protecting powers, states like Sweden and Switzerland. The threat of a world war which might involve all states forces us to recognize how indispensable it is to have a category of persons absolutely and inviolably neutral. Even as things are now, under present conditions of international and ideological conflict, the impartial mediatorial ministrations of a perman-ent neutral respected on all sides are urgently needed. We have no such neutrals today, only so-called unaligned countries. We try to pretend that the United Nations is a neutral agency, but we know quite well that it is not, since

it is not distinct from the contending states and groups of
states. With the Servant-Nation, however, we will have a
world agency equally serving all peoples, with no axe to grind
and no territory to defend, which cannot take sides in any
dispute, and which, therefore, can be an acceptable mediator.

There is a continually expressed desire that there should
be a world agency of this kind, to preside at international
conferences, supervise the implementation of agreements,
promote disarmament, undertake the dispensation of aid to
underprivileged countries, giving service 'without strings'
with no motive of self-interest or sectional advantage. Such
an agency is required also to promote all policies for the
common good of humanity, on land, beneath the seas, and
in outer space. It would be desirable that all the Specialized
Agencies of the United Nations should be staffed exclusively
with world citizens, and that the Servant-Nation should be
the repository of all international treaties and conventions.
As affecting human rights and the rights of minorities the
Servant-Nation could exercise trusteeship and be a kind of
ombudsman for mankind. It would be almost impossible for
the states to create such an agency, but they could thankfully
use its good offices in a hundred ways once it was functionally
available.

Above and beyond current problems the Servant-Nation
will be inspiring and encouraging all nations to live up to the
highest professions of their constitutions internally and in
their external relations. Standing for a peaceful united world
community its aim will be to set a living example of nationhood at its best, to investigate and experiment with policies
making for closer cooperation and integration, until it can
appear by common consent what form of planetary society
is most suitable, not as a power-structure, but on a basis of
mutual fellowship. Through its universality of distribution
the Servant-Nation in this respect can be used creatively in
the character of an experimental working-model.

With all the hardness and intransigence there is in the
world the Servant-Nation has to manifest itself Messianically
'as a green shoot out of a dry ground.' We may truly say,
'This is the Lord's doing; it is marvellous in our eyes. This is

the day which the Lord hath made; we will rejoice and be glad in it.'[12]

We are constantly being treated to surprises, some of them breath-taking, some of them alarming. But there is one surprise for which in man's hour of crisis each one of us deep down within us has been longing and waiting, whether we are statesmen, philosophers, or simple working people. We could not give a name or a form to what we were expecting; for we did not know in what way, from what quarter, or in what guise it would come. We could not readily justify our faith by reason. But we felt instinctively that something wonderful ought to happen progressively to change the sorry, sordid, savage aspect of Society.

Now that its nature stands revealed, we can surely give voice to a heartfelt '*Hallelujah!*'

NOTES AND REFERENCES

1. I. Cor. xiii. 11.
2. See Zech. xi.
3. See the Appendix to this volume.
4. See R. F. Wright, *Medieval Internationalism*.
5. Rev. P. T. R. Kirk, *Christianity and the Crisis* (Symposium).
6. Rev. Stanley Jones, *Christ and Present World Issues*.
7. Rev. Dr. Howard Masterman, Bishop of Plymouth, in *Christianity and the Crisis*.
8. For a fuller quotation see Part Two, chapter 3.
9. See Josephus, *Antiq.* Bk. XIV. x, and Radin, *The Jews among the Greeks and Romans*.
10. Eusebius, *Ecclesiastical History*, Bk. I. ch. iv.
11. The modern technique of simulation also furnishes a suggestive comparison. By reproducing under controlled conditions circumstances liable to be encountered defects can be rectified in advance and every kind of contingency that might arise can be studied experimentally.
12. Ps. cxviii. 23–24. This is the last of the *Hallel* psalms sung at the ancient Jewish Pilgrim Festivals.

7

Plan in Progress

THE annunciation concerning the Servant-Nation took place
on Monday the 26th September 1938. I have related the
circumstances in the Prologue. From a human angle the
coming of a People of Peace could not have been heralded
at a less propitious moment. With Hitler's insatiable demands, at that time on Czechoslovakia, no one knew what a
day would bring forth. The world was on the brink of another
world war, and the Munich pact would bring only a brief
uneasy respite. The evil doctrine of mastery over human
minds, bodies and souls was in the ascendant, exhibiting a
particular virulence. There was a horrible pitilessness and
bestial use of mass-psychology in the power-drunk systems
of the time, which did far more than shatter peace: they
overturned sanity. It was as if a malignant spirit stalked the
earth, broadcasting the germs of a hideous political disease.
The League of Nations was helpless before it. All democratic
peoples went in fear of it. It was a sickness so dire that it
seemed as if only a spiritual means in complete contrast could
wholly defeat it.

After years of suffering and destruction the immediate
danger was overcome; but the spirit behind it had not been
eradicated, only temporarily subdued. The revelation had
therefore been right, that the evil could not be cast out by
summoning force to meet force, employing power to combat
power, but only by the much stronger unarmed and despised
weak things of the world, love, compassion and selfless service.

But the Servant-Nation in its new expression had yet to
be born, and then to experience all the pains and difficulties
and disciplines of growing up. It has taken thirty years for
it to reach maturity, so that it would be ready and equipped
for its mission. That moment has only now arrived, and this
is why the message is going out in a manner and to an extent
that was not previously possible.

The full story of the formative years may never, perhaps,
be written, because there are very few still living who are
acquainted with the details. But it is needful to record the
course of events sufficiently for those whom the message will
reach, so that those who will now enter the Servant-Nation
and those who will have to take account of it may alike be
aware of what lies behind the emergence of this strange
enterprise on behalf of humanity.

Speaking for myself, as instrumentally the prime mover,
I am most deeply and humbly grateful to that nucleus of men
and women who united their lives with this adventure
without knowing very much about its origin, and who
sustained it with their courage, their loyalty and their
limited means when the obstacles to its success appeared to
be overwhelming and the chances of its coming to full
fruition seemed extremely remote. They believed that what
it signified was valid, and ought to be supported, even though
there was much they could not fully grasp, and much that
bewildered them about how to proceed.

It was comparatively easy for me, who had had the vision,
to be confident that what had been signified would come to
pass. Although the whole project, on the face of it, gave an
impression of fantasy, I knew inwardly that I had only to be
faithful to what was disclosed and the thing would happen
despite setbacks and what would be said and done to obstruct development. I cannot pretend that all that would be
encountered was comfortable to bear. There have been
times when the hurt of gainsaying and active opposition was
almost unendurable; but I have never been in doubt of the
outcome. On occasions when everything looked like defeat
it was always possible to effect a rally and to go forward.
The circumstances have been very like the wilderness

journey of the earliest members of the Chosen People.

The task was one which from the very beginning was deemed impossible, and experienced workers in the peace and world government movements did not hesitate to say so when apprised of what was proposed. I felt my own insufficiency very keenly. How and in what way did one start to create a new nation, especially one of this unique type and composition? I was little known. I had never undertaken any leadership. My acquaintance with political science and international law was slender. Most people were preoccupied with the immediate threat of war. I had a living to earn, and a growing family to support. The conditions seemed anything but propitious.

I am still not sure how it came about. Someone must have spoken about me. But one day I received an invitation to be a speaker at an international spiritual Peace Conference convened at Lytchett Minster in Dorset by Lady Madeleine Lees. I recall that another speaker was Sir Francis Young-husband, founder of the World Congress of Faiths. I addressed the Conference on 'The Divine Plan of World Government' and afterwards printed the text for circulation. The effect was immediate. There was soon a small group meeting at our London home to discuss this thinking, which resulted in the formation of a little Society for the Constitution of a Holy Nation. The members came together in different houses in rooms darkened by wartime blackouts, often reaching their destination during air raids, sheltering on the way in porches when bombs were falling and there was a rain of shrapnel from the anti-aircraft guns.

I was able to address various groups, and write a number of articles, which brought new recruits from the provinces and even surprisingly enough from overseas. The Society became the Service-Nation Movement, and from 1941 a magazine *The World Citizen* began regular publication. Boldly in 1944 a leaflet was sent to the Allied and Neutral Governments advising them of the intention to bring the new nation into being. In the meantime there had been a great deal of study and research, which helped to clarify a good many issues.

The next date of importance was Armistice Day, 11th November 1950. I had felt a strong prompting to go into action, and circulated an invitation to a conference at a West End hotel. It was here that the Servant-Nation acquired definition, and was named the Commonwealth of World Citizens.

It was a puny infant, with a total weight of about forty people. But at this time an unexpected opportunity presented itself. In Europe a plan had been devised to promote a Peoples' World Congress, signifying impatience that the United Nations was not moving towards world government. The idea of world citizenship had caught on, through the activities of men like Garry Davis. An International Registry of World Citizens had been established, based on Paris. All who wished to do so could obtain a registration card, which entitled them to a vote in Peoples' Congress elections. A massive gathering was organized for December 1950 at Geneva. Two delegates were sent to represent the Commonwealth of World Citizens, and this was the first occasion on which it appeared as a people in its own right. The fact aroused great interest and comment, and brought in a number of additional adherents.

The following year it was possible to hold a first General Assembly of citizens in Paris, and a Drafting Commission was appointed to begin work on the preparation of the Servant-Nation's Constitution. I had a great deal to do with the preparation of the text, which had to meet the peculiar requirements and relationships of the new people distributed throughout different countries. A first draft was ready for presentation to the second General Assembly, which met in London in 1953, and it was then agreed that it should be sent to every adherent for study and suggestions. The views expressed were analysed and those proposed alterations which had considerable support were incorporated in a revised text. This was again circulated, and further amendments were debated and voted upon at the third General Assembly held in September 1955. The text as finalized was then unanimously approved to go forward for adoption by a duly convened Constituent Assembly. The Constitution, however, was described as Provisional. It was fully appreci-

ated that revision would in due course be required in the
light of experience.

During these preparatory years there was a steady
augmentation of the number of citizens. These were acquired
largely through personal contacts and correspondence, and
a few Press notices. What people were joining was not a
membership movement: they were becoming world citizens
in the context of the new Commonwealth. This was a
serious life commitment, not to be undertaken in a momen-
tary enthusiasm. At no time, therefore, was anyone directly
asked to join. Nevertheless, by 1952 there were citizens in
14 countries, by 1954 in 25 countries, and by 1955 in 30
countries.

The Constituent Assembly was planned to be held at the
end of August 1956. The chosen venue was the Temple of
Peace and Health at Cardiff in the Principality of Wales.
Here was the headquarters of the United Nations Association
in Wales. This splendid building had been erected by the
munificence of Lord Davies of Llandinam, whom I had
known personally, as the 'first edifice in Great Britain
specifically intended to secure the advancement of the great
cause of World Peace.' It was therefore most suitable for the
unique event which was to take place within its walls.

This was to be the *barmitzvah* (confirmation) of the
Servant-Nation, when the Commonwealth of World Citizens
would be proclaimed in being *de facto*. The great Assembly
Hall was packed with citizens, who in many instances had
travelled hundreds and even thousands of miles to be present,
some of them working their way by stages. There were
numerous representatives of organizations who had been
invited as observers, and among state officials were the
Deputy High Commissioner of Ceylon and the United
States Consul in Cardiff. There were reporters from various
newspapers and the main events were covered by radio and
television.

The bare facts cannot convey the emotional atmosphere,
but the proceedings were conducted with a decorous
solemnity. Everyone was acutely conscious of the implications of what was being done. The hour of decision came

on the morning of August 29th. The hand-written copy of the Constitution was brought in on a cushion by a boy and girl, and presented to the gathering for formal adoption. Every right hand was lifted in acceptance, and to the offering of prayer for blessing the flag of the Servant-Nation was hoisted and unfurled on the roof of the Temple of Peace.

Prior to the Assembly a copy of the Constitution had been transmitted to the Secretary-General of the United Nations and to all Governments, and at the close of the proceedings a Council was elected to prepare the way for the first experimental Parliament. All who had become citizens before constitution were required within six months to ratify their citizenship under the Constitution.

The problem of organizing world-wide elections was no easy one, but at a meeting of the Council in Paris in 1957 a method was agreed upon. Constituencies were created, not according to countries but to zones of concentration of citizens. Candidates, in some cases as many as four, were adopted for each zone, and their qualifications communicated on the zone voting papers. Voters would number these in the order of their preference, and election was by the method of the single transferable vote. The ballot was conducted postally by an independent body, the Proportional Representation Society, which scrutinized and counted all votes and declared the results for every zone. All canvassing by candidates was prohibited.

It was considered advisable, to avoid any suggestion of partisanship, that the elected Chamber of Deputies should meet in a neutral country. Facilities were available in Austria, and by courtesy of its Government the Servant-Nation's Parliament assembled in Vienna in May 1959. Here it elected its first ministers, and the Commonwealth's initiator was invited to act as President. At this Parliament the Commonwealth of World Citizens assumed the distinctive title of *La Mondcivitana Respublico* by translation into the international language Esperanto. Consequently the body-politic of the nation became thenceforth commonly known as the Mondcivitan Republic and its citizens as Mondcivi-

tans. It was not considered practicable, however, to adopt
an official language.

The formation of a Government was important because it
facilitated communication with the state Governments.
Mondcivitan ministers could correspond with their opposite
numbers in the different countries according to protocol and
receive replies appropriately. Indeed, it was remarkable how
readily in many cases the existence of the Mondcivitan
Republic was accepted unquestioningly. Had the citizens
in general been more acclimatized to their new status the
effect would have been much greater and much more could
have been achieved. Occasionally there were amusing
incidents when various officials vainly studied the map to
find in which part of the globe the Mondcivitan Republic
was located, and it was not uncommon to receive mail
directed to our Commercial or Cultural Attaché.

Helpful initiatives were taken during the life of the first
Parliament to promote world peace and international
understanding, both directly and by preparing resolutions
for sponsorship by states in the General Assembly of the
United Nations. It will suffice here to give three examples as
illustrations.

The Servant-Nation originated a proposal for the convening of a Third Hague Peace Conference to review the
whole world position in the light of all the developments
since 1907 when the Second Conference met. This had the
backing of a number of bodies, and especially of the International Arbitration League which acted as co-sponsor. The
I.A.L. had been influential in fostering the convening of the
First Hague Conference of 1899.

Later, in September 1961, the Mondcivitan Republic
transmitted to the member states of NATO and the Warsaw
Pact 'An Urgent Call on behalf of Humanity.' This was in
connection with the dangers of fallout resulting from the
testing of nuclear weapons. Part of the text reads:

'The Mondcivitan Republic (Commonwealth of World
Citizens) . . . asserts as an incontrovertible fact that no
Government in the world has been invested with a mandate

which permits it to exercise, or attempt to exercise, the power of life and death over any peoples not legitimately subject to its jurisdiction. This not only excludes all acts of coercion and aggression involving the people of any other country or countries, but any action, such as the testing of nuclear or other weapons, which may be a danger to them or inflict injury upon them.'

Resolutions adopted by the General Assembly of the United Nations in October and November 1961 gave effect to the substance of the Servant-Nation's 'Urgent Call' in similar language. The issue has more recently arisen again in connection with Chemical and Bacteriological weapons.

The following year the Mondcivitan Republic intervened over the Cuban Crisis. As President I communicated personally with President Kennedy and Chairman Kruschchev on October 25th. The letters were in identical terms and the text was as follows:

'The U.S.S.R. and the U.S.A. in their power and dignity have given the firmest pledges of their will to work for a peaceful world, only practicable, as is evident to all nations, if these two great countries cooperate with each other and combine their efforts.

'Consequently, since all mankind looks to them for leadership, and since both understand in their hearts that the highest and noblest duty devolves upon them, it is unthinkable that they should be deflected from it by any circumstances, however unhappily arising or from whatever causes, which would manoeuvre them into horrifying and fatal conflict.

'Rather, when such circumstances appear as now, must it be their concern to intensify activity to reach mutual understanding and concord, and resolutely refuse to yield to all persuasions and impulses which might dictate any other course, even though these may be prompted not by low motives or the believed antagonistic intentions of the other, but by the purest and most honourable considerations.

'What is right to be done need not be in any doubt when

such clear responsibility towards the whole human race is seen to transcend national and even ideological obligations.'

How influential this letter proved cannot for certain be known; but I am now making it public because of what transpired, and because it is the fact that Mr. Kruschchev in his concluding letter to President Kennedy on October 28th substantially echoed my words and thoughts.

That same year, 1962, the International Arbitration League took the decision to merge with the Mondcivitan Republic as best qualified to continue its work. The League had been initiated in 1870 by Sir William Randal Cremer, who in 1903 was awarded the Nobel Peace Prize. He was also instrumental in bringing into being the Inter-Parliamentary Union. It was as a tribute to him that one of his admirers, Andrew Carnegie, donated funds towards the building of the Peace Palace at the Hague, to be the home of the Permanent Court of International Arbitration, and later of the International Court of Justice. He died in 1908 at the age of eighty.

The next year the second Parliament of the Servant-Nation met at the Temple of Peace at Cardiff, the place of its Constituent Assembly. In accordance with the Constitution a Praesidium of five was elected under the name of the Supreme Council, each member of which would hold the office of President for one year in turn. At this time the Mondcivitan Republic had its citizens in 60 countries, but they were still not very numerous.

It is needful here to say on what basis the Servant-Nation operates internationally. The Constitution states clearly its obligations to labour in the cause of mediation and reconciliation (Article 5), to maintain a strict impartiality in all international disputes and conflicts (Article 13), and without prejudice and in no antagonistic spirit to direct the attention of governments and authorities to any violations of the fundamental human rights, or to conduct prejudicial to world order and good relations, or calculated to endanger peace, acting in such matters in the name of and on behalf of humanity (Article 14). It has been the practice not to

intervene unless first hand knowledge of the circumstances
has been obtained and a proposal for a settlement has been
arrived at which is equally fair to both sides. Normally such
proposals have not been made public. What has so far been
done gives only the promise of what can be achieved as the
Servant-Nation gains fully qualified and dedicated citizens
and wins the trust and respect of the nations it seeks to serve.

The time has now come when the world mission of the
Servant-Nation must begin in earnest, and therefore both
for the sake of mankind and of those who will be led to join
it the lessons of the formative years must be stated and taken
to heart. Unlike what many would assume the retarding
factors have not been external but internal. There has been a
much greater readiness for Governments to take the
Mondcivitan Republic at its face value than for its own
adherents. Partly this has been due to the fact that very few had
been in public life or were at all at home in matters political
and economic, and could not therefore contribute usefully
to planning and executing policies. A much greater impact
would already have been made if the initial citizens had been
better qualified and able to be more completely identified
with their undertaking.

A new people of this unique type, equipped for all needs,
does not come into being automatically. It has to evolve,
become conscious of kinship and its own way of life. This
process takes a considerable time even when those concerned
share a common country, language and culture. It is bound
to be a much slower and far more difficult process when the
citizens are from a variety of backgrounds and are widely
distributed over the world. It is greatly to the credit of so
many unsophisticated but valuable citizens that hopefully
and trustfully they have hung on tenaciously through the
hardest years, giving of their time and often very slender
means, because world citizenship was a reality to them and
because they believed in the principle of service. They
enrolled because they were of this mind, the finest kind of
people in the world today.

These men and women had thought out a great deal for
themselves before they joined. Mostly they were connected

with various societies working for good causes, peace, world
government, international friendship and understanding,
service to the underprivileged and needy. They had broken
down barriers, but frequently they retained their previous
interests and approaches. They could see the Servant-Nation
as one activity in the cause of world peace and unity, but not
as a rule as a top priority. Some were party political-minded,
ranging from right to left, while a few were anarchistically
inclined. Some believed in working to change the policies of
their own states, by representations and demonstration,
while others believed in direct world action by the people to
bring pressure on all states. Some were very spiritually-
minded, while others were humanists or agnostics. Feeling
the desperate condition of world affairs, most were people in
a hurry, driven by a sense of urgency to get results before it
should be too late, impatient of slow progress, and allying
themselves with whatever seemed to promise the speediest
means of achievement.

The Servant-Nation was thus regarded commonly as a
second-string, to supplement other efforts rather than
replacing them. This attitude no less operated against
concentration on the task of making the Servant-Nation
fully functional. It appeared to narrow down the field of
operations too much. Surely the field was the world. Why,
then, put everything into building a nation, even a Servant-
Nation, when we were trying to get beyond all nationalism?

This failure of understanding has been by far the hardest
challenge to meet. It has been almost crippling at times.
Only a handful of people could bring themselves to visualize
the organic structure of the new nation, to work at planning
its internal economy. This was not only because of inexpert-
ness and lack of imagination, but also because of some
reservations as to whether the whole enterprise was really
essential to the ends citizens had in view. Additionally, there
were all the difficulties of novelty. It was like cutting a ship
adrift from its moorings to take its chance in unknown seas,
with a motley crew on board untrained in seamanship trying
in a fumbling way to obey commands which they did not
comprehend how to execute. But miraculously, as it might

seem, the ship remained afloat, weathered storms, and made progress towards the ultimate haven no human eye had ever seen.

The parliaments and ministerial offices were not just play-acting and makebelieve, as some would say. They were indispensable to the recognition of the Mondcivitan Republic for the furtherance of its mediatorial and service functions internationally. They were also experimental disciplines to promote integration and identification and gain practical experience of autonomy. They might seem pretentious, when little more than a thousand persons were involved. But these trial runs could teach much to those willing to learn, and give promise of what could be done when the time would come for the influx of multitudes who from the first would see the character and need of the Servant-Nation more clearly, and bring to its development their vision, their zeal, and their practical equipment. We had to be what we said we were from the start, looking to the future to make it meaningful. All honour to those pioneers, who overcame their misgivings and stuck it out in the days when it was hardest to have faith, and so prepared the way for others to reap the harvest of their sowing.

I have given both sides of the picture honestly and straightforwardly, to illustrate the potentialities for those who have the courage and insight to make the Politics of God their own, and to warn the timid and the dubious that they should not get mixed up with this adventure. Better that they should profit by the ministrations of the Servant-Nation than they should cause confusion by coming into it. There is no personal advantage or self-satisfaction to be gained by being a Mondcivitan, so that people should want to become one for any glory the status confers. Boastfulness is excluded. Mondcivitans are not perfectionists, and neither worthier nor better than their fellows. But they do have to be stable, reliable and gregarious.

On various occasions it has been my privilege to address Mondcivitan gatherings. In bringing this exposition to a close I find words I need in some of these speeches, and I would like to use them here as making them again my own.

Involved as we all are, it is not easy to see things clearly. Evidently we are being called upon to transform ourselves into planetary beings with harmonious universal relationships. But we find that the majority shrink from such an enlargement of consciousness: they cling to the narrower familiar ways of life, now made more precious and desirable because they are threatened by inevitable change. Security is the word we continually hear. False values are attached to the noble idea of patriotism. There is emphasis on class solidarity, race solidarity, ideological solidarity, defensive pacts and blocs.

Who will give us back our littlenesses, our little isolated segregated worlds in which we feel safe, and which we understand? No one! Presently the former things will be no more, the exclusive patterns of our planet's past will be extinguished. It takes high courage and bold imagination to face this, to embrace this new existence of the future, to press forward and not to look back with vain regrets. As yet there are comparatively few who are capable of it. Even among those who have the vision, many who realize that we must have a united world and live as world citizens want to see that world conforming as closely as possible to what they have liked and thought best. The bigger home is to be stocked with most of the old furniture.

Of course everything is not to be discarded. That would be greater folly. But what we take forward with us must not so much be institutions as the living things which evolve as we evolve. There is no short-cut to our goal. That is why I speak of evolution, not of revolution. It is of no profit to have a change of names without a change of nature, to alter systems without altering behaviour. It is not for us to overturn with ruthlessness, but to identify ourselves with the heart of life, which is love, that we may grow up and through the existing orders and bear flower and fruit everywhere upon the earth.

This is the way of the Servant-Nation. It is not our function to sway masses, to exercise material power and authority. It is not our business to cry in the streets, to denounce and pass judgment upon rulers, but rather to

cultivate the capacity for insight and impartiality in ourselves, so that we may have that to offer which will be of real
service to others. This is why we have to be informed on all
that relates to human history, personality and experience.
This is why we have to be a training ground to live forward
in advance of our generation. This is why we have to undertake experiments with ourselves as the subjects, so that our
influence may stem from our example, and that we may
pioneer a good and desirable road for all mankind to follow.
We have no motives of self-interest or ambition for power.
We do not aim to govern the world, but to govern ourselves
throughout the world. We incorporate only those who
voluntarily accept the responsibilities we have undertaken,
who care so much for human welfare that they cannot do
other than join us. But it is our desire that what we demonstrate may act as an inspiration and incentive to all peoples,
so that they in turn may find the will to unite and achieve
harmony and well-being.

The opportunity that is ours beggars description for its
potentialities of fruitful service to mankind. World community is now the goal, and an almost feverish search is being
made for solutions to the pressing problems with which
humanity is confronted. Everywhere men and women are
awakening to the curiously lit dawn of an unprecedented
day. When that day comes it will see world peace taken
permanently off the danger-list, and permit the energies and
adventurous spirit of youth to find an outlet in tasks sufficiently hazardous but untainted by the guilt of blood.

What a programme lies ahead! Millions in all continents
have progressively to be brought into active participation in
the organized life of the world community. All the resources
of the planet, and eventually of the solar system, have to be
harnessed and canalized to meet the expansion of human
needs. The great enemy Waste has to be vanquished. War is
waste. Want is waste. Disease is waste. Destruction of
consumable commodities is waste. All barriers to free
intercourse and association have to be broken down, and a
pattern of world society created to coordinate rather than
to rule, to cooperate instead of to exploit.

The ancient myths agree that before paradise could exist chaos had to be conquered. The ending of traffic-blocks and bottle-necks in production and distribution, and in all relationships of human kind at all levels, is the indispensable preliminary to anything faintly approaching a heaven on earth. At present technological invention is far outstripping moral elevation. The soul has to soar as well as the rocket. It falls to the Servant-Nation, as the People of God and the People of Man, to explore and corporately to express the good life for the general benefit. In our day and age, in accordance with the Divine Plan, it is being re-formed and re-animated for this exacting and arduous Messianic purpose. Pray God, it will not fail this time!

Epilogue

To the best of my ability, and only too conscious of my inadequacies, I have carried out my assignment. It has been both a rewarding and a punishing experience, with moments of great happiness and of intense agony of spirit. If I had not been upheld I could never have endured. Mercifully, I have been kept and preserved, and permitted to live to see so much accomplished that in contemplation seemed humanly-speaking improbable, if not impossible. My heart is therefore filled with great thankfulness. I can hand over my charge with the vision fresh and unclouded, and made so much more certain in my mind as the years have disclosed its inherent rightness theoretically and practically. It has been a continual joy to find as I went ahead with study and activity that the discoveries I was making for myself provided new enlightenment and confirmation, reinforcing what initially had been an electrifying intimation without substantiating detail.

But it is not of myself that I am chiefly thinking; it is of those in all their diversity who have to face the painfulness of adjustment to the perspectives of the Politics of God.

First there are the lineal heirs of the vision, Jews and Christians. The message creates a basis on which at long last they can come together. The Divine Plan for mankind, represented in the Bible, called for a dedicated Priestly People by means of which all the nations would be blessed. Humanity would be enabled to be delivered from its troubles through a nation-Messiah. This proposition, for Christians, necessarily involves a change of dogmatic emphasis, and gives the task of Jesus as personal Messiah its true value. The function of the personal Messiah was related to the nation-Messiah, as servant and exemplar, as was that of the nation-Messiah to mankind. This is why the concept of the Messiah appears to be both individual and collective, and why both the king of Israel and the people of Israel are termed Son of God in the Bible.

It follows for Christians that if they were to continue after the fashion of pagan antiquity to ascribe deity to the man Christ Jesus (Christ meaning Messiah) they must equally ascribe deity to the nation-Messiah; for Israel was called the Beloved Son of God hundreds of years before the birth of Jesus. This should help Christians to straighten out their doctrines, by recognizing, what I have described in my two previous volumes, the special circumstances in the early Church which gave rise to its complex theology. Already it is evident that modern Christian thought no longer considers Jesus to be divine in any other sense than as a man who best expressed what God wants man to be as made in his image. Similarly they must be prepared to see that the Servant-Nation must best express what God wants all nations to be.

The task of Jesus as the Christ, in the providence of God, was to renew in his people the consciousness of the character required by their calling. This is why he said that he was not sent except to the lost sheep of the house of Israel. Christianity's chief contribution was the extension to believing Gentiles of membership of the Servant-Nation, thus bringing the world obligations of Israel to the forefront and correcting the tendency to national self-interest. The existence of Israel was not for itself, or for its own sake, but for mankind.

This is what has now to come home to Jews, so that they cease to be on the defensive or isolationist. Largely they have abandoned belief in the coming of a personal Messiah; but with it for all practical purposes they have also abandoned the belief that they were a Chosen People. In prayers and sermons lip service is still paid to that concept, but it does not govern the policies of the state of Israel, or of the Jewish communities in general. Of course it is right that a personal Messiah would now be an anachronism, and that no one could now hope to establish a claim to be he. But Jews are wrong in surrendering the chief justification for their survival. To them must come the new understanding of the real Jesus, divorced from the peculiarities of Christian doctrine, to enable them to see sympathetically how true to the fundamental significance of Messiahship this Jewish descendant of David was, and through his example not to have any change of religion, but a change of heart, so that there is regained and revived the impetus to fulfil the Servant-Nation's mission to the world.

As John the Baptist is said to have put it, 'Think not to say within yourselves, We have Abraham as father: for I say unto you, that God is able of these stones to raise up children unto Abraham.' If Jews and Christians, as communities of the People of God, opt out of their mutual mission to the nations, God's will for mankind will still be done. He can and is raising up the Servant-Nation of today to come to the aid of humanity; and Jews and Christians, who desire to do God's will, will come forward to claim their rightful citizenship.

That citizenship, however, is now open freely to all, of all faiths and tongues and races, who receive the message and embrace it. No one is excluded who wishes to enter. It is not needful to become either Jew or Christian. The Servant-Nation makes no distinctions, and has no preferences, but it does require dedication and devotion to its singular function.

Under the names of Romanism and Messianism I have endeavoured to make clear the differences of approach to world problems represented by the politics of men and the Politics of God. The former enslaves, while the latter serves. The one compels, while the other persuades. The one destroys men's lives, while the other saves them.

Either in the coming era, commencing now, or at some future time if service is again rejected, the Divine Plan will be fulfilled, because that purpose and design embodies the principles which raise men up to the stature of Children o1

God. It is for each one of us to choose whether we will make God's will our own today. But let each be clear about his motives. Just as self-interest and personal ambition is excluded, so is fadism and fanaticism. The task is not for the peddlers of pet nostrums, but for those who are capable of looking at everything freshly in the light of a new identity.

The present success of the Servant-Nation vitally concerns all mankind. For the solution of contemporary problems everything depends on the outcome of this venture. Will the Moncivitan Republic stand up to the test? Here in miniature, in microcosm, is the whole world community, which has to acquire a conscious kinship and peaceful harmony. If on the small scale it fails, how shall it work on the full scale? If this people cannot govern itself wisely and cooperatively throughout the world, what chance is there of peaceful and equitable World Government?

The Messianic New Jerusalem was to be a cosmopolis, with all nations flowing into it, not a Romanist megalopolis, keeping the nations in thrall by naked force. Godness has decreed for us, 'Not by power, not by might, but by my Spirit.' Who is ready to respond?

Appendix

THE MONDCIVITAN CONSTITUTION:
PREAMBLE AND PRINCIPLES

The Preamble

BELIEVING that in due time the peoples of the world shall be united for their common good and well-being, and that there shall be peace throughout the Earth:

WE men and women of different lands, races and nationalities, see clearly that it is now required of some part of mankind to give social and political expression to such unity, as an example and incentive to our fellows, and as a means of promoting a true and universal comradeship.

ACCORDINGLY, we have joined together to create from ourselves and from all who shall be likeminded with us a new and independent people, whose prior allegiance and service is given to humanity, and whose character is representative of citizenship of the world.

WE are embarked upon this course for compelling reasons. We are moved first of all by compassion for our fellows, whose peace of mind has been taken away by the perils, conflicts and uncertainties, of a period of unprecedented change in the conditions of life on this planet. We are conscious of the grave, but not insuperable, problems of adjustment to the requirements of living under a democratic world order. We see how new resources, means of transport and communication, of great benefit to mankind, have been converted through fear and suspicion into terrible instruments of hostility and mass destruction. We see the temporary submergence of a sense of the real worth of every individual and the value of human life in a futile and selfdefeating struggle both for sectional mastery and personal advantage. But we see also in many connections and institutions, national and international, an expression of the highest aspirations, much nobility and concern for human needs and sufferings, and desire for peace, understanding, and mutual concord.

CONFIDENT that men will not endure subservience to any conditions, authorities, or systems, which impose upon them unnatural actions and restrictions of fellowship, and will always quest for a right application of knowledge to collective existence, we take courage to attempt, however fallibly and imperfectly, to establish at the level of government within the world of nations an AGENCY universal in its scope, impartial and just in its relations, defenceless in terms of armed force, designed exclusively for the wellbeing of all peoples without distinction.

WE therefore, commending our enterprise to the goodwill of all persons and authorities, do now adopt this our Constitution, and proclaim in being as from this day and date the COMMONWEALTH OF WORLD CITIZENS.

Principles

1. The Commonwealth of World Citizens acknowledges none as enemies, no matter what they may do; for to admit the existence of an enemy is to create a barrier, darkening understanding, breeding hatred, and giving encouragement and licence to cruelty and inhumanity.

2. The Commonwealth of World Citizens recognizes none as foreigners, or of a lower dignity, since all belong to the same human race. There shall be identical treatment of those outside the Commonwealth as of those within it, treatment that is founded on reverence for the human personality.

3. The Commonwealth of World Citizens shall ever promote and actively assist measures for the welfare and

equitable unification of mankind, and shall at all times respond to the extent of its ability to calls for aid in emergency or catastrophe.

4. Neither the Commonwealth, nor any of its citizens, shall under any circumstances engage in war or in preparation for war, or in aggression, oppression, or wilful misrepresentation. The Commonwealth of World Citizens shall ever hold itself free from all alliances, agreements and contractual obligations, whether open or secret, which can have the effect of favouring any group, party, section, or state, or any interests whatever, to the hurt or detriment of any others.

5. The Commonwealth of World Citizens shall study to be impartial in all its relations and judgments, and shall labour in the cause of mediation and reconciliation.

6. The character of the Commonwealth is democratic and cooperative, based on mutual service and respect, holding all men in honour in public and private.

7. In its government and internal economy the Commonwealth of World Citizens shall continually seek to cultivate and display those standards of conduct which are equitable and just.

A Questionnaire and Application Form for Citizenship (printed in English) is obtainable from The Mondcivitan Republic, 27 Delancey Street, London, N.W.1. Requests must be accompanied by an International Reply Coupon obtainable at any Post Office.

Index